The Oppositional Imagination

Feminism, critique, and political theory

The Oppositional Imagination

Feminism, critique, and political theory

Joan Cocks

ROUTLEDGE
London and New York

First published 1989 by Routledge
11 New Fetter Lane, London EC4P 4EE
29 West 35th Street, New York, NY 10001

Data conversion/typesetting
by Columns of Reading

Printed in Great Britain by
Richard Clay Ltd, Bungay, Suffolk

British Library Cataloguing in Publication Data

Cocks, Joan
The oppositional imagination:
feminism, critique,
and political theory
1. Political science
I. Title
320

Library of Congress Cataloging in Publication Data

Cocks, Joan
The oppositional imagination:
feminism, critique,
and political theory
1. Political science
I. Title
320.19

ISBN 0–415–01512–X
0–415–03206–7

For my parents

Contents

Acknowledgements

Over the years, many students at Mount Holyoke College and in the Social Thought and Political Economy Program at the University of Massachusetts have kept up animated conversations with me on political theory and feminism. In an important sense, this book is really for them.

It would be possible but not, I think, entirely desirable to mention by name all the friends whom I enticed into arguments on what became the key questions of the pages to follow. Heated debates stretching late into the night seem to be a prelude to the development of critical theory. I hope the wear and tear on personal relationships has not been prohibitively high.

While I cannot thank individually all the colleagues who gave me thoughtful encouragement on this manuscript, I do want to make special mention of the members of The Donner Foundation Project on Gender in Context, who provided an alert audience for early versions of my chapters on Masculine/feminine. I also am indebted to Linda Nicholson for her many intelligent and helpful comments on the same chapters, and to Kristina Rolin, who sent from Finland a highly astute and sympathetic commentary on pages I had sent her.

There is no adequate way to thank my friend and colleague Meredith Michaels for the sensitive attention she has given this manuscript. She wrote perceptive comments on many chapters, in many versions, and in our frequent talks together she mulled over the twists and turns of my arguments with a lucid and generous understanding.

The three people who have been most central of all to this project are Karen Struening, Peter Cocks, and Craig Malone. I have spent years in pleasurable conversation with each of them on questions of politics, theory and feminism. These conversations have meant as much to me as my attempts to put my consequent thoughts on the page. Each has read and responded to large sections of the manuscript with great critical and political intelligence. Each, finally, has played a distinctive part in inspiring my description of figures who go against the grain. I must add a special note of appreciation to Craig Malone for his dedicated theoretical attention to this book in all of its phases. He pushed me hard on the conceptualization of my arguments, and he also inspected my sentences with a sharp editorial eye. To Peter Cocks, a different kind of appreciation for being his usual humorous and affectionate self even while living in close quarters with a writer at work on a book.

It is a pleasure to express my gratitude to the Rockefeller Foundation for awarding me a Humanities Fellowship near the start of this project, and to Mount Holyoke College for awarding me a Faculty Fellowship near the finish. Both gave me the privilege of thinking and writing in relative solitude. Gretchen de Roos assisted me with my footnotes at almost a moment's notice. Finally, I would like to thank my very incisive and articulate editor, Nancy Marten.

Introduction

Things in Two's are Sometimes, but not Always, Dichotomies

This is a book about opposites. My preoccupations hinge on the tension point between philosophy and poetry, abstract thought and concrete experience, culture and counter-culture, objective and subjective force, domination and rebellion, and last but not at all least, masculine and feminine. Some of these oppositions I mean to preserve, some to reconcile, some to dissolve, and some to break into fragments.

Perhaps the most prominent opposition here is that between political theory and practical life. The nexus joining the two elements of this classic pair is notoriously complex. If political theory lives off the practical circumstances of ruling, serving, warring and uniting, the questions it asks are set free by those circumstances rather than being directly about them. Sometimes they are set almost entirely free, so that the political theorist seems to resemble a philosopher inquiring into a universal order of things. Sometimes they are set hardly free at all, so that the theorist seems more like an historian immersed in a welter of once-lived details. In fact, however, the political theorist occupies a distinctly third place – provoked by particular conditions and events to think about the right conceptualization, or real significance, or underlying logic, or moral or historical value, of all conditions and events that are broadly like or interestingly unlike them.

Paradoxically, the contributions that political theory has to offer to life depend on its achieving a partial distance from life. They depend on its agility in beginning with what actually is and then moving in all sorts of directions beyond it. There, theory can work to unearth the hidden complexities of the "what is." It can speculate about what else there could be, or should be, besides it. It can determine how possibility might be transformed into actuality, and which social groups would be most likely to carry that transformation out. It also can choose to theorize not directly on the basis of social life but through commenting on prior political–philosophical commentaries or even through working off portrayals of society that are explicitly fictional. The possibilities for political theory's movement are almost endless. The one danger to those possibilities is that theory can lose altogether its connection and even its desire for a connection to actual political affairs. This it does when it embraces its own professional–philosophical texts as its only proper object of attention, and when it insists that the study of living ideas and practices is not political theory at all but some coarser and cruder activity.

It has been my intention here neither to collapse the distinction nor to snap the connection between political theory and the practical world. Moreover, it is the most abstract and idealist kind of theory that I have wanted to join to the most mundane and bodily aspects of actual life and to the most politically committed practices of resistance. In the book's first part, I discuss a kind of theory that attends to power as it is radiated through culture rather than as it is governmentally imposed. This is a power entrenched in ordinary linguistic distinctions, literary and imagistic representations, and habits of practice; as well as a counter-power emergent in distinctions, representations, and practices that are extraordinary and iconolastic. In the book's second part, I try to come to grips with a specific cultural order that rules over the sexed body (an order I call "the regime of Masculine/feminine"[1]); a counter-cultural formation that has risen up against that regime (a formation which calls itself "radical feminism"); and, finally, figures and episodes of life in antithesis to both power andcounter-power which are too fragmentary, multiple or fleeting to be summed up by a single name.

Now, I have said that a political theoretical investigation typically begins at the point of some problem in practical life and then becomes a search for the categories and method by which the problem can be understood. The line of movement thus is from the concrete to the abstract, and to the illumination of the concrete by the abstract. Nevertheless, when the theorist comes to write about that illumination, the procedure very often is reversed. On the page, the theorist tends to begin with what Hegel would call "the idea of the idea" rather than with the idea of the concrete thing. That is, she begins with a discourse on the categories and method she will use in making sense of the problem at hand. This difference between the procedure of investigation and the procedure of presentation reflects the twin facts that the practical world provides political theory with its original inspiration, while the search for a way to comprehend the world is theory's original condition and distinguishing mark. And one should note that from a theoretical point of view, it cannot be said that the inspiration is more important than the search, that the thing is more important than the idea; that the comprehension of the world is more important than the method of comprehension. It cannot be said, that is, that the worldly object is the end for theory and the abstract thought of the object merely the means. The equality of treatment of object and idea, indeed, is another point separating political theory from classical philosophy, which favors the idea, and from history, which favors the object.

The main body of this book follows this typical order of theoretical presentation, moving from a discussion of categories and method to a consideration of certain problems of sex and power in their light. The remarks below, however, follow the line of my initial investigation. They introduce the central questions of this book in the order in which they first posed themselves to me.

1.

If what is meant by "an extremity," a "margin," or "periphery," is something at an edge rather than a center – a set of practices that go against the grain, a point of view outside the range of all permissible points, tastes that are perversions of the normal – then I will be exploring extremities and centers of two antithetical sorts. First, I intend to probe a segment of feminism which, as a practical movement, proclaims itself radically opposed to the established order of sex and gender; and which, as an interpretation (and it is as an interpretation that it most concerns me here) understands that order in terms beyond the pale of common sense and all traditional intellectual musings. Now, if one looks at sex and gender no longer as people ordinarily and conventionally do, nor even from a respectable avant-garde position, but from this far periphery, what one sees is a tightly organized system of sex-based, malignant social power, exploitation and hatred where a loose arrangement of natural or customary power, mutual dependence and love had been seen before. Radical feminism has been determined to pierce through the hypocrisies and romanticizations with which it claims the center has cloaked its rules and dictations. We will see how sharp and bright radical feminism's own gaze has been.

What remains at the same time obscured from both peripheral and conventional view are life-forms that negate, if not the center's authority, at least the breadth and depth of its control. Such life-forms include evasions of that control that subsist not apart from and against but in the interstices of the ordinary and everyday, and that are often tacit rather than overt, understated rather than overscored; and subversions that have attained a more definitive counter-existence, but that are still unmarked or are actively secretive. It equally will be my purpose to illuminate those figures, aspects of socio-sexual relations, and moments of actually lived life which lie outside not only the established rule of sex and gender but also radical feminism's counter-rule. Some examples of these are the male figure who is not at all a living condensation of egoism, self-aggrandizement and aggression; the female figure who, out of autonomy and strength rather than men's manipulations of her, her resentment and envy of men, or her own acclimatization to a "male mode" of behavior, acts with viciousness and cruelty; the male and female bodies that resemble each other more closely than they resemble "exemplar" bodies of their own sex; the erotic command that is issued through not the brutal but the delicate physical movement; the character who is a thoroughly polyglot mix of "masculine" and "feminine" traits.

In the past, studies that began at the margins of life were likely to be branded as being of secondary interest and importance, "not the main thing," irregular, trivial, and idiosyncratic. At the present moment, marginality happens to be something of a fashionable theme. While there is nothing much to be said in favor of fashion for its own sake, there are two things to be said on this particular fashion's behalf.[2] The political advantage in looking at peripheries and extremities is that power is exposed in what it drives from the center of life to the edges, and in what it incites as its own antitheses. But the generic advantage is compelling too: that peripheries and extremities are worth the intellectual detour simply for the shock and oddity of what is likely to turn up. As to why there is a magnetism to shock and oddity that can make detours too dangerous to take, so that the traveller sticks even more closely to the main route – for the moment, I must leave that question to the reader's private reflections.

It will be clear that I am signifying something fairly exclusive by "the center," if I mean to pose radical feminism as "the extremity" rather than some different kind of cultural formation, political group, or radical vantage point; and if I mean to consider as figures concealed all around, the man who does not instantiate the masculine, the erotic command issued through the delicate physical movement, the body that escapes given gender assignments, as opposed to some entirely different series of liminal types. What I mean by "the center" here is an order of sex and gender inclusive of the established phallocentric discourse on the meaning of the body (a discourse of words, but also of mannerisms, gestures, bodily costumes and decoration, cultivated proclivities and tastes), the elaboration of the "masculine" and the "feminine" personality, the sexual division of labor, the social orchestration of biological reproduction, the assignments of public and domestic power and subjection made on the basis of genital type. The whole, massive weight of this will be treated as comprising an entrenched and hegemonic regime.

This is not at all to suggest that it is the only regime there is to social life. It is not to say that there are no other axes along which power spins itself out, or that this one is more important than the rest. Surely there is no reason why one power relation must be fundamental, why there must be only one right description of what lies at the heart of things: "It is class," "It is race," "It is sex." The human mind, which tolerates the idea of profusion when it comes to sensation, accident, poverty and wealth, should be able to tolerate the idea of profusion when it comes to power, with which, as unpleasant a fact as it is, social life is so evidently over-rich. On the other hand, it also is not to say that power has no rhyme or reason to it, that it is inexplicable, chaotic, unorganized, but only that there may be multiple organizations of it that are vigorously effective at one and the same time. I want to emphasize this quite clearly at the start, so that there will be no mistaken conflation of radical feminism's notion of the center and my own. I will not be treating power as if there must be a primary power relation from which all others spring, or with respect to which all others are secondary contradictions or delusory antagonisms, or compared to which all others are lesser versions, as if power relations were stretched tight on a single, parsimonious continuum. Power will not, then, be considered as some fixed quantity that, if it appears with force along one axis, must be that much less forceful along the others. It will not be assumed to be something that is identical with horror, so that the less horror there is the less power there must be, and the more power there is the more horror there must be. Power will not be presumed to come from a single origin, either diachronically or synchronically, as if all its forms and instances had to be identically indebted. Finally, and to match a notion of power that even in these preliminary ways is highly fractured, it will be assumed (and isn't it a reasonable assumption?) that individual persons can occupy different positions along different axes of power at one and the same time. People are complicated enough, alas, to enjoy the various pleasures of domination while simultaneously suffering all the insults and injuries that subordination brings in its wake.

In sum, I will assume that there are as many legitimate descriptions of the center as there are axes of social power, and that individuals will have at least as many distinct relations to the center as there are such descriptions. This book does no more, when it is being specific, than probe one sort of center–extremity relation. But to the extent that there are certain resemblances of predicament among different such relations, the reader, I hope, will find enough stimulation here to make the comparative move on her own. I do mean my investigation of radical feminism to raise, at least implicitly, questions to do with the progress any cultural–political formation against any established order is likely to make, as well as the paradoxes and difficulties in which it is likely to become mired. Its most predictable kind of progress is bound to be its break to some degree with conventional, entrenched ideas and practices. Its most intractable paradox will be its repetition in reverse of dominant terms, principles, and assertions. Its most fascinating problems will occur if it forges a new mode of life in opposition to the old. For then, it will be poised to give birth to the twin tendencies of the Liberator, who for emancipation's sake pits itself against all old dictations, prohibitions and repressions; and the Censor, who for the sake of protecting the purity of the emergent mode of life, issues dictations, prohibitions, and repressions of its own. An important question, then, concerns the ways in which marginal cultural–political groups generate such progressions, paradoxes, and problems for themselves. There is, too, the question of whether such groups must gravitate towards a monolithic and conspiratorial view of the Oppressor, a romantic view of the Oppressed, and a belief in the possibility of an earthly utopia. Can a militant oppositional effort be sparked by complex, not simple, ideas? Or is the power of simple ideas a necessary stimulus to rebellion? Is disillusionment, then – when life ultimately is found to be complicated, not simple – rebellion's necessary end?

If by "center" I mean to evoke the idea of an entrenched system of sex, gender, and power, what do I mean by "radical feminism"? The term can refer in the North American context to a specific political current of the feminist movement in the 1970s and 1980s, with identifiable although shifting organizations and objectives.[3] More complexly, it can refer to specific ideas about women, men, sexuality, history, civilization, nature, and the good life. These ideas may appear in the writings of such feminist "organic intellectuals" as Adrienne Rich, Mary Daly, Susan Griffin, Kathleen Barry, Andrea Dworkin, and Catherine MacKinnon. They may inform women's newspapers, pamphlets, broadsides, and song lyrics. They may manifest themselves as unwritten principles and mores of feminist therapy, pedagogy, and athletics; tacit policies of acquisition and display on the part of women's bookstores and art exhibits; particular strategies of political action and criteria for selecting which causes to be political about. They may appear more intangibly still as the gist of women's casual conversations, as shared presumptions among friends, and as rules for the living of everyday life – rules regulating who is welcome to social gatherings, what kinds of clothes it is permissible to wear, what foods appropriate to eat, and above all what kinds of people should arouse one's sexual desires and how those desires should play themselves out. When they appear in full force, these ideas, presumptions, and rules constitute a world view that is coherent, detailed, and explicit. But they also may crop up less methodically, more sporadically, in the thinking of women who would not claim to be committed to any world view at all. More than a few of these ideas are familiar elements of much feminist thinking in America; a certain few are familiar elements in the feminist world at large.[4]

Then again, "radical feminism" can connote living women's communities on the boundaries of contemporary society. These vibrant and visible, if also marginal, ways of life are made of meeting-places such as bars, cafes and restaurants; life-supporting institutions such as shelters, health clinics, rape crisis centers; cultural institutions such as bookstores, small publishing companies, educational workshops, dance troupes; political activities such as organizing against wife- and child-battering, the sexual domination of women, militarism, and environmental destruction; public events such as music festivals, dances and lectures; and finally, at the least formalized ground level, networks of households, love affairs, friendships, and social acquaintances.

In my own work, I will be focusing on radical feminism as principles of thought, sympathy and valuation, and as permissions and prohibitions for action. This is not to underemphasize the fact that such principles and rules have their ground in actual, marginal practice, nor that they have implications for the reordering of social practice as a whole. Quite to the contrary. Radical feminism as an organism of ideas warrants our attention in large part because of its tight, generative connection to a real – if unstable and very possibly transitory – counter-cultural formation. At least in the United States, where feminism at present is most practically if not most theoretically advanced, radical feminist thought has had, through this connection, a greater effect on the living of life than has, say, socialist-feminism, which is the more intellectually and theoretically sophisticated, or radical black feminism, which is the more politically and culturally astute. At the same time, radical feminism has not been characterized by the failure of nerve of liberal feminism, which, by the same token that it has had the most sweeping impact of all on society at large, has suffered a near-total lack of imagination, an inability to think past every received habit of thought and practice except one.

What will we find if we look at radical feminism as an organism of ideas connected, in this way, to a marginal mode of life? We will find, first of all, the presumption that the primary division in society is one between women and men. All other divisions – of economic class, nationality, race, and so on – are derivative, or delusory, or secondary in significance and effect. Second, we will find the presumption that the self's interior is seared thoroughly and absolutely by the particular sex to which the self belongs. Each and every point of that interior is believed to express, if not necessarily the biological fact of maleness or femaleness, at least the way in which that fact has been given a particular psycho-cultural existence, as well as, in the case of women, a deep truth that contradicts psycho-cultural dictations and constraints. Third, not only each and every one of the self's interior points but what it exhibits of itself in its connections to others – the words it speaks, the sentences it writes, the emotions it displays, the actions it takes, and the objects it fabricates – are through and through characteristic of one of two positions in the socio-sexual dynamic.

The most telling feature of this socio-sexual dynamic is declared to be men's tyrannical power over women. Men may have attained their power at the close of pre-history through brute force, but they have preserved it over the course of history not only through violence but through customary and political–legal authority, and through the manipulation of women's desires, purposes, and beliefs. By controlling the means of cultural production, dissemination, and implantation, and hence the stock of available and effective interpretations of "male" and "female," men have been able to orchestrate women's embrace of their own subordination. The substance of that subordination is massive and multiple. In the interests of increasing their pleasure, assuaging the anxiety in their relations with other autonomous and masterful men, and gratifying their impulse to dominate, men have made women into objects for men. And it is into that most delightful kind of object, to use de Beauvoir's famous words, that women are made: an object who is also a subject and so actively can desire her own object-status, who can adore, attend to, comfort, and voluntarily prostrate herself in front of the pure subject, Man. Men have fashioned a passive female eroticism as a compliant complement for their own active desire. Men have taken command of women's child-bearing capacities, usurping a control over the reproduction of the species that biology refused them. Men have forced women to engage on men's behalf in biologically necessary toil, thereby disentangling themselves from an enslavement to the requirements of the body and freeing themselves to enter onto the stage of history and civilization. In part, to be sure, men enter onto that stage to compensate for their being merely secondary figures in the creation of life and unwanted third terms to the unity of mother and child. But they go as adventurers, not as exiles, in search of virgin territory on which to exercise their will to power. The ascendance of historical over cyclical time, and civilization over organic nature, are signs of the triumph of that will.

Men's rule over women and the historical–cultural world has been so perfectly monolithic and self-identical across time and space as to be labelled simply, and completely, "the patriarchy." Women's affirmation of their own subordination (to the extent that they do affirm it), and their love for their male master (to the extent that they do love him) testify to their blindness and victimization under patriarchal law. It is as such blind victims that women are rallied by men to take sides in wars, imperial adventures, industrial strikes, and political revolutions – all instigated by some men against other men for men's own interest and sake.

Against both the patriarchal self and the feminine self that is its subject-creature, radical feminism posits the idea of a true female self – what women are in essence and would be if they existed in a free state. In contrast with the patriarchal self, women are held to be relational and empathetic in their connection with the world, rather than egotistical and impersonal. They are claimed to see things as organic wholes, understanding them intuitively, receptively, and sensuously, rather than knowing things through definition, dissection, and logical analysis. Women do not act through imposing their own purposes and will on everything around them but respect the integrity and natural impulse of things in themselves. They look to care for, not master, the other and so lean in all relations towards harmony, not conflict. In contrast with the feminine self, undomesticated women are held to be self-loving selves, not in that they are narcissists, but in that they refuse to negate themselves by worshiping and abasing themselves before a male master. Instead, they love themselves as autonomous, free beings, and they love other women as equal beings with themselves. Finally, in contrast with both the patriarchal self and the feminine self, women have, in their truth, a deep, organic tie to wild, natural forces, which pits them against the predations of civilization, reason, and science.

Well, later on we will plunge into the more arrestingly problematic details of this socio-sexual critique and trace out its secret origins, theoretical implications, and political significance. But we should be clear at the start on radical feminism's truly novel and inspirational offerings. The most startling are its militance and courage. It is less than any other point of view caught up in sentimentalizing heterosexual relations, and more than any other, willing to denounce some of the most sacrosanct aspects of social life. The very single-mindedness of its concerns, and its absence of all hesitation and qualification, lend it a fierce and admirable intensity. Then, too, against modern culture's glorification of scientific reason and technique, its alienation from organic and sensuous life, and its desiccated habits of thinking, speaking, and writing, radical feminism stands as a great romantic Refusal. Among the other post-Enlightenment refusals (not all of them "romantic" by any means), it is unique in its sexual thematic, in its being not merely an intellectual position but a living practice, and in its rhetorical power at not only substantively defending but also stylistically evoking spontaneous emotion and the sensuousness of physical things. What distinguishes radical feminism, too, and not merely from other critics of technocratic society, is its contempt for the pretensions and pomposities of authority. It is supremely scornful of men's obsession with great men, with leadership, with military discipline. It pokes fun at men's rush to do obeisance before those who are higher up in some line of hierarchy, and their insistence on receiving obeisance from those lower down. It laughs at men's sanctimonious stress on the need for obedience, at their worship of canonical texts, at their idolatry of heroes, and at their solemn reverence for every sort of father: the father of the family, the town father, the fathers of the nation, the fathers of the Constitution, the father of an invention, or a genre, or an epoch.

But radical feminism's real stroke of genius, it seems to me, has been its exposure of the intersection of politics, culture, and sexuality as the dead center of relations between women and men – even if those relations are not, as it thinks, the dead center of the world. It got the angle from which to look at sex and gender exactly right, or at least it showed how much that is key could be seen from that angle.[5] By keeping its eye trained on sex and gender as a distinct system of political power, and on the cultural force that system brings to bear in its constitution, domination, and exploitation of the feminine, radical feminism thus illuminates a territory with its own autonomous integrity, with respect to which the political stances of criticism and resistance, not, say, the therapeutic stances of confession and cure, are appropriate and imperative.

And yet, at the same time that radical feminism exposes a territory for critical investigation, it provides no real method for making one's way intellectually across it. It has been unable to account with any persuasiveness not only for dominative power's advances and slippages in the sexual domain, but for feminism's own appearance and development as an oppositional tendency. In its revelations and denunciations, it has leaned very heavily on poetry and polemics – a potent enough mixture for shaking up common-sense convictions, but hardly suitable for the task of comprehending and articulating how and why power works as it does, or, for that matter, what it is. Thus it is that radical feminism's unveiling of a key subject-matter for critical attention, its own existence as a counter-cultural formation, and its highly metaphorical-hyperbolical account of that subject and that existence, make up as much the pieces of, as the answer to, the puzzle of sex, gender and power.

2.

If we choose to work that puzzle out – if we choose to come to theoretical terms with cultural power and resistance in the domain of sex and gender – we very quickly will be forced to backtrack to solve an anterior problem. How do we come to theoretical terms with cultural power and resistance per se?

This proves to be a very large question, and a search of feminist quarters does not uncover a good answer to it. Certainly, the two developed strands of feminist theory already firmly in place, materialism and psychoanalysis, contribute much to our understanding of the system of sex and power but not enough to our understanding of the cultural–political features of that system, and very little to our understanding of cultural power and resistance in the abstract.

Materialist feminism, for a start, is most adept at revealing the economic functions women serve and the punishments they suffer as the subordinate sex; the variability of those punishments and functions under different modes of production and from one class to another within each mode; and the universal facts of biological sex that provide the raw material for socially and historically particular ways of organizing species reproduction, gender differentiation, and the production, distribution, and consumption of goods. But materialist feminism takes as its first premise rather than its first question the distinction between "woman" and "man." It investigates material punishments, functions, limitations, and allowances that are levelled as injuries and benefits on biological creatures designated as having one sex/gender identity or the other. Indeed, they are levellable as injuries and benefits of a system of power only because that designation already has been made. Of course, such material punishments, functions, limitations, and allowances perform a double service for that system. They do not merely injure and benefit women and men, but they also, in the same stroke, help to elaborate, exacerbate, and embellish the truth of the distinction between "masculine" and "feminine." This second service, however, is not a material but an ideal, symbolic, or discursive one, and to the extent that feminism attends to it, it does not do so as a strictly materialist feminism at all.[6] Likewise, to the extent that we wish to investigate the mechanisms by which brute bodily life is made, and resists being made, into masculine and feminine life, we must move from what typically are called "materialist" to what traditionally have been called "idealist" preoccupations.

Psychoanalytic feminism, for its part, highlights precisely the question of how the brute body is fashioned into the "woman" and the "man." But it pitches its answer alternately at too low and too high a level to suit our particular needs. At the microscopic level, it seeks to discover how the individual child psychologically becomes the little girl or little boy, who then becomes the woman or the man. At the macroscopic level, it speculates about how culture is forced out of biological being, and how society is forced out of the mother-infant dyad. What it does not do is to reveal at the political level how a mode of social life imposes the rule of Masculine/feminine on the sexed body, how it orchestrates the legitimation of this rule, and how it elaborates and enforces the specific content of masculine and feminine selves that psychoanalysis presumes when it charts that content's inscription on the androgynous child. And when psychoanalytic feminism takes up the representation of masculinity and femininity in cultural artifacts and forms, it does so to uncover and decipher there the themes of pre-oedipal and oedipal experience. It does so, that is, in primarily a psychoanalytic and not a political way.

Nevertheless, both cultural–political theory and psychoanalysis emphasize the significance and force of language and meaning, the ideational and the symbolic, desire, understanding and intention. It is because of this common emphasis that we need to be clear about what cultural–political theory is distinctively to do that psychoanalysis does not and would not.

Most obviously, cultural–political theory inquires primarily into consciously lived life, rather than primarily into the unconscious with conscious life treated as a signpost to that. I do not mean that cultural–political inquiry accepts on trust all the breezy, self-deceptive, and self-serving accounts of conscious experience that any self is all too willing and able to give. It always must search out and make plain forbidden as well as acceptable desires, suppressed as well as confessed allegiances, contradictory as well as coherent beliefs. But in its central descriptions of those forbidden desires, suppressed allegiances and contradictory beliefs, it must draw on the same kind of language a self would use to describe reflectively its conscious experience at the level of that experience, not at the level of its unconscious processes – with which, by definition, its conscious experience can never be identical. Cultural–political theory, for example, must treat admiration, envy, and hatred in the main as admiration, envy, and hatred, and not transform them into expressions of cathexis, demands of the super-ego, or reaction-formations.

Of course, the language of consciously experienced life may not be entirely separate from the language of psychoanalysis. Direct experience may have incorporated, to some extent, a psychoanalytic interpretation of experience into itself. This is most likely to happen in a widespread and facile way in a culture in which psychoanalysis has become popularized, and in a sophisticated way among individuals who are highly trained in that school of thought. But the life that is experienced directly entirely in psychoanalytic terms would be an impossible life to live out. It would be life lived always at one step removed from itself, a life of passions instantly reduced to the more fundamental forces thought to be behind them. My point is not at all that direct experience is necessarily unreflective experience, but rather that the reflective intelligence belonging to it operates at a different logical level than the intelligence of the psychoanalytic point of view. This is why some of the finest analysts where that reflective intelligence is concerned are not Freud, Klein, and Lacan, but Woolf, James, and Morrison; and why it is not the intelligence of doctors as distinguished from the blindnesses of their patients, but the intelligence that authors bring to light in their characters. It is because the world of culture and politics is a consciously experienced world (whatever else it may be), and because conscious experience is always much more complex, detailed, and varied than the starker unconscious processes that may be said to provoke it, that an ability to describe consciousness at the level of consciousness is so essential to all cultural–political investigations.

Almost as obviously, what such investigations at the same time must do is to ferret out the seeds of desire, the causes of loyalties and betrayals, the impetus for a set of beliefs, in so far as they derive from the thought and action of a vast multiplicity of selves with whom the single self may have little familiarity and absolutely no personal connection. That is, a cultural–political inquiry makes its major moves back and forth between some individual train of thought or action or sensibility and the larger, collective political and cultural world. It understands that world, in turn, as it is not only infused with but determined by purposes and projects of individuals and groups that are, in the main, conscious ones – but also as it is not determined by purposes and projects at all, conscious or unconscious. The sheer historicity, sociality, and objectivity of practice must prepare one to expect that, not only may individuals be constrained by a mode of practice regardless of their own wishes, but that mode of practice may owe its debt of origin to none of its participants' wishes at all and instead may exert an independent, generative force on them. Of course, the language required to capture this generative force on thought and action will not be identical with the language of immediately experienced life. But this is because it will refer to social limits and pressures on experienced wishes, hopes, and aims that may not be immediately visible to the individual self, and not because it reduces those wishes, hopes, and aims to a different categorical level which purports to be their deeper truth.

It is in part to compensate for the recent psychoanalytic turn in feminist theory that I want to take the cultural–political turn instead. But it would be disingenuous of me were I to claim that I have chosen this route solely to fill a gap and right a balance, as if otherwise there would be every reason to go the other way. It seems quite clear to me that the existence of overweening social power (barring any purely naturalistic explanation of it) always will require a political theory for its understanding, which will not be necessarily incompatible with psychoanalytic probings but will be necessarily different from them. And to the extent that overweening social power is not restricted to the relation between citizen and state, a political theory will have to address itself not only to what classically, in the West, has been known as "politics," but to axes of power and resistance as they have become synonymous with, say, the gradations of bureaucratic organization, the division of labor, the shadings of the human skin, and the differences in genitalia and reproductive organs. In those instances in which dominative power and the resistances to it assert themselves through imposing interpretative grids on the human body, as they do with respect to both race and sex, a political theory will be fundamentally a cultural theory as well.

If we look outside the bounds of feminist discourse, we will find cultural power taken up as a theoretical problem by several distinct intellectual and political tendencies. These all refer back to Hegel, the great idealist philosopher ("out of the concept, comes the world") and Marx, the radical investigator of systematic and mystified power ("the truth of social life is concealed, and that concealment works on behalf of domination"). To be sure, Hegel and Marx may flit across these tendencies as silently as ghosts, so that the debt owed to the two may rest only in a determination to suspect the self-images of an age, to be on the look-out for the operations of power and the way those operations are concealed, and to ally with social forces of criticism and resistance. Still, I want to use the phrases "critical philosophy" and "critical theory" interchangeably to embrace all such suspicious and rebellious varieties of thought. Therefore I mean to take in by them much more than either Marxist theory (which is what Antonio Gramsci most specifically meant by "critical philosophy") or the contributions of the Frankfurt School (which is what people most often mean by "critical theory" today).[7]

What is significant for us are the ways critical philosophy has broadened its interests, shifted its focus, and modified its sensibilities over the last fifty years.

The most prominent strand of critical philosophy is, of course, Marxism, which in its most classical form praises the powers of theoretical reason, attends to the objective features of especially the capitalist mode of production, and insists on the primary political importance of the oppression and emancipation of the working class. Its emphasis on the historical significance of material conditions has been matched from the very start by its concentration on questions of class consciousness and ideology, so that only in its worst reductive moments can Marxism be accused of underestimating the confluence of culture and power. It is, then, in addition to its permanent interest in that confluence that western Marxism in the twentieth century has become fixated on cultural questions, a fixation that begins with Gramsci in the 1920s and 1930s and continues with increasing intensity into our own day. This fixation is a response to the fact that late capitalist practices of production and consumption have become so entrenched as the foundation of everyday life, and the habits of thought and valuation associated with those practices so identical with the limits of common sense, that a popular commitment to capitalist society is now as much a guarantee of its vitality as are the exploitation of labor and accumulation of profit.[8] The prominence of the cultural theme in the work of contemporary Marxists such as Raymond Williams is re-affirmed by the fact that quite pivotal profit-making enterprises in the late twentieth century engage specifically in cultural production. The fabrication of ideas, images, and cultural artifacts has become an enormous and highly centralized industry, which in turn enjoys, through mass communications techniques, saturating power over the collective scene.

Internationally, meanwhile, the global expansion of capital has been accompanied by a cultural imperialism of a corrosive/productive sort. The attempts to reconstitute the Third World on the one hand in the West's own image, and on the other as its negative reflection; and the cultural incursions into Canada, Britain, and Continental Europe by what has been until very recently the most successful capitalist country in the twentieth century, have been formidable enough that any strictly material analysis of capital cannot do justice to it. By the same token that dominative power is seen to have invaded the constitution of desire, self-image and everyday understanding, the idea of the subordinated subject expands to include, in layers overlaid on the traditional industrial working class and the economically imperialized nation, the whole culturally captivated population in the West, and all culturally colonized populations in the Third World. At the point at which Marxism becomes sensitive not only to the cultural power of advanced capitalism but to the cultural dimensions of the imperial and neo-imperial relation, it comes up against the edge of the second major tendency of critical theory in our age. This is the tendency of post-colonial criticism. The near fusion of cultural Marxism and post-colonial criticism is nowhere more well-illustrated than in the work of Edward Said. Said explicitly traces out the line that runs from Marx to Gramsci to Williams. He also extends it into the entirely new terrain of the cultural–political relation between the Western Subject and its Other, the East. But Said performs one last act of theoretical synthesis in his analysis of Orientalism as a subjugating discourse, as well as in his essays on theory, culture, and politics. He gathers together with the strands of Marxism and post-colonial criticism the third strand of critical philosophy that will be of great interest to us.[9]

This third strand is really a set of separate breaks with the fundamental premises of the Enlightenment tradition. The liberal side of that tradition had touted reason as an objective and universal thing, which after wrenching itself free from the chains of medieval custom and superstition initiated the modern age and grew afterwards in a quantitative way. The radical side of that tradition had touted reason as a potentiality developing over the course of history through contradiction and the synthesis of opposites. But both sides declared reason to be the benchmark of progress, the guarantee of the ultimate triumph of freedom, and the foundation of science which in turn was declared to be the foundation of truth. By the mid-twentieth century, however, the idea of reason's linear progress had been discredited by the rise of fascism. The idea of its dialectical progress had been stymied by Stalinism and the incorporation of the working class into the late capitalist state. The notion that scientific reason was the pinnacle of civilized achievement was delivered a great blow when science invented, as its supreme creation, the means of absolute annihilation. These debacles formed the historical backdrop against which some thinkers began to argue that one could not talk with certainty about reason, goodness, historical movement, and truth, while others declared that a will to power lay veiled behind any such talk at all. Writers as intellectually, temperamentally, and geographically foreign to one another as Stuart Hampshire and Michel Foucault concurred in seeing the truth and goodness of particular identities not as trans-epochal, trans-cultural, and objective but as products of particular and transitory modes of social life with particular habits of conceptualization, belief, and action. Where thinkers like Foucault went much further than thinkers like Hampshire was in denouncing truth, reason, and goodness as ideas produced inside a mode of life in order to ratify it, and in exposing distinctions between the rational and irrational, truth and illusion, freedom and constraint, along with their companion insitutions and practices, as operating for power's sake.

Thus, from its earlier economistic, and/or politically monistic, and/or rationalistic position, critical theory has moved along a course of developing a multifaceted analysis of cultural power. At the same time, it has moved within sighting distance of feminism's own horizons. It has come in close enough range for feminism to be able to give critical theory the sort of intellectual pleasure in which it so likes to indulge – if only it could be hedonistic enough to take some of its delights from feminism. Feminism, after all, has uncovered a whole new set of power relations for critical theory to track down, demystify, and denounce – a whole new world, or rather the old world of class exploitation, colonial domination, and scientific desiccation complicated in an enticing new way, for it to penetrate, interpret, and deconstruct. The opportunities for intellectual adventure generated out of feminism's critique of the sex/gender system would be only half of what theory could enjoy, the other half's being all the paradoxes and promises in particularly radical feminism's own development as oppositional thought and practice. And how much, in return, would critical theory offer to radical feminism – this time to enhance not its pleasures but its understanding of power's complex operations in the cultural domain. It could do so were radical feminism not adamant that all established ways of understanding anything are intrinsically "male" – were it not, that is, strangely enamored of the view that the genitalia are linked internally to thinking along any particular line, that a mode of analysis devised by a person of one anatomical type must bear the stamp of that type, that the body leaves its impress automatically on the idea and the word. Were radical feminism less sure as well, not that the will to know the logic of male domination and female subordination must have a privileged connection to women's will (for this seems incontrovertibly the case), but that the content of knowledge must come solely out of "women's experience" as some sanctified and truth-producing zone.

These missed pleasures and chances mean that critical theory loses an opportunity to come to grips with one of the most recalcitrant axes of social power and to connect itself to living arguments and struggles. Radical feminism, on its side, can continue to hold to a blunt and crude understanding of power – which, given radical feminism's political commitment, is bound to have practical reverberations. Of course, blunt and crude representations of dominative power have been resorted to often enough before in history for strategic reasons by leaders mobilizing masses. But a movement that succumbs at its most as well as its least theoretical moments to the magic of simple ideas hardly can triumph as an emancipatory movement in any meaningful way. Gramsci surely was right in declaring that any popular radical movement must aspire on behalf of all ordinary people, and so quite emphatically on behalf of its organic intellectuals, to the highest possible level of thought. That aspiration partly is to complex thought as a means by which the movement can grasp the given order of things and partly to complex thought as an end. An emancipatory movement, after all, must seek to create a good mode of life as much as it seeks to undermine a bad one, and the notion of good must signify not only an absence (the absence of oppression, the absence of exploitation, and so on) but a presence. That all people think at the highest possible level is one compelling idea of what is present in a good mode of life. This is not to say that must be the only good, or the highest good, or a good appropriate in every situation or context.[10]

Both radical feminism and critical theory exhibit a preoccupation with dominative power and resistance. Radical feminism and certain strands of critical theory exhibit a distaste for technocratic society, a disenchantment with scientific truth, and a horror of the idea of reason-in-history. But their most promising new point of coalescence, it seems to me, would come through radical feminism's focus on critical theory's transmogrification of the old idealist principle: "out of the concept, comes the world." In its benign form, this is the principle that all identity is produced inside classificatory orders that are basic rather than superstructural parts of limited and transitory modes of social life. The principle becomes more malignant when the claim is added to it that classificatory orders and their supporting institutions and practices constitute tyrannical regimes of truth which produce identity through disciplining the human body. Thus we are given the theoretical means to say that men's domination over women, notwithstanding all its material dimensions (men's exploitation of women's labor, their control of women's reproductive capacities, their sexual use of women's bodies, and so on), does not issue out of the combustion of essential male and female identities fixed in male and female bodies. It is not the logical function, that is, of any underlying material fact. However male dominance happened historically or "pre-historically" to arise, and however crucial to it various facets of bodily difference at various times may have been made to be, it rests at base not on differences in the brute sexed body, but on the harsh, systematic fashioning of brute bodies into masculine and feminine selves.

This idea of course has a fine pedigree in feminist discourse itself. Simone de Beauvoir had argued in *The Second Sex* that Masculine/feminine only appears to identify two distinct and opposite real entities, but in truth is, *à la* Hegel, a "self-identical whole" made of two contrary parts that provides the basis of a system of power.[11] Gayle Rubin had declared in "The traffic in women" that there is no essential truth of the sexed body that that system conceals or distorts.[12] Kate Millett had intimated in *Sexual Politics* that there is nothing more foundational to masculine and feminine than the cultural representations of them, as those representations are elaborated, objectified, and extended in inanimate and living "texts."[13] Thus a use of the elements of cultural-political analysis will allow us to develop what are in fact classic feminist ideas.[14]

If we follow the direction pointed out to us by critical philosophy on the one side and these classic feminist works on the other, we will be led to these initial observations about power, culture, and sex. The system of sexual domination and subordination is as strongly affected by the hold of the mass communications industry over public discriminations and associations as the system of class in advanced capitalist society. It is as deeply marked by the cultural legislation of the distinctive characteristics of Self and Other as the order born out of cultural colonialism. But culture and power are bound together in sexual domination and subordination more intimately still. For the system of sexual power works by imposing an interpretive grid on the human body. The production of meaning is logically primary, which is not to say historically prior, to power's operations in this case.

To write from two different intellectual positions is to write for two different audiences of readers. I mean to be writing for all women who are interested in feminist questions inside the academy and, indirectly, out. I also mean to be writing for social and political theorists who are interested broadly in cultural power and resistance, and, more broadly still, in the nature of political theory.

Of course, different sets of flesh and blood readers are often far more difficult to reconcile than different sets of ideas, and my intended readers are more intractably at odds with each other than most. Except for the few who cross over into both camps, feminists tend to be highly suspicious of theory, and social and political theorists indifferent or hostile to sex, gender, and feminism as objects of intellectual attention. To the extent that the suspicion on the one side and indifference on the other are signs that both occupy separate positions in a system of power, the problems in writing for these contrary audiences cannot be resolved through writing alone. Still, one audience may be tempted not to read a book that opens with a discussion of theory, and the other not to read a book that closes with a discussion of Masculine/feminine. To ward off what would be for any book an unpleasant end, I invite feminists who are impatient with anything that does not bear obviously on sex and gender to begin their reading with Part Two and work backwards. Theorists who are distressed by the subject of sex and gender should begin with Part One – something might ease up along the way. Emphatically, this is not to say that Part One is for political theorists and Part Two for feminists, as if feminists need not bother grappling with general problems of conceptualization and theoretical method, and political theorists need not attend to sex and gender as a key site of power and resistance.

A more peculiar complication to do with audience arises when I come to address the topic of erotic desire in the second part of the book. Feminists have looked on eroticism as a key question for study and debate, and their discussions of the subject are generally extremely frank, extremely adventurous, and extremely graphic. If there is humor as well as seriousness in those discussions, it is of the open, not the snickering kind. Political theorists, on the other hand, are not used to treating sexual desire as an intellectual question at all. Now, the feminist theorist always is faced with the problem of how to write about erotic life without being positivistic on the one hand or confessional on the other – without, that is, being overly external or overly internal in her approach. Also she is faced always with the problem of how to write about erotic life in a language that evokes its subject-matter without inciting in the reader a simply voyeuristic attitude. This second problem becomes acute when one is speaking to one audience that eagerly awaits every new idea about eroticism, especially female eroticism; and another audience that is profoundly embarrassed by the question of eroticism when it is given a political–intellectual cast – above all, I suspect, when it is given that cast by a woman. I mention this partly to warn readers from the second audience of what they will be reading about, and partly to indicate all around the predicaments that are apt to surface as soon as one tries to talk across sharply drawn lines. But I mention it, too, because the problem of how to speak and write about eroticism is one particular instance of the general dilemma of how to use words to say things. This is as important, it seems to me, as the dilemma of what things to say.

The dilemma of how to use words to say things raises the great question of whether it is possible to unite critical theory with an evocative and imaginative prose. Can a kind of thinking that abstracts from experience, not to reject it altogether for some detached and universal point of view but to decipher its secret causes and dimensions, still converse when appropriate in a language that is sensuous and concrete? And can critical theory not only reveal what is hidden in actually lived life, but release from it new possibilities of conception, desire, and action? A second question, in a sense the same question posed at the level of substance rather than style, is this: Can the idea that objective conditions give rise to and constrict particular kinds of human subjects be fused with the idea that those subjects may evade the full weight of those conditions?

Part One

On Theory

1

Consciousness and Culture

The elements that will help us compose an analysis of cultural power descend from a number of grand theoretical approaches that are different and even, at times, antagonistic, yet are complementary in important ways too. Some are complementary because they are in fact transfigurations of what Edward Said has called a "traveling theory": one that has been beckoned from its place of origin into distant geographical locations, altered historical situations, and novel political circumstances – and has been both revised and preserved along the way.[1] The line that begins with Marx and leads from Antonio Gramsci to Raymond Williams marks the route that one such traveling theory takes. Other approaches are complementary through being more tangentially connected. They have been mapped out in the same intellectual epoch, with the same concatenation of thoughts in the air; or there have been criss-crossing influences among their key authors, who either are eclectic enough to have drawn on a variety of other thinkers or are idiosyncratic enough for a variety of other thinkers to have drawn upon them. All these approaches, finally, can be said to have a certain commonality to them through having been fed off the same large reel of historical dilemmas.

Thus Stuart Hampshire, Edward Said, Michel Foucault, and Gramsci-Williams (taken, for a moment, together as one) do not write out of what even in the most attenuated way can be called a single tradition. They do not set the same mood or strike the same attitude in their work. They do not direct their attention to the same domains of inquiry. They do not begin with identical methodological presuppositions, and except in the vaguest of ways their political allegiances do not overlap. Yet there are among them certain striking thematic repetitions, certain similar analytical obsessions – certain ways, too, in which their separate arguments and insights are reciprocally illuminating. What is flawed in each argument alone, moreover, is improved by the selective combination of the arguments together. For in some cases there is too great a faith in subjective agency, in others too great an emphasis on objective determination. Some defend an overly centrist strategy of resistance, others an overly localist one. In certain arguments we find a naive esteem for a final harmony in social relations, and in others, a hypertrophied sensitivity to the possibilities of repression in any collective way of life.

1.

Two basic principles on which all our theorists agree are, first, that the world receives its order, and objects in the world their identity, from schemes of classification rooted in transient modes of social life; and second, that those classificatory schemes reflect and support specific ensembles of social interests, intentions, and desires. These principles pave the way for a general preoccupation with what can be called, very broadly, "cultural–political" questions, or at least with questions directly antecedent to them. Such questions concern the way in which human consciousness is constituted socially and historically, rather than universally and transcendentally; the process by which ideas become solidified and rigidly fixed, and the counter-process by which engrained habits of thought lose their social potency and hold over the individual mind; the relation of the genius of an individual thinker or idea or cultural product to discursive impositions of substantive truth, style, theme, and allusion; the identity and location of groups, institutions, and movements that generate and protect, or challenge and attempt to replace, dominant efforts of knowledge and imagination; the dynamic of entrenchment, extension, erosion, degeneration, and collapse of a socio-cultural whole.

In pursuing these questions, all of the theorists have poised themselves on a tightrope between opposite kinds of analysis. One kind inflates culture to an expression of the eternal presence or immanent development of a universal "Spirit" or "Mind." The other reduces it to a superstructural effect of a material base. Our theorists keep their balance between the two, first, by insisting on the concrete materiality of things to do with cultural life. They understand this materiality variously, to be sure: as the situated nature of all thinking, which always occurs in a world of objects of which the thinker is necessarily one; as the prominence of the human body as a target of cultural–political intervention and discipline; as the intimate connection between scholarly activity and geo-imperial adventure; as the tie of culture to a ruling class or to a subaltern class challenging its rule; as the correspondence between contemporary institutions of cultural production and massively centralized economic power and interests. But second, our theorists show a strong, clear disdain for what Gramsci – the one to find the perfect phrase – called the "metaphysics of matter."[2] All of them stand against the notion that the world as it is physically given, and apart from any sense or thing humans make of it, is the sole or primary or even secondary-but-still-crucial respository of truth.

It is with the notion of a general "anti-metaphysics " that I want to begin assembling the theoretical elements offered to us by Gramsci, Hampshire, Williams, Foucault and Said. It is an appropriate beginning, given my larger project. For isn't a key question feminism poses to the contemporary age whether the function of culture has been not to create Beauty, articulate Truth, and accumulate Knowledge, but to elaborate and impose the rule of masculine over feminine? And isn't a key question feminism poses to itself whether the rule and the culture enforcing it have their root cause in the body – in the male and female bodies as physiological repositories of essential truths?

In his *Prison Notebooks*, Gramsci supposes, and surely he must be right, that religion is the origin of the belief that the objective reality of the world lies outside all human theoretical and practical labor upon it. The religious teaching that "the world, nature, the universe were created by God before the creation of man, and therefore man found the world already made, catalogued, and defined once and for all. . . has become an iron fact of 'common sense' and survives with the same solidity even if religious feeling is dead or asleep."[3] Against religion, common sense, and (his real target here) vulgar Marxism, Gramsci states that objectivity is unintelligible apart from the specific way it is constituted by the intellectuality of "man," which abstractly is guaranteed by his being a user of language, and concretely is given its content by the particular form of society in which he lives. With an emphasis that will have everything to do with his assessment of culture's importance for revolutionary politics, Gramsci declares that all people, quite apart from what they do "professionally" in their economic function, are philosophers with particular conceptions of the world, artists with particular tastes, moral theorists with a conscious line of moral conduct.[4] "Spon-aneous philosophy" is "proper to everybody"[5] – not only through everyone's participation in some discourse of common sense, popular religion, or critical thinking, but more fundamentally still. For "even in the slightest manifestation of any intellectual activity whatever, in 'language,' there is contained a specific conception of the world."[6] Such world conceptions are rooted always in a particular mode of practice, and a social context, and a civilization. The belief that man can achieve some external, cosmic standpoint from which to view the world "objectively" must be another "hangover of the concept of God."[7] What is "objectively real"[8] can mean only "humanly objective," which means "historically subjective:"[9] "no more than a conventional, that is, 'historico-cultural' construction."[10]

It was the political implications of such an anti-metaphysics of matter and truth that most interested Gramsci, and in any case he did not always follow the philosophical ones consistently through. If we want to be sure of what those philosophical implications are, then, we will have to look elsewhere. Let us turn our sights just for the moment from fascist Italy to postwar England, from Marxist revolutionary politics to academic linguistic analysis, and from Gramsci's *Prison Notebooks* to, say, Stuart Hampshire's *Thought and Action* – a text that, while wedded to the philosophy of mind and the vantage point of the individual "man," presents starting-principles for cultural–political theory in the general spirit of Gramsci's own.[11] The first of these principles is a far more detailed and radical restatement of Gramsci's notion that human intellectuality gives specific form to the world. Hampshire attacks the assumption that convention and artificiality rest on a more fundamental "tier of basic and natural discriminations which is independent of any institution of social life."[12] "Reality is not divided into units that are identifiable apart from some particular system of classification";[13] there is no system which is most in tune with any real or true divisions of the world; the description of reality is essentially "inexhaustible," in that "[t]here is no theoretically determinable limit to the variety of new types of classification that may be introduced."[14] It is the development of new interests, new purposes, new kinds of knowledge, new practical needs, new forms of social life which give rise to new types of classification, and what these new forms and types will be there is no way of specifying in advance.

The secret of language, in sum, does not lie in some objective truth external to it which it identifies for thought and speech. That secret lies rather first in reality's being an open field for interpretation. It lies second in language's own internal function, which is to divide that field into identifiable, recurrent segments.[15] It lies finally in the ensemble of social and historical purposes, interests, and needs with which the divisions inevitably are fused, since it is humans' intentionality as active agents in the world that provides them with the impulse to discriminate among one object and another, their sociality that provides them with the impulse to speech, and their historicity which provides them with an inheritance of discriminations already in place. Hampshire too hints at the religious lineage of the belief in an objectively true reality knowable from an elevated and disinterested god-point, and while it is the pretensions of traditional philosophy, not of vulgar Marxism, that he is out to deflate, the case he makes is very close to Gramsci's own.[16] Observation and description are undertaken by people situated in, not above, the world, and a particular classificatory scheme, fostering and fostered by particular social purposes and needs, already has divided that world into a particular array of objects before any single effort of observation and description begins. The paradoxical nature of language becomes apparent here. Its function of imposing specific rules of identity or individuation and resemblance or classification has a necessity to it: thought cannot occur unless relatively persisting things of different kinds and types can be thought about. But the system of discriminations linguistically imposed is always fundamentally contingent. Thus it is that, by "fixing" the world conceptually, language at once frees thought to think and permits it to think in only one of an infinite number of logically possible ways.

Thought, then, has a double relation to language, being indebted to and constrained by it. If I can anticipate an analytic move we have yet to prepare ourselves to make, in any struggle between established and marginal cultural orders, indebtedness and constraint will be the twin antagonistic themes. Both sorts of orders, of course, will declare that their antagonism is that of the other's falsity against their own truth. But what the dominant discourse has distinctively to offer on its own behalf are conceptual discriminations that are elaborate, evocative, and refined, because of the long and vital history in which they have had time to build up. The marginal schemes, being either mustier or cruder (depending on whether they are residues of some now defunct mode of life or are only just coming into being) will have a different kind of advantage. Through their very marginality to most people's routine sense of the world, they hold out a promise to emancipate thought from encrusted habits of reflection, criticism, and imagination. Now there are, theoretically speaking, an infinite number of ways to make sense of the world that the dominant way rules out. In practical terms, however, any way that arises from inside a mode of life to challenge the dominant scheme will come from the relatively few schemes that are not utterly bizarre but share in many of the old conceptual presuppositions. That is, in actual practice, the emancipation of thought from its old habits – which, being simultaneously its induction into new ones, is not at all the same thing as a pure or final emancipation – will be extended in the name of not a weirdly strange world (for how could such a world be thought up or understood?) but the familiar world transfigured in ways that are at least vaguely comprehensible and, for exactly that reason, politically more than psychologically threatening to it. Conversely, while the established scheme prohibits in the abstract every possible kind of conceptual seduction, practically it stands against terms at once at odds with and closely resembling, in certain ways, its own. Cultural struggles, in short, are waged in and over what for everyone is partly the same conceptual field, which is not to say that a startlingly new field unimaginable to everyone may not be the struggle's distant result.

But we have jumped straight from human intellectuality and the "intellectualization" of the world to collective cultural antagonisms. We must backtrack to ask ourselves how conceptual schemes are intertwined not simply with ideas but with practice, so that "culture" can have the sense of a "whole mode of life," and cultural antagonisms a palpable significance.

Here, too, Hampshire helps us out with a philosophical discussion of what for him is an entirely intimate relationship between thought and action. In establishing the types of things there are in the world, language establishes the types of things towards which it is possible to have active intentions. The limits of what people are able to think set the limits of what they can think to try to do. Action on its side manifests a particular direction of intelligence – it is not "bisectable" from the individual's particular intention, the given cultural range of possible intentions, and conventional norms of what counts as what kind of action in what circumstances. This is not at all to say that there is nothing else to action but the intentionality of the actor; the impersonal, objective force of established classificatory habits; and of course physical movement. An individual's unconscious motivations, social groups that seek to manipulate individuals' beliefs and actions in various ways, and logics of practice that confine the thought and action of dominant and subordinate alike, may be doing their own secret work. But the internal relation of thought to action is not in any way diminished as a consequence.

That relation is even more complex still, for what also cannot be separated sharply from the individual act and the entire domain of action is what Hampshire calls "the whole person" and what I will call "sensibility." This is the current of taste, judgment, desire, and sympathy that an individual shows not merely (and not always directly) through the single action but over the much longer run, and which gives the single action a dense reference to the life of consciousness that an action would not have if there were only one discrete purpose or meaning behind it. The sensibility expressed in or (for this can happen too) exaggerated, corrupted, suspended, or betrayed by a single act includes the way a person

> thinks and expresses his thoughts and feelings, the things that he notices and neglects, the attitudes that he adopts, the feelings that he restrains and the feelings to which he allows free play, the words that he chooses to use or that he uses unreflectingly, the gestures and physical reactions that he controls or suppresses, the plans that he makes and the sudden impulses that occur to him.[17]

Once again to move beyond Hampshire's scale of analysis: if a culture as a whole mode of life includes specific habits of thought and possibilities for action, it also includes a certain range of characteristic sensibilities, although any real individual, being an individual, will be more complicated than any type of sensibility would suggest. This given range of sensibilities a marginal culture will be sure to contest, as it contests the given range of thought and action more discretely defined.

Individuals acquire at birth, then, a particular system of classification and with it particular ranges of possible interests, intentions, actions, and sensibilities. This cultural inheritance is not the product of any individual's will but instead is the context within which "he exercises his will, and makes choices,"[18] and as such it is bound to seem natural to him. Whether it is truly natural or artificial, Hampshire says it is "pointless" to ask, as it is the nature of man to think and act conventionally.[19] The opposite way to put the claim is that any particular order of thought, action, and virtue "contains an element of legislation or prescription."[20] That specific "human powers and activities" count as "normal and customary" is as much an imposition as it is a necessary condition of developed cultural life.[21] Not any malignance of a ruling social group, nor even any malignance of an impersonal cultural order, but the inevitable limitations of cultural upbringing, the social weight of the conventionally given, plus in every individual life, the sheer "inertia of habit,"[22] will ensure that humans begin living life within a relatively narrow circle of thought, interests, and action, the boundaries of which will be very hard to see, no less to see beyond. At its extreme pole, this comparative confinement and habituality of conventional life become a mean narrowness of thought and dullness of action. Hampshire calls this degenerated condition "the unreflecting state of a morality left to itself"[23] – when purposes "harden into habit and heedlessness, when comparison and reflection die . . . and . . . intentions are fixed, always formulated . . . in the same narrow set of terms,"[24] when there is "a naive confidence in established classifications of specific situations, actions and mental processes as being the permanently obvious and self-justifying classifications."[25]

Hampshire's idea of an unreflecting state of morality left to itself will turn out to bear a distant resemblance to Raymond Williams' notion, which we shall meet head on a bit later, of a "selective tradition." This is the plucking and sanctifying of a society's "meaningful past" out of a much wider and richer actual array of habits of thought, practices, and events, the social memory of the whole array being's, through that plucking and sanctifying, suppressed.[26] Such a shrinkage of the past is done in the present interests of social domination. But however much it may be the case that a selective tradition, by restricting the knowledge of real lived variety, tends to replicate on a larger scale and encourage on its own an unreflecting state of morality, the point as Hampshire makes it has a more general and fundamental significance. For Hampshire, the reduced horizons of unreflecting morality refer back, in an exaggerated way, to the nature of human intellectuality and culture *per se* as a reduction. This reduction is a logical necessity rather than a political contingency. It is grounded in the fact that while the world is theoretically an infinitude of possibility, any human experience of it must be finite and so depends on some finite way of representing the world's having been selected out.

We find a similar emphasis on the restrictive/permissive doubleness of any culture when we move to what will be the more political discussions of Williams and Gramsci. In *Marxism and Literature*,

Williams describes "culture" most generally as a basic, constitutive process that creates specific and different ways of life – a "whole, lived social process"[27] by which people generate (not necessarily intentionally or self-reflectively) self-interpretations and their interpretations of others in directly personal relationships; their understanding of the natural world and their place in it; their use of material resources for what contemporary society "specializes to 'leisure' and 'entertainment' and 'art'."[28] Culture is a determinative force in the negative sense that it sets limits but also in the positive sense that it exerts pressures – that is, it is forceful both by saying "No" and by saying "Yes." Its positive determinations are not only or even primarily those that press against established limits but are also and very centrally "pressures derived from the formation and momentum of a given social mode: in effect a compulsion to act in ways that maintain and renew it. They are also . . . pressures exerted by new formations, with their as yet unrealized intentions and demands."[29] Once internalized, these pressures become "individual wills."[30]

In his emphasis on culture Williams is greatly indebted to Gramsci, who had gone so far (for a Marxist) as to declare that, while economic crises in themselves can produce a more favorable terrain for fundamental historical events, what is decisive for those events is "the dissemination of certain modes of thought and certain ways of posing and resolving questions involving the entire subsequent development of national life."[31] Gramsci is better able than Williams to convey a specific sense of culture as a directed and imposing process by drawing on Hegel's largest notion of the State as a formative and educative socio-cultural whole that creates and maintains a particular kind of civilization and citizen. The disadvantage of this concept of the State for most contemporary minds is that it smacks of idealism in much too old-fashioned a form, but also, and more importantly, that it suggests a monolithic and intentional rule. But its strong advantage, which any critical theory of culture will have to find some other way to retain, is that it evokes the sense of a diffusion of the means and a broadening of the meaning of rule beyond governmental institutions and the making and enforcing of laws to socio-cultural practice and the dictations of moral right and customary norm. This concept of the State (and by implication, its attendant critical theory) embraces both "political society," which by means of law imposes compulsory obligations on the individual, and "civil society," which by means of morality and custom "exerts a collective pressure and obtains objective results in the form of an evolution of customs, ways of thinking and acting, morality, etc."[32] Through law, morality, and custom, the State applies pressure on single individuals, eliminates certain attitudes and practices and disseminates others – is, in short, an "educator" that "urges, incites, solicits and 'punishes' . . ."[33]

2.

That all human beings are intellectuals who act with a certain conception of the world, and that a collective culture sets limits and exerts pressures on thought and action, which never can occur abstractly but must be always the product of some set of limits and pressures or other – these twin principles lead Gramsci and Williams (as well as Said and Foucault) to pay special attention to the processes by which conceptions of the world, broadly speaking, solidify, are refined, transformed, replaced; to the specific sites at which such conceptions are produced and given practical weight; to the social groups which think and live according to received ideas in normal times and according to radically different ideas at unusual moments in history; and, finally, to the social groups that function as professional intellectuals – including, on Gramsci's list, scientists, philosophers, religious ideologists, scholars and political theorists. It is important, Gramsci writes from the silence and isolation of his cell, "to study concretely the forms of cultural organization which keep the ideological world in movement within a given country":[34] to examine the relationship between cultural workers and the population as a whole, and institutions and organs such as the school, church, newspapers, magazines, the book trade, private educational institutions, the university, and the specialized cultural activities of the medical and legal professions.

Williams for his part identifies the various structural aspects of the cultural process which give body to culture's being a determinative force, quite apart from any association that culture might have with specific relations of social domination. This is not to say that certain of these aspects will not be most effective in societies in which social power is massively centralized; or that they have not been born out of specific relations of social domination but now have a more autonomous existence and significance. Williams orders these structural aspects of cultural life according to whether they are more or less formal, palpable, and fixed. At the "most" end of the spectrum is the *institution*, on which Gramsci had focused above: the family, the school, the church, the workplace, the community, as well as, in contemporary times, the major communications systems, including the press, cinema, radio, and television.[35] The prominence of these massive communications systems signals, in advanced capitalist societies, the fusion of cultural production and capitalist economic power. Having penetrated small-scale and hence what had seemed to be independent cultural enterprise, having become a locus of international capitalist investment, and having been integrated with other forms of capitalist production and distribution, large-scale institutions of cultural production are now both intellectually and economically central to capitalism.[36]

But, as Williams reminds us, a culture is always much more than its formal institutions. It includes, very crucially, *tradition* – not "a relatively inert, historicized segment of a social structure" but "an intentionally selective version of a shaping past and a pre-shaped present, which is then powerfully operative in the process of social and cultural definition and identification."[37] The making significant of certain meanings and practices from the past is then an aspect of contemporary social and cultural organization, which wields its power simultaneously backward over the past and outward over and into the present social whole. A third aspect of cultural life is the *formation*, which Williams defines as an effective, conscious movement in intellectual and artistic life (literary, philosophical, scientific, and so on) having an influence on the active development of a culture (hence not backward-referring as the tradition), with no direct or manifest institutional realization of its own, and with a "variable," sometimes "oblique," sometimes positively contrasting relation to formal institutions.[38] According to Williams, such formations play, in developed, complex society, an increasingly important role. Finally, to evoke the least visible dimension of cultural life, and to remind us of the fact that part of human cultural activity is not reducible to its fixed forms and finished products, Williams introduces the category of *structure of feeling*. By this he means to signify a social experience "still in process" or "of a present kind"[39] – "a kind of feeling and thinking which is indeed social and material, but each in an embryonic phase before it can become fully articulate and defined exchange."[40] The structure of feeling is not, on the one side, entirely chaotic or in complete flux; but is not, on the other, congealed enough to be acknowledgeable by name. At most it is the pre-emergent stage of some new, as of yet indistinguishable, formation. It is not intimated by and therefore recognizable and expectable in terms of a tradition, and it is as far as it is possible to be and still be *something* from the institution – the very physicality of whose buildings and grounds announce its solidity to the world at large.

Because it is "at the very edge of semantic availability," Williams tells us, the structure of feeling is often felt or misunderstood as a simply "inner," "individual," "subjective," and "private" experience.[41] This conflation of the inchoate with the subjective is one example of a whole series of mistaken conceptual distinctions dividing off the social from that which is relatively fluid and unfixed in social life. One consequence of the mistake, to follow on from Williams' argument here, is that socio-political theory concentrates its attention, when it has any kind of a choice, on the more rather than less solidified form: on the institution rather than the formation; on the act rather than the thought of the act; on the part of the thought that is "factually substantive," rather than the part that is not bolted down to a fact but is "fanciful," "metaphorical," "merely" a matter of style and so on. Thus theory too easily reduces the important contents of consciousness to "knowledge," when in fact the imagination is just as essentially and seamlessly a part of conscious life and so of conscious political life. The imagination, in turn, is reduced to the "inner" and "subjective," when in fact it is – as are all forms of thought, and as is the imagination as an element of all forms of thought – a creature of cultural limits and pressures. Imaginative writing, finally, is reduced to "fiction," when in fact all writing, having fundamentally to do not only with stylistic proprieties, generic rules and the like, but with language (that maker of the world as a world filled with *this* sort of entity and *this* and *this*), is imaginative at its very core.

It is against this whole series of received reductions, and in what will turn out to be the political if not entirely the intellectual spirit of Williams and Gramsci, that Edward Said in *Orientalism* takes up and makes use of the category of *discourse*.[42] We would do well to add it to Williams' list of the structural aspects of cultural life. Said acquires this category most directly from contemporary French theory and above all from Foucault. Its distant point of origin, however, is German philosophy and most notably Hegelian idealism. Hegel portrays the Idea as an Absolute Subject that creates its object out of itself and then sees the object as a separate, independent entity. Hegel takes the various objective self-elaborations of the Idea to be, quite literally, everything. Said, descending intellectually as he does not only from Hegel but from Marx, portrays a discourse as a coherent and forceful system of written and spoken ideas with no grand Absolute Idea behind it. There are only mere human beings – above all, for Said, those Gramsci would call "professional intellectuals" – and they are not really behind the discourse but are authored by it as much as authors of it. Their particular habits of thought are passively received before they actively refine, embellish, deepen, and extend them. What these intellectuals are authored by includes an established vocabulary, a classification system already in place, unquestionable doctrines, time-honored images, also precedents of reference and allusion, rules of argumentation, criteria of truthfulness, standards for distinguishing between mediocre and excellent work – a whole ideational body that has acquired a solidity, authority and imposing presence into which the individual intellectual is absorbed. But a discourse includes as well a set of supporting institutions – for example, the academy, libraries, government foundations, research centers, scholarly associations. Finally it includes – really, is trained upon as its entire reason for being – a specific object which it creates in a host of representations out of itself. The most crucial of these representations is that the object as it is represented has its existence independent of the discourse. The discourse adorns the object with a wealth of descriptive phrases that purport to disclose the object's "true," "real," and "secret" self, which the discourse, seeking the truth of the object, has labored to discover and know.

The imposing nature of a discourse over the individuals who think, write, and speak in its terms; representation as discursive activity; and the presentation of representation as truth, Said shows us, must be taken up altogether as a central and active facet of cultural life. Quite obviously, discursive activity as Said takes it up is closely related to the conceptual constitution of the world that Hampshire analyses. It is, however, more pointed and specific, distinguished by its focus on some particular object or set of objects; a particular sort of doctrine, images, and procedural rules; particular locations and institutional supports, which may or may not be primarily scholarly; and finally, although Said does not mention it himself, particular sorts of products which may or may not be confined to forms we usually think of as "cultural artifacts." And what we usually think of as artifacts are scholarly texts, works of "art," advertisements – that is, to fabrications detached and detachable from the human body itself.

For a final note on the cultural question in general, let us return to Gramsci, with his love of the grand sweep. It is the task of the critical theorist, he tells us (and while by "critical theorist" he means the Marxist theorist, the point can be more broadly intended), to study the entire philosophy of an epoch. And since all people are at the least spontaneous philosophers, the philosophy of an epoch will include not only all the philosophical tendencies of the professional philosophers but the views of "restricted ruling groups," and, lastly, popular philosophy – that is, the conception of the world that is implicit in the practical activity of the "great masses."[43] It is the solidity of popular convictions, after all, that often have "the same energy as a material force."[44] Such attention to philosophy, in what must be one of the most expansive and implicitly political senses given to it, will be well served if one also keeps an eye on what we already have seen that Said calls "traveling theory." Any philosophy of an age is sure to be partly made of ideas and theories and (Gramsci and Williams would add) concepts that have come from a different time, place, and situation – and that, passing "through the pressure of various contexts" are variously accepted, or resisted, or misread.[45] Misreadings are, Said notes, "part of a historical transfer of ideas and theories from one setting to another."[46] That it is the nature of ideas to move, be taken up, revised, transformed, and put to new uses is, for Said, a point against all charges and counter-charges concerning the orthodoxy or revisionism of any particular reading of a theory or idea. But the point also tells against all temptations to collapse a theory or idea back into its point of origin so that every characteristic of its origin becomes an innate characteristic of the theory or idea: an idea is irrevocably Western, for example, because it first emerged in a Western geographical context to address a Western predicament, or it is irrelevant to matters to do with sex and gender because at the start it was formulated with class or race in mind, or it is male because someone with a male body first thought it up.

2

Dominative Power

1.

Thus far we have been circling around but managing to avoid the political question in our discussion of culture and consciousness. Now it is time to take up that question directly. We will find that four of our five theorists see power as infusing social life in ways that traditional political theory is unable to grasp. Gramsci, Williams, Said, and Foucault take their first departure from that theory by de-emphasizing power as it is exerted through the imposition of legal right and the monopolization of the means of physical violence. This is not, importantly, to say that they show no appreciation for the mechanisms and weight of state force. Above all, Gramsci paints an imposing picture of "political society" or "the sphere of positive law," which is distinguished from "civil society" through its operating by means of direct domination and authoritative command. Political society or the state in the small sense of the term is the "armour of coercion" of the State in the grand, Hegelian sense – it is its "repressive and negative educator," which effects a correspondence between individual acts and social ends through its courts, prisons, and police.[1] In normal times its force is turned against groups that do not consent spontaneously to the social order. In times of crisis, when that order threatens to disintegrate and mass spontaneous consent begins to fail, the state's target broadens to include the population as a whole.

To the coercive capacities of juridical government, the other theorists make brief but respectful bows. Williams refers us right back to Gramsci's notion of "'rule' (dominio)" which is "expressed in directly political forms and in times of crisis by direct or effective coercion."[2] If Williams dwells no further on power as political rule, it is because he can count not merely on Gramsci but on traditional theory's already having trained everyone's attention sufficiently on it. He himself will be concerned with power of a more elusive sort. Like Williams, Said draws on Gramsci's notion of "political society" principally to separate out from it a kind of power that will surface elsewhere than in the army, the central bureaucracy, and the police, and in another way than that of direct domination. Yet he still is very careful to make clear that "political society" often has an instigative connection to that other power. Political circumstances impinge, for example, on academic discourse and its judgments of truth at least obliquely. The British scholar, say, who is an Orientalist cannot but come to his subject-matter aware, "however dimly," that he belongs to a political power in a geographical region with definite interests and a history of imperial involvement in the Orient.[3] More immediately, "political society in Gramsci's sense reaches into such realms of civil society as the academy and saturates them with significance of direct concern to it."[4] The political state is invested in certain fields of specialization, it encourages certain directions of research through the dispensing of money, public awards, and the prestige that comes from a proximity to dominative power; it makes direct requests to or demands on professional intellectuals when political interests require.

Foucault, for his part, does not touch even lightly on such connective pressures between political state and civil society. His obsession with the prison and the army, which most obviously would seem to be institutions attached to juridical government through their functions of protecting property and enforcing the law, is emphatically not an obsession with the prison and the army in that attachment or those functions at all. Even so, Foucault is hardly blind to the legal– coercive power of the modern state. He pays tribute to that power when he berates Marxists for seeking state control, which can only lead, Foucault declares, to their enjoyment of the pleasures of centralized political domination.[5]

Nevertheless, the main argument as all these theorists wish to make it is that power in the modern age requires, for its understanding, a shifting of sights away from the radiations of political society as they extend outward onto the citizen population, to the forcefulness in what at least Gramsci and Said after him call "civil society." Williams will prefer to "civil society" another Gramscian term, "hegemony," that Williams uses to evoke the sense of a power confined to no delimited sphere but rather socio–cultural–political all at once. Foucault, finally, urges a shift in sights that is essentially functional rather than spatial, from juridical power – which does, by definition, have a specific location at the "top" of and overlooking society – to "normalizing power," which inserts itself in "public" and "private" institutions of all different levels and sorts (the prison, the hospital, the school, the family), so that the distinction between "political" and "civil" society no longer is an especially acute one.

But let us follow Gramsci rather than Foucault in insisting on the initial usefulness of that distinction. It allows us to speak of a power that originates "in society" rather than in the rule of a political state over society, and that exhibits itself in normal times through the spontaneous consent rather than the coerced obedience of a whole population. What that whole population consents to is "the general direction imposed on social life by the dominant fundamental group."[6] For Gramsci, this fundamental group is an economic class, which as a result of its position and function in the world of production enjoys a prestige that wins mass allegiance magnetically, so to speak, to the rules of conduct helping that world continue to be what it is. But it is not at all hard to imagine other groups that would be dominant along different axes of power than the one emerging out of productive relations: groups that become "fundamental" when social life is divided up according to different schemes of classification than those to do with productive property, tools, labor, class divisions and the like. Such schemes of classification identify things in the world for the sake of different social purposes than those of material production and consumption – different in the sense of "incommensurate," not in the sense of "competing" or "opposing."

Whatever the fundamental group turns out to be when the world is subjected to some other central classificatory scheme (and a scheme rooting itself in the life of the sexed body is, after all, only one of several), Gramsci's overarching point holds true. In civil society, a conformity of individual action to social ends as they serve the interests of that fundamental group is produced by morality, custom, and intellectual suasion, not by law; through the school and tradition, not the courts and prisons; and in the form of the individual's free consent to the social order, not the individual's coerced obedience to it – or, to put it another way, in the form of the coercion of the individual's desires and goals by public opinion and moral climate, not of the individual's actions by governmental decree.[7]

In civil society we see the positive rather than the negative side of the project of the State in the grand sense of the term: the creation and expansion of a particular cultural–moral civilization. This is the creation and expansion of at once a particular world and a popular embrace of that world, so that through the simple process of everyone's living life out, the norms of conduct constitutive of that world will be affirmed and preserved. The winning of mass intellectual and behavioral consent to a form of civilization manifesting the ethos of a fundamental social group signals the triumph of what Gramsci calls power as hegemony. It is precisely because the spontaneous consent on which hegemony depends must be gotten from the mind and the heart that "[e]very relationship of 'hegemony' is necessarily an educational relationship."[8] And to politicize a point Hampshire made earlier, the first stage of that education is the habituation of the mass of people to a classificatory order of the world that, although it expresses the point of view of the fundamental social group and so is not only conventional but reflective of a position of power, comes to seem to have "crystallised" from the "point of view of a hypothetical . . . man in general."[9]

To refer to the whole complex of power that weaves back and forth in its exertions between two very different forms – one legal–political and based at root on physical coercion, one moral–cultural and based on habituation and spontaneous consent – Said and Williams speak of "hegemony" and "domination" interchangeably. A slight shift in the lines of Gramsci's terminological map, perhaps, but not in his conceptual one. Both thinkers follow Gramsci and if anything go further than he does in naming culture as the dimension of hegemonic power that is especially active and key. In his own work Said concentrates almost solely on the activity by which the fundamental group (for Said, the European–occidental population) secures a cultural predominance of certain images and ideas through which it foists the principle of its own superior identity onto a larger population. As both the privilege and the condition of that superior identity, this fundamental group, through its professional intellectuals, takes charge of creating the major aesthetic–veridical discourses on the characteristics and relations of the social and geographical world. Said focuses on the power of representation as it is wielded primarily by "high culture" philosophers, historians, painters, novelists, and so on, but his analysis of how that power works pertains to representation in its crassest as well as its most elevated forms. The target of discursive power according to him is a population whose subordinate identity is being textually etched out as a counter to and foil for the fundamental group.

The resulting relation of subordinate to superior identity, importantly, is not in any way analogous to the relation of a subject population to a king. The power that is wielded discursively, first of all, falls not directly over the target population but rather over the cultural universe of identifications, meanings, stipulations of truth. It is the power of rule in the sense not of law ("This is forbidden, this is required") but of measure or norm ("This is what being Oriental means, this is the true Oriental, this is the aberration, this is what the Oriental nature cannot be or do".) Second, the power that is wielded by the fundamental group through the proxy of its professional intellectuals is not an independent, external power of mastery over the hegemonic discourse, but a power that that discourse fabricates and constantly renews: the self-identity of the fundamental group as distinct from the target population in such and such a way is produced by the same discourse that that group, through its intellectuals, spins out. In the main, discursive power is infinitely grander, longer-lived, and more imperious than any of the individuals who actively generate or passively are benefited by its terms. That power rules them, in crucial ways, rather than the other way around.

For this reason, "fundamental group" turns out to be a much happier phrase than "ruling class" for Gramsci to have used in denoting that part of a population that culturally has imposed itself on the rest. After all, when Said tells us that "saturating hegemonic systems" are as effective as they are because "their internal constraints upon writers and thinkers . . . [are] productive, not unilaterally inhibiting,"[10] he obviously means his point to apply not to the target population (in this case, those whom the discourse marks out as "the Orientals") but to the wielders of discursive power: the human authors of the discourse who are paradoxically, by the same token, authored or enabled by it in quite specific ways. They are, that is, educated by its other thinkers and writers, provided a starting place by its presumptions, stimulated by its images, pressed down the avenues of reflection it has carved out, enticed to solve the perplexities it has created – their imagination determined as much by the doors swinging open one after another before them as by the doors shut and locked along the way. Said is very adamant on this score: it is the professional intellectuals and, by extension, the fundamental social group to which they are attached who are the first casualties of hegemonic power as representation, although they will not, of course, be the worst. The whole question of spontaneous consent in its relation to hegemony is thus revealed to be newly complicated here. What turns out to be an essential characteristic of cultural hegemony is not only the free consent of a subordinate population to the given cultural order (or, to put it more bleakly, the coercion of its habits of conceptualization, reflection, and imagination), but the more active consent of a fundamental group's intellectuals to the terms of a discourse more fundamental – in the sense of being prior to and more powerful than – themselves.

For reasons to do with his particular subject-matter, Said chooses to fix on cultural production as "high" intellectuals engage in it. He illuminates high culture, of course, in a very different light from the way it illuminates itself. He shows it to be yes, sophisticated, vivid and complex, but also throughly invested by power, whereas it shows itself to be thoroughly disinterested and propelled only by the search for beauty and truth. Williams, on his part, treats the abstract question of culture and power much more broadly, making mention of "high" and "mass" cultural institutions, traditions and formations – the sheer structural variety of them being one source of cultural tension and contradiction. By studying all of these, Williams would hope to chart the habituation of a whole populace to patterns of classification, valuation, and conduct that add up to a particular hegemonic form of life. We will see later on, however, that Williams is hyper-alert to the ways in which established patterns are interrupted, evaded and undermined. Williams' treatment of hegemonic culture is almost anthropological in scope. He means to include within its purview the entire project by which humans shape and define their lives: not only political and economic activity, not only articulated meanings and ideas, but "the whole substance of lived identities and relationships."[11] Anthropological in scope, but political in purpose, as the "whole lived social process" is to be looked at as it is organized by dominant meanings and values, permeated by "specific distributions of power and influence,"[12] and "saturated" by "relations of domination and subordination."[13]

Gramsci's description of the hegemonic relationship as an educative one and the endpoint of that education as the spontaneous consent of a subordinate group, Williams restates this way: that the true condition of hegemony is the positive self-identification of a population with hegemonic forms, or at least a complete resignation to those forms as being necessary and natural. Thus what are in fact the "pressures and limits of what can ultimately be seen as a specific economic, political and cultural system" seem to be the "pressures and limits of simple experience and common sense."[14] The entirety of lived life over which power extends Williams describes in terms thoroughly collective and deeply political – terms that in other ways, however, echo Hampshire's account of the "whole person" as comprising sensibility, thought, and action. It includes "a whole body of practices and expectations, over the whole of living: our senses and assignments of energy, our shaping perceptions of ourselves and our world. It is a lived system of meanings and values – constitutive and constituting – which as they are experienced as practices appear as reciprocally confirming. It thus constitutes a sense of reality for most people in the society, a sense of absolute because experienced reality beyond which it is very difficult for most members of the society to move, in most areas of their lives."[15]

2.

Our theorists' first departure from traditional political theory, in sum, has been their locating of power largely outside the boundaries of the juridical state. But they make two other breaks as well which already have begun to become evident for us. One concerns the operations of dominative power. Williams, Said, and Foucault will move away from the notion that power is exercised from top to bottom, by a ruler or ruling class as master over a subjugated group. The other break concerns the function of power, which political theory, according to our theorists, characteristically has represented as that of denial, prohibition, suppression. In Gramsci's straightforward way of putting things, power is positive and educative as well as negative and repressive. For Williams, power is permissive, constitutive, exerting pressure as well as imposing limits. Said declares that power is productive as well as inhibiting. Foucault, finally, states that power does not merely censor, block, exclude, but produces desire, knowledge, truth. Foucault's attack on traditional theory's conception both of how and what power does is eloquent and concise enough to be worth our brief review, before we go on to see what conception our authors will put in its place.

With a particular interest in power as it is exerted over sex, Foucault asks in *The History of Sexuality*, vol. 1 how power in general has tended to be understood. He declares that it is represented always as moving downward from a "unique source of sovereignty" onto a passive, obedient subject, and outwards from a massive center to local, "capillary" points, achieving omnipresence through "consolidating everything under its invincible unity."[16] The purest case of such power is to be found in the relation between legislating monarch and those submitting to his law. Foucault claims, indeed, that the whole top-down, center–capillary conception of power has descended to us from the monarchical age and is altogether inappropriate to the conditions of modernity. We should note that he makes his argument against the monarchical code of power not on the grounds that contemporary power is located fundamentally in society rather than in the radiations of a juridical state. Foucault would be sympathetic enough with the point, but it does not, for him, hit quite home. This is because the idea of power as something wielded by a sovereign is perfectly able to migrate from political to civil society and seems almost harder than the concentration of attention on the political state for modern theorists of power to give up. Thus, for example, the analysis not of hegemony *per se* but of its working through the machinations of a unified, dominant class is but a transfiguration of the "power of the king," in which "hegemonic power" is wielded by a collective rather than a single individual, having its seat in the civil as well as the political sphere.

The classic idea that the "conditions of possibility" for power are found in the "primary existence of a central point"[17] is, according to Foucault, closely connected to although not identical with the idea that power has only "the force of the negative on its side."[18] Power traditionally is said to assert its prerogatives by imposing on society a binary system of the licit and illicit, the permitted and forbidden. Such power acts by saying "No" – by demanding the renunciation of desire and will. It censors, suppresses, and denies that which seeks to have its own active existence. Thus it is "basically anti-energy . . . incapable of doing anything, except to render what it dominates incapable of doing anything either, except what this power allows it to do."[19] This traditional notion of what power does, in combination with the notion of how it does it, makes for a "strangely restrictive" mechanics of power that is "poor in resources, sparing of its methods, monotonous in the tactics it utilizes, incapable of invention, and seemingly doomed always to repeat itself."[20]

How is such an inadequate mechanics of power to be replaced? Let us take up the question of the operation of dominative power first. Williams provides us with one aspect of the answer, through presenting "hegemonic power" in a way that does not force it down a channel from "ruler" to "ruled." He notes that the idea of a ruling class is based on "much earlier and simpler historical phases,"[21] while hegemonic forms of dominance and subordination capture the normal life of organization and control in developed societies. What Williams means by "hegemonic forms" are thought and practices that reproduce the dominance in society of a particular class and the dominance in culture of that class's particular ethos, without being purposefully designed by that class and inflicted by it on its powerless subordinates. Hegemonic power does not exert itself from a central point downwards through suppressing a subject population's antithetical desire and will, but diffusely, from a mass of particular points throughout the entire population, through a "lived system of meanings and values . . . which as they are experienced as practices appear as reciprocally confirming."[22] Hegemonic power is identical with the established limits of everyday experience and common sense. It is precisely because of "the depth and thoroughness at which any cultural hegemony is lived"[23] that the idea of a ruling class in and over society is off the mark: that depth and thoroughness is lived, after all, on everyone's part. Thus the dominant social class is not the given order's master but its creature at least as much as the subordinate class is; while the subordinate class is no less likely than the dominant to be desirous, willful and committed in bolstering the given order. This is not to say that the particular hegemonic activities in which the subordinate class engages will not be different from those of the dominant group, or that bolstering the hegemonic order is all it is able to do. It is only that passivity and impotence will be no more than activity and energy its characteristic way of living on the entrenched side of things.

For reasons to do with his focus on power as representation, Said, for his part, refuses to say how the subordinate group *actually* lives life at all. But, as we have seen, he pushes the point of the dominant group's captivity by hegemonic ideas and practices very, very far. At least the professional intellectuals aligned with that group are thoroughly and deeply authored by the discourses they maintain and extend. Power's operations as Said shows them here are convoluted rather than direct. The power of representation, for a start, is wielded not by the fundamental social group as a unified center, but by intellectuals associated with that group in ways that are bound to be circuitous and, in some cases, attenuated. Then, too, the production and reproduction of hegemonic images and ideas operate much more as a massive discursive power bearing over these intellectuals than as a power they enjoy in an originative and independent way.

It is Foucault who most strenuously is out to supplant the top-down, center–capillary account of how power works. This is not only through his according professional intellectuals even less real agency in their discursive activity than does Said,[24] who still acknowledges against Foucault, to whom he is otherwise quite openly indebted, "the determining imprint of individual writers upon the otherwise anonymous collective body of texts constituting a discursive formation."[25] Foucault goes so far in denying the capacity for agency in everyone that if one were to go all the way with him, any talk, not of dominative power but of dominating social groups would be extremely hard to sustain.

Luckily we are not obliged to follow Foucault this far in order to take from him a few good tips concerning power's operations. The first is exactly the tip Said already has offered to us, having taken it himself from Foucault:[26] that impersonal forces of control must be separated analytically from human aims and objectives and given priority in any account of great systems of power in modern life. Entrenched discourses and the institutions that arise to support them are prototypical here. More prototypical still, at least for us, is the overall coherence to which the multiplicity of "local" thoughts, actions, discourses, and institutions may add up: a coherence that, having congealed out of all the local situations, turns back to impose its own pressures and limits on them. Such impositions are like the consequences of a logic, rather than devices which some ruling subject has dreamed up – a logic tightly worked out although no one has designed it, and effective although no one brandishes it over anyone's head. All of this is not to say that human intentionality is entirely irrelevant to power in modern life. It is present at the molecular level – everyone acts with aims and objectives, after all. But given the pressure of impersonal forces on that level, intentionality will not be all-determinant there, and it is absent entirely at the level of the system as a whole. There is no large, directing intelligence behind that system orchestrating its general features and local events.

If the first note we can take from Foucault here is that of the non-subjectivity of modern power, the second is that of power's local rather than central origins and instigations. Power is exercised from "innumerable points";[27] it originates in the molecular situation and, through the multiplication of all the different effects of those situations, works its way up to the collective level. Major systems of domination, political rule, large-scale social cleavages – all will be the "terminal forms that power takes."[28] While the "hegemonic effects" sustained by local relations are weighty, relatively rigid, overbearingly "inert," the local relations themselves will be "unbalanced, heterogeneous, unstable and tense."[29] There is, in other words, a vitality to power at the molecular level and a fixity to it at the grand one, so that approaching it theoretically from the bottom is the surer way not to miss its variations, reversals, and diversions. And when it comes to the local detail, one must be ready, if not quite for anything, at least for many unpredictable and surprising things. Whatever the great situation, this particular one, being particular, might bend in all sorts of ways – towards some new and intensified form of the power prevailing on the grand scale, or towards some humbled version of it, or towards its deterioration, or towards its inversion. Exactly how the local situation bends is the interesting question for what it illuminates not merely about life on the molecular level but about life on the grand scale. Molecular details that begin to diverge in increasing numbers from the massive fact eventually will add up to a different massive fact, after all.

To make one's first approach to "power" in the form of the collective fact, on the contrary, is to be set in the direction afterwards of facing the molecular detail as its more or less perfect manifestation – to look at the world as if it were made of the grand fact replicated by miniature facsimiles of itself (except for the "insignificant aberration") at every particular point. And as that grand fact has to do with some major dominating force, one will almost as surely be tempted to read it as literally bearing down in that force on the particular detail, which becomes then not only the manifestation but the causally determined product of power in its systemic form. If there is a danger that approaching power "from the bottom up" allows us to avoid, then, it is the danger of reifying "hegemony" and "domination" – of freezing the statement of them into tyrannically determining truths. It allows us to avoid this by presenting power relations not as "static forms of distribution" but as "matrices of transformation," characterized by "constant modifications, continual shifts."[30] But one can only push the point so far. "Transformations, modifications and shifts" either must refer back to some specifiable and *relatively* fixed system of social power as a whole, into which they are to be counted as inroads (its total collapse being the end of *them*); or they must signify pure flux, the endless play of power without any substantively limited shape and point to it. In this second case, power itself becomes the grand fact: a sort of Absolute Spirit pervading every and any particular detail, as if abstract particularity were its base condition and not particularity in certain of its socially and historically specific aspects. Foucault's intentions are, I think, ambiguous here. When he declares that power is omnipresent because it "is produced from one moment to the next, at every point, or rather in every relation from one point to another" – because power "comes from everywhere" – is it the vitality and integrity of the local situation he means to affirm, or the status of power as an all-pervasive, ontological truth?[31]

Well, *we* at least must make sure to combine an appreciation of modern hegemony as crystallizing out of a multiplicity of molecular situations with two other points. One is the point that the power originating locally is indebted to social, historical life, not to life as sheer being. The other is the point that the relatively inert, grand fact of social hegemony is not undone by its having crystallized out of a multiplicity of mobile little ones. One must be equally alert, therefore, to hegemonic impositions and local instigations and variations.

Foucault's next note on power's operations is less sympathetic for our other theorists than his rejection of power as sovereignty and his insistence on the importance of local relations. Gramsci does not hold to it at all, Williams only hints at it vaguely, and Said embraces it without providing it with any explicit theoretical support. This is the principle of the fragmentation of power, which requires that the concept of hegemony be opened up, not, this time, vertically to make room for the local situation as well as the grand fact, but horizontally to make room for the multiple axes on which power in society inevitably turns. A single mode of life, that is, can be organized hegemonically in a variety of ways at once, each way becoming salient and clear when that mode of life is looked at through one of its several different key classificatory schemes.

Much more than the mere multiplication of axes of power is indicated here. The principle of power's fragmentation leaves us no reason to suppose that all of those axes are reducible to one, or that one is the cause of the others or the logically primary axis at a particular historical point or the original model after which the others have fashioned themselves. There is no reason to suppose, in short, a single center to the life of social power – not, this time, because there is "no king," but because (if we may misbehave for a moment and continue to use an antiquated and inappropriate metaphor) there is, in the same geographical territory, more than one king and more than one kingdom. In its most radical interpretation, the principle denies not only any reductive connection, but any necessary logical or historical connection at all between such different organizations of power. In such a radical interpretation, the search for capitalism's real relation to patriarchy (and "patriarchy," unlike "capitalism," is a king-term, that evokes exactly the wrong way in which modern power operates) might just as well be dropped as continued. There would be no particular reason to expect to find any coherent relation of either active correspondence or meaningful contradiction between the two, as opposed to the merely accidental ways in which they may work with or against each other.

Foucault's final point about the operation of power is this: that whether it exerts itself molecularly or on the grand scale, and whether, if on the grand scale, it takes the form of sovereign rule or hegemonic pressures and limits, it will have, in addition to any large-scale consequences, "capillary" effects. Power passes through "fine channels" and should be attended to analytically there, at its "extremities," its "ultimate destinations":[32] not only in its regional and local forms, but right down to the point at which it "reaches into the very grain of individuals, touches their bodies and inserts itself into their actions and attitudes, their discourses, learning processes and everyday lives."[33] If an example of power's great effects is the co-ordinated movement of an army across a geographical terrain, an example of its capillary ones are the reflexes of the individual soldier as they have been induced through the disciplining of his body. Indeed, the human body in all of its actually or potentially differentiated forms is power's most palpable fine target.

3.

Before we can say anything more about power and the body, we must examine the third break that Gramsci, Williams, Said, and Foucault make with traditional political theory. Besides shifting their sights away from power in the juridical state, and besides rejecting a simple "top-down" notion of power's operations, they all declare that power's function is not merely prohibitive and repressive but productive, positive, educative. But what precisely does power produce? We have been given already some general answers: a whole type of civilization, a moral–political ethos and direction to social life; the limits of common sense and everyday practice; the object of discourse. Now I want to describe power's productivity via three more highly specified notions: Williams' idea of a selective tradition; Said's account of the representation of Self and Other; Foucault's declaration that power produces truth, and modern power, truth as the norm.

A hegemonic culture, according to Williams, asserts itself in the form of an entrenched and bounded mode of life beyond which it is difficult for most people to move, but even so it is never uniform or static. It is made of a vital and often contradictory "complex of experiences"; it generates, in the changing circumstances that typify all life, "changing pressures and limits"; it has "continually to be renewed, recreated, defended, and modified."[34] This renewal has to do most obviously with the present's reaching forward into the future but also, paradoxically, with its moving backward into the past. That past is made of meanings, actions, and events far more eclectic and various than any hegemonic culture would be eager to tolerate were the past to become present, or, and this is the real worry, were it to become actively a source of inspiration for the future. Thus for its own protection, such a culture is impelled to create out of its variegated history a much narrower but also differently varying "significant" past, by selecting only certain meanings and events for emphasis and celebration; isolating others for the purposes of revilement and stigmatization; neglecting or excluding others; and diluting or converting the rest into non-threatening forms.[35] This renovation of the past for the sake of connecting it with and affirming relations of power in the present has no end to it – that present always is turning into more past, after all. The continual working through of its own once-lived life then makes the hegemonic culture powerful but vulnerable too, through the exertion it takes to attend to a past that is never complete, and through the real record of that past's being always "effectively recoverable."[36]

That there is a "real record" to be recovered means that a selective tradition operates not only positively but negatively, suppressing the memory of active tendencies of thought and practice that are antipathetic to itself. In this sense at least, Williams' account of cultural power *vis à vis* a society's own history moves in a more classic way than Said's account of cultural power *vis à vis* an alien society. The hegemonic power of Western culture exerts itself over the "strange world" of the East, Said declares, by generating first of all a whole series of representations of it including, very crucially, the representations of that world as incompetent to represent itself, and of the West as intellectually and morally equipped to know and reveal its truth. While these two formal or procedural claims can be called quite unabashedly "lies and deceptions," the same terms cannot be used for the West's substantive descriptions of the East. Substantive truth, with respect to the kinds of entities into which the world is divided and their defining qualities and relations, is always, for Said, an internal function of representation. There is nothing "truly true" outside of some system of representation or another, and so no "truth of the East" to show up Western discourse as definitively false. By the same token, Western discourse does not operate by means of suppression, distortion, and concealment, but at least originally through production alone.

As to what such power produces – the discourse of Orientalism with which Said is concerned creates, through the splitting off of specific qualities, propensities and desires from an abstract idea of the human subject, a delimited and concretely elaborated idea of the Western Subject on the one side and on the other, the figure of the East, in which the split-off qualities have been invested. This discursively created "double" of the Western Self (Said calls the Orient "almost a European invention," one of Europe's "deepest and most recurrent images of the Other,"[37] its "surrogate and even underground self"[38]) which is conjured into being by exactly the same process through which the Western Self comes to study, know, and artistically render it, is represented by the West (more exactly, by "a very large mass of writers, among whom are poets, novelists, philosophers, political theorists, economists, and" – last of all – "imperial administrators"[39] as having an entirely separate and independent existence. Through its control over the discourse of Orientalism, the West is in the strategic position here, assuming the place of the sovereign Self inside the Occident–Orient relation it portrays. It is not, however, absolute master of the discourse, as it owes and does not know that it owes its sense of itself to its own discursive fabrications.

What is originally telling about Orientalism is not its correspondence to some real Oriental and Occident world, but its internal coherence as a system of ideas, the imaginativeness of those ideas (about the "sensuous," "cruel," "despotic," "languorous," and "feminine" Orient), and the presumption of its writers to have privileged insight into the Orient through their Occidental status, which putatively embues them with an impartial, high-minded, rational and mature intelligence. Thus it was, Said tells us, out of the "unchallenged centrality" of a "sovereign Western consciousness" that an "Oriental world emerged," over which Western power was wielded in and through representation.[40] This representational power in the imaginative field was connected to but not at all a mere function of economic and political power in the practical field. Through that connection, the Western power of representing the East – a power exerted first of all over the *Western* imagination – expanded to include the negative methods of political coercion and the positive methods of cultural domination over an actual "Eastern" population. Orientalism's significance, then, lay in its being at once a coherent, imaginative, durable body of ideas with presumptions to veridicality, and a "sign of Euro-Atlantic power over the Orient."[41]

In sum, what power in this case produced positively was an entire imaginative field, including inside it the figures of the European Self and Oriental Other; a geographical map marking out the familiar and strange territories inhabited by these two figures; a knowledge of the truth of the Other and the Strange; and the verbal and visual texts in which such knowledge was preserved. Power produced, secondly, a host of institutions with cultural authority, in the West, over the subject of "the Orient" – universities, research organizations, libraries, journals, museums and the like. Generating a compelling vision of the Orient by such efforts along with a vision of the Occidental mission, power produced thirdly a political interest in and ethos of imperial domination of Occident over Orient. Thus cultural forces along with "brute political, economic and military rationales" fueled the practical organization of the political, economic, military, and cultural rule over "the East."[42]

On the notion that power produces identity, truth, and desire – the identity of the individual object (for example, East and West), the truth of the object (for example, Oriental despotism, cruelty, and splendor), and the practical desires generated in a world of objects like those (for example, the impulse towards political domination) – no one is more insistent than Foucault. For him there is neither transcendental nor historically immanent truth, but only socially specific regimes of truth made up of particular rules of true identity and difference, criteria of evidence of truth, the discourses accepted as true, and the power effects that attach themselves to the true in a host of different ways.[43] Power and truth are primordially and inextricably bound together, first of all, in that the very stipulation of "domains of objects and rituals of truth"[44] is the act by which power makes, in the classificatory sense of the term "make," the world.

They are bound together, second of all, in that for there to be potency in any act inside this world, the object's stipulated truth must be known in advance of the act, and the object must be able to be forced, through the operations of power, to "speak" it.

One way in which truth is stipulated and elicited by power that once was pre-eminent but no longer is so, and is salutory for no longer being so, is the way characteristic of sovereign rule. In the opening section of *Discipline and Punish*, Foucault provides us with its illustration in the torturing of a subject who transgresses the law of the king. Two truths are elicited by torture out of the body of the transgressing subject. First there is the truth of the crime, which the tortured body "confesses" in a secret trial to royal interrogators, and "admits" and portrays (by means of particular tortures that mimic his crime) in a public spectacle, where torture becomes no longer the means of extracting proof of the crime but the means of executing its punishment. Second, there is the truth of the majesty and omnipresence of sovereign power, which the tortured body proclaims in the same spectacle to the population at large.

In modern times, to the contrary, power most characteristically works through "normalization" rather than through sovereign rule. The body of the individual is forced by power to speak the truth, not of crime and the law but of deviation and the norm. The forcing is done not primarily through state coercion but through the collusion of scientific knowledges, "normalizing institutions" (the army, prison, school, psychiatric clinic, family), and, we would add, the typifications produced and disseminated by the massive centers of public culture. The truth of the deviation is elicited from the individual by a variety of scientific experts and is "treated" in a variety of institutions that also operate to insure normalcy and prevent deviation before it occurs. The truth of the norm is publicized to the population at large through advertisements, bowdlerized scientific reports, social survey results, "popular" films, magazines, and self-help books. Finally, normalizing power is individualized not in its source, where there is characteristically impersonality and anonymity or at least individuals whose identities are of no historic importance.[45] It is individualized rather in the most recalcitrant and, to add to Foucault, the most obedient targets of power's effects: in the deviants from and the ideal specimens of the norm. These deviants and specimens, whose relation to the norm is, most importantly, one not of mere intellectual agreement or disagreement but of bodily correspondence or divergence, are given a sort of minor immortality in the case study, the medical record, the biography, the published diaries, and the "docu-drama."

With this account of the truth function of both sovereign and normalizing power, we meet up once again with Foucault's description of the body as power's finest target. In insisting that the body is "in the grip of very strict powers,"[46] Foucault stands out from all our other theorists, whose interests in the body are at best indirect. He also, at least at first glance, contributes to a general "anti-metaphysics" when he claims that everything above and beyond the brute, raw body that appears to be either some natural expression or extension of it, or, on the contrary, some feature of a personality, soul or self housed in but otherwise independent of it, is in actuality a marking on the body made by power relations in a "political field."[47] We need not be as theoretically stingy as Foucault is when he claims that "it is largely as a force of production that the body is invested with relations of power and domination";[48] or as severe as he is in stressing the body's utter subjection to power; or for that matter as secretly metaphysical as he is in making power into an abstract subject which ubiquitously and indiscriminantly pervades every particular instance in human life. We still can preserve what for us will be a crucial point: that the body at least in part is an artifact of specific configurations of power in its physical development, shape, bulk, ornamentation, pleasures, antipathies, self-denials, capacities, and weaknesses.

We also can appreciate Foucault's distinction between sovereign and normalizing power, as well as his counter-intuitive but quite apt declaration that modern normalizing power has a much broader target than had the old sovereign law. (The Law, it should be noted, has not disappeared in modern times but has moved over, along with the Text or Tradition, to make room for the authority of the Norm.[49]) The "normalizing judgement" directs itself towards "a mass of behavior that the relative indifference of the great systems of [monarchical] punishment had allowed to escape" – that is, towards that which "does not measure up to the rule, that departs from it. . .[t]he whole indefinite domain of the non-conforming. . ."[50] To the "universal reign of the normative," each individual submits "his body, his gestures, his behaviour, his aptitudes, his achievements."[51] "He" does this, we might add, whether he belongs to a socially dominant or subordinate group.

What distinguishes the modern from the traditional reign of the conventionally required and proscribed? Traditional convention, after all, is probably nowhere more exacting than in the small-scale, face-to-face community at the opposite pole from the anonymous power that Foucault describes. Well, the two may not be as utterly unlike as Foucault would have us believe. But one unique characteristic of the modern norm is that it asserts itself as an empirical truth revealed through the observation of behavior, the interpretation of talk, the statistical analysis of social tendencies – not as a moral truth revealed by the sheer length of time in which the norm has held good, or through the intuitive or speculative knowledge of essences, or through some divine, monarchical, or patriarchal pronouncement. Another unique characteristic is that the modern norm is imposed through its being impersonally and methodically worked up in the object, not commanded to the object by a tangible and familiar authority whose dictations may be haphazard, arbitrary, or capricious. Finally, the modern norm is enforced by multiple and usually large-scale institutions, which together, and as a result of technical advances in record-keeping, communications, and transportation, can "cover" massive populations with great breadth, consistency, and attention to detail.

But our own concern is with something more specific than, and rather different from, the body *per se* as it is subjected to normalizing judgment, scientific discipline, and institutional control. What does Foucault have to say about the sexed body in the modern age as it is a fine target for power – or at least, what does he open the way to saying that we must go on to say for ourselves? The argument of Foucault's that will be of most use to us is that out of the inchoate interplay of sensations and pleasures on the body, discursive power creates the object "sexuality," which it specifies according to a battery of distinctions between normal and pathological desire. Modern power over the body as a field of and for pleasurable sensation operates by bringing "sexuality" medically, psychiatrically, pedagogically, economically into being; representing it as "'by nature' a domain susceptible to pathological processes"[52]; inciting it to speak about itself (in, for example, the therapeutic session, the court trial, the public interview); observing and classifying, analysing, treating, and curing it; selling it, for the gratification of its "normal" and "perverted" tastes, licit and illicit delights; also, we would add, simultaneously stimulating and regimenting it through incessant depictions of it on the cultural screen.

Foucault is explicit and clear. Modern power creates and incites sexuality, and it has a far greater capacity for self-aggrandizement through doing so than it would have if it merely prohibited and repressed a sexuality initially independent of it. Yet he falls strangely silent just when the reader expects him to identify the central and mammoth organizing principle by which the sexed body is made positively into *this* sort of body, with *this* sexuality, distinguished into *this* normal form and *these* deviations, eager after *these* kinds of pleasures, and warranting *these* satisfactions. Was it some residual attachment to a natural order of classification, some secret interest in preserving the entrenched regime of truth, or merely a distaste for stating the obvious fact, that stopped him from declaring that the inchoately and diffusely desirous body is formed into one of two highly delineated sexual types through the imposition of the norm of "masculine" or "feminine" upon it? Surely "masculine–feminine" is the most fundamental truth that the sexed body is forced to tell, as if its raw physiology gave rise in the most exact, detailed, and far-reaching way to particular propensities, enjoyments, dislikes, gestures, even to "normal" pathologies, with sadism's being the normal masculine pathology and masochism the normal feminine. It is above all on the creation, incitement, and refinement of these stipulated truths that power over the sexed body expands itself and thrives.

If Foucault's first telling but incomplete point about the sexed body has to do with the discursive creation of its "truth," his second has to do with the shift in power's primary ground in the general field of sexual relations, from kinship ties to bodily pleasure. Foucault argues that the pre-eminence of the "deployment of alliance," in which power in sexual relations works off a system of marriage, family structure, the "transmission of names and possessions," gives way in the modern age to the pre-eminence of the "deployment of sexuality," in which power enlarges itself on the basis of bodily sensation, the "quality of pleasures," the enjoyments of the flesh.[53] Whatever vitality remains to the modern deployment of alliance is given to it through its being a field for the deployment of sexuality: the family becomes a major theater of sexualization, where the psychoanalytic, sociological, legal, cinematic, and literary eye can peer in on the heterosexual couple and its sexual initiations, difficulties and peccadillos; on the Oedipal passions of the child; and on the pre-, extra-, and post-marital course of desire.

But the deployment of sexuality spreads itself out over a much wider terrain than this. It does so, if we can be plain where Foucault is cryptic (and plain in ways perhaps not altogether faithful to him), on the heels of three related historical developments. The first is the deployment of alliance's loss of economic force, through production's being reorganized outside the domestic sphere and on a far more colossal scale than any kinship network could cover. The second is the deployment of alliance's loss of moral-prohibitive force, through the decay of its internal structure of authority and the release of eventually all its members from the restrictive household and kinship network out into the great public spaces opened up by the industrial age.[54] The domestic spaces to which people return, by the same token, become more and more individualized, less and less the residual locus of hierarchical authority. The third and most recent development is prompted by a productive process that, at some turning point, no longer seeks to press the desire of the working population in cramped, reproductively regimented directions in order to assure for itself a maximum number of labor hours and laborers. It no longer simply calls for, *à la* Foucault, the drawing out and strict management of bourgeois sexual desire for the sake of safeguarding that class's biological well-being. Instead, a process of infinite production demands and tries to work up increasingly on everyone's part[55] a desire for pleasure expanded infinitely in the quantitative sense but qualitatively harnessed to the cause of consumption – a desire provoked and satisfied in public no less than in domestic quarters.[56] The body and its pleasures become a fine target for power, in sum, to the extent that, on the one hand, toil and moral–familial discipline no longer are the great haunting facts of social existence; and, on the other, a capitalist productive process comes to depend on an endless arousal, satiation, and new arousal of desire that takes place, promiscuously, everywhere. What recedes as a target for power at the same time – recedes but does not at all disappear – is the body as it engages in the twin labors of species reproduction, organized inside a hierarchical familial order, and material production, organized first inside that order, later out.

Two moves in Foucault's own explicit argument should be distinguished here. One is the logical separating out of the body as it is engaged in species reproduction and familial alliance, from the body as it is a field of sensation and desire. The other is the claim of a chronological shift from the reproductive–familial body to the desirous body as a primary ground for power.[57] Through the first move, Foucault disentangles two kinds of dramas that are almost always mistaken for one, partly because of the way in which the body – to some extent, the very same parts of the body – figure centrally in each, and partly because of the way in which the desirous body traditionally has been yoked to the cause of alliance. Through the second move, Foucault opens up the possibility of conceiving that different operating principles of power may prevail in the general field of sexual relations at different times, even while the sexes continue to occupy the same relative positions of dominance and subordination.

To take complete advantage of this disentanglement and opening, however, we will have to go further than Foucault does. For after attributing largely to economic causes the shift from the deployment of alliance to the deployment of sexuality, Foucault stops short once again, leaving us to discover the key to the configuration of power looming up at either end. Given that the general field in which the shift occurs is one of sexual relations, we can expect *this* key to be sexual, not economic. And indeed, don't we find at the center of the deployment of alliance, power's concentration in the patriarchal father? Don't we find at the center of the deployment of sexuality, power's different concentration in the phallic desirous self? It is exactly the patriarchal and phallic figures who must become clear as two figures for us, if we want, against Foucault in his reticence, to bring the deployments of power into their fullest relief; and if we want, against feminist tendencies towards simplification, to admit a certain nimbleness and variety to power in the field of sexual relations.

You will remember that Foucault points the way to saying, but refuses to say, that normalizing power works off the body and its pleasures to create an object "sexuality" differentiated into "masculine" and "feminine" types, representing them as if they emanated out of the body itself. Now, analogously, Foucault points the way to saying, but refuses to say, that while power in the deployment of alliance is concentrated in the male as he occupies a specific place in the family structure, power in the deployment of sexuality is concentrated in the male as he enjoys a masculine eroticism. Now, masculine desire has been represented already by normalizing power as a direct emanation out of the body. Mastery inside the deployment of sexuality thus will be represented as a bodily emanation as well.

Thus the modern regime of truth of Masculine/feminine becomes pre-eminently a drama not of lineal connection, inheritance rights, and familial authority and obligation, but of sexual personality, prowess, and impulse. Its characters are marked out not on the structural basis (one step removed from the body although, of course, partly a function of bodily difference) of family position, with sovereignty invested in a patriarch ruling over wife, sons, daughters, servants and other underlings; but on the literal basis of raw physiology, with mastery invested in the masculine self as a function of his genital arrangement. Patriarchal sovereignty had asserted itself through the imposition of a moral-prohibitive law that negatively constrained the independent desire and will of all family members. Phallic mastery, on the contrary, asserts itself through the imperious demands for the positive satisfaction of masculine desire, the right to the satisfaction of desire in every possible sense traceable back to a right to the satisfaction of desire in its narrow sexual sense. As for the female body – the regime of truth of Masculine/feminine sees nothing positively present on it to warrant the registration of *its* existence as an equivalently desirous self. The female body is noted terminologically merely as an absence or lack: as the body "without a phallus." It is declared through that deficiency to be incapable of exerting active or independent force. The "reign of the Norm" of Masculine/feminine thus becomes a double reign over the female body. If it imposes on each of the two kinds of bodies a particular norm and characteristic deviations, it imposes on all bodies the rule that masculinity is the norm of active desire and femininity is active desire's deviation.

These "true meanings of the body" initially are attached to it in the family. In performing this crucial service for the deployment of sexuality, what is left of the deployment of alliance still functions vigorously enough. The meaning of the body is reiterated didactically in the church and school. Rebellious bodies may be punished by coercive-legal methods but more frequently are treated medically and therapeutically. The distinction between obedient and dissident bodies is made use of and thus affirmed economically: on its basis is spawned a whole industry for the production and sale of licit and illicit services and paraphernalia. But it is most fundamentally through the cultural production and dissemination of ideas and images that the regime of truth of Masculine/feminine is held up. Notwithstanding the unconscious constitution of gender identity and scientific–therapeutic interventions in the cases where that constitution has "gone wrong," it is the imaginative–conceptual–figurative dimension of modern culture (including, of course, psychoanalysis and medical science in their imaginative–conceptual–figurative capacities) that elaborates that truth in its logically primary form. It is what Gramsci would call moral–intellectual activity that, in its constant churning out of vivid and popularly compelling portraits of masculine and feminine types, wins the spontaneous consent of individuals to them. It weds those individuals to a system of classification; habituates them to the established direction of socio-cultural life; confines them inside the limits of common sense and everyday practice; upholds the position and ethos of the fundamental socio-sexual group; insures masculinity as the norm for one kind of body and femininity as the norm for the other, and phallic presence and absence as, respectively, the Norm and Deviation for the desirous body *per se* – maintains, in sum, Masculine/feminine as a cultural–political regime of mutually confirming ideas and practices.

3

Criticism and Resistance

We have been dwelling on what Hampshire would call the weight of an established mode of life, and what Gramsci, Williams, Said, and Foucault would call the impositions of dominative power. Inevitably, perhaps, given our subject-matter, we have conjured up the idea of something all-embracing, totalistic, and triumphant. But in fact, of our five theorists only Foucault paints a picture of power that is as bleak as this, and he is not thoroughly bleak every step of the way. As for the rest, if they have cultivated a "pessimism of the intellect," to use Gramsci's famous phrase, they have done so for realism's, not fatalism's, sake. Even Foucault, in an extremely ambiguous and limited way (being, as he is, so very nearly a fatalist); Said, cautiously but emphatically; and Hampshire, Gramsci, and Williams most energetically of all, are determined to find and theoretically mark out the grounds of criticism and resistance.

Certain of those grounds that our theorists identify are so fundamental as to be almost synonymous with the conditions of thought and action *per se*. These underpin the purposeful challenge to and strike against an established order but also underpin the idea and movement that go spontaneously and unintentionally against the grain. The first such condition is one Hampshire discusses in great detail: that no particular mode of life can subsume within itself every abstract possibility of thought and action. What makes it particular is precisely that it closes off a near infinity of possibilities for conceptualization, valuation, and practice. That closure is necessary if there is to be any coherent, comprehensible social life at all, but the particular possibilities foreclosed are contingent, being the vastly larger flip side of the possibilities specified and permitted. By the same token that a mode of life rules out these possibilities for thought and action, however, it also points silently to them. In a world "always open to conceptual rearrangement,"[1] the very limits of any given arrangement provide the boundary beyond which thought and action can venture out.

Williams and Said make an argument almost analogous to Hampshire's own when they claim that every dominant culture by definition is selective and exclusive, not all-inclusive. "[N]o dominant culture ever in reality includes or exhausts all human practice, human energy, and human intention," Williams declares,[2] and Said echoes him: "In human history there is always something beyond the reach of dominating systems, no matter how deeply they saturate society."[3] There are always experiences to which "fixed forms" do not speak, aspects of actual consciousness diverging from "official consciousness."[4] The existence of experience not entirely vanquished by dominating systems is how we know they are dominating, after all. Williams and Said are referring not just to possibilities but to actualities that a dominant culture denies, ignores or suppresses. But Hampshire would not be unsympathetic to the expanded point. He himself describes the way in which inchoate experiences having no recognized status inside a conceptually specified range of possible kinds of experiences always can well up and press hard against it, for the logical reason that any limited range entails the possibility of something happening beyond the limit. Thus we must expect not only the possibility but the actuality of experience to be richer than any given articulation of experience allows. The circumscription of any order is what makes it a weight (a weight, as Williams and Said argue, that becomes doubly onerous when it dictates the subordination of some specified social group) but paradoxically also is what prevents it from exercising a total sort of tyranny. The possibility it rules out always may be activated, the actuality it does not recognize always may force itself into public view.

The first condition of criticism and resistance, then, has to do with the fact that any system or mode or order is a contingent reduction of a much greater possibility. The second condition has to do with the fact that any present order is studded with deposits left by a past that to a larger or lesser extent was under the sway of a different conceptualization of the world, a different regime of truth, perhaps the ethos of a different fundamental social group. The very historicity of social life, which no act of legal–political coercion can obliterate (however much it can succeed to obliterating a particular building, or archive, even a particular population), guarantees that elements from the past will live on inside and in at least passive tension with the present. Gramsci alludes to the living presence of the past when he describes how a new linguistic order replaces an old one by taking over its forms and using them in its own different way. It absorbs "in metaphorical form the words of previous civilisations and cultures,"[5] so that "language is at the same time a living thing and a museum of fossils of life and civilisations."[6] The presence of these fossils means that the present order on the one hand is powerful enough to turn what had been taken as literal truths into metaphorical ones, but on the other hand is not at all of a single piece, nor is it all of pieces of its own design. It is made in part of elements that, when practical circumstances are unsettled enough, can go off like little time bombs, suddenly becoming proofs of and pointers to a different way of life. Now, certain marginal social groups all along may have followed quite literally that way, living it in enclaves within the larger population. Williams will call such groups "residual cultures." But for the population as a whole, the crystallized deposits of the past not merely in language but in institutions and social practices are potential points of aggravation in the present scheme of things.

As Hampshire, Gramsci, and Williams all are more eager to tell us, the future is also a ground for criticism and resistance. Here again the very historicity of human life is the enabling condition of resistance, producing it now out of developments reaching from the present into the future rather than out of deposits secreted in the present by the past. New needs, interests, and practices may arise out of the present mode of life that it cannot accommodate through incorporation, suppression, or control. Such contradictions in a mode of life may be a function of its own internal dynamic, or they may issue from some accidental sequence of decisions and actions, or they may emerge through the pressure of external phenomena, such as a natural disaster or foreign invasion. But more fundamentally still, they may have their origin in the sheer confusion, creativity, and vitality of human life. Out of *this* can be thrown up the most unpredictable combinations of conditions and events that may leave no permanent trace behind them, but that alternatively may congeal into long-lived situations spawning needs and interests that never were there before, and that, without any special negative impulse on anyone's part, resist all efforts of domestication. It may be that a new way of life will arise in the cracks and crevices of the old, refracting these developments in their most advanced and explicit form. Williams will call such ways of life "emergent cultures." New developments may remain concentrated – and isolated – there. Then again, they may spread out from such points of concentration to lend their weight, in the rare case, to the collapse of the larger order, or to its slow decomposition and reformation.

Perhaps the most curious ground of criticism and resistance is one Said unwittingly suggests to us when he notes that ideas and theories can be misread in their historical transfer from one setting to another. For surely misreadings are not confined to new ideas imported into a society from the outside. The most familiar principles of a dominant order can come to be misunderstood in special circumstances by large sectors of its population. Such misunderstandings may be undramatic, fragmentary and multiple, signifying only that the order is less than perfect in its wielding of ideological control. But it also may be the case that a whole popular mass misinterprets – but then the better term here might be "re-interprets" – dominant principles in broadly the same way: a mass that is sincere, steadfast, and self-righteous in its attachment to the established regime and yet also is fervently on the side of what in fact is a drastic revaluation of values. Here we will see a movement at once loyal, radical, and tidal.

And then there is the ever-present promise of a break in the hold of a dominant order that is made by the relatively unfixed and fluid aspects of social life. At any given moment, as Williams already has told us, there are meanings and values actively lived and felt but not crystallized into definitive form: feelings still inchoate, ideas not yet articulated, experiences only vaguely registered or understood. Precisely in their being too elusive to be institutionalized, too shapeless to be ground into a tradition, too mute to be sanctified, such aspects of social life offer potential openings of resistance to the entrenched order of things. They have yet to develop and congeal, and so there is still the chance of their going in an off-beat, not conventional, direction.

Thus far our discussion has had as much to do with spontaneously, as with intentionally, "negative" thought and action. There is one final enabling but also constituting condition of spontaneous resistance that we should note. It is Gramsci who provides us with the relevant distinction this time, between thought that is thought and thought that is acted: that is, between the conception of the world that is "logically affirmed as an intellectual choice," and the conception emerging "from the real activity of each man, which is implicit in his mode of action."[7] Now, if one had to choose between the two, one might guess it would be "thought that is thought" that would be more likely to be iconoclastic, while "thought that is acted," being exterior, hence discoverable and punishable, would be more likely to be conformist, out of the actor's caution or cowardice (how hard to draw the line between the two!). But Gramsci wants to argue that there are situations in which thought that is acted can be radically oppositional, while the explicit intellectual conception lags behind.

Gramsci begins his argument with a description of "normal times," when a subaltern social group thinks and acts according to a conception which "is not its own," but which it has adopted "for reasons of submission and intellectual subordination" from another group.[8] This subaltern group is likely to see the world in deterministic, mechanistic, fatalistic terms, and to see itself in the world as a mere "thing" – the servant of God's will, the creature of life as it always has been and always will be, the victim of nature or fortune. And indeed, this "naive philosophy of the masses"[9] is an opaque reflection of the fact that their political position is weak and their conduct not independent or autonomously determined. But either sporadically or as part of some greater historical transformation, there are times when everyday life is suddenly disrupted and subaltern individuals find themselves unhinged from their normal constrictions. In such "unusual times," they enter onto the historical stage as protagonists and agents, to act in "directive" and transformative ways.[10] It is unusual times, then, that present the enabling ground for criticism and resistance in action but not necessarily, Gramsci adds, in thought. For while the conception of the world manifested in the practice of subaltern individuals is now their own "embryonic" conception, their "superficially explicit or verbal" conception may still be the one "inherited from the past and uncritically absorbed."[11] The subaltern individual at this point can be described as having "no clear theoretical consciousness of his practice," or "one contradictory consciousness," or "two theoretical consciousnesses."[12] The verbal theoretical consciousness, Gramsci warns, is not without its consequences, as it continues to hold together the subaltern group, influences its conduct and the direction of its will, and can induce in it a renewed political passivity. He adds that it is understandable for this group to cling to received ideas of determinism and fatalism, even when it is being directive and self-acting, out of theoretical naiveté. It is "idiotic," on the other hand, for intellectuals to construct in a self-conscious way a deterministic theory out of ideas that are so much the residue of religious resignation and that bend so far towards political quiescence.[13]

The distinction between a naive and a self-conscious adoption of ideas brings us straight to that pivotal condition dividing off intentional from spontaneous criticism and resistance. For it is the possibility of moving from an uncritical acceptance of received ideas to a reflective consideration of them that enables one purposefully and knowingly to think against a regime of truth, a hegemonic culture, a whole mode of life. This is not to say that reflectivity is either a necessary or a sufficient condition of opposition. We just have seen that there can be opposition without self-consciousness having come first and, equally, there can be self-consciousness without opposition being its consequence. It is only that achieving a distance from inherited ideas in order to weigh, judge, and think about rather than through them, opens up the multiple possibilities of returning to embrace old ideas with a new understanding of their origins, significance, and logic; of repudiating those ideas through that understanding instead; or of taking any number of half steps that lead in both directions at once – of revising, synthesizing, or transforming ideas that had been merely passively accepted before. In each case, one is pushed beyond old intellectual horizons to entertain different kinds of conceptual discriminations, new ways of viewing old situations, hence new possibilities for action.

From this pushing past comes a greater freedom of thought – a freedom that Hampshire and Gramsci call "philosophical." Importantly, both writers describe the line of philosophy's movement as starting always in the given, concrete situation of the particular thinker and stretching out towards a more and more reflective intelligence about it – what counts as "the situation" enlarging in breadth and depth by the same stroke.[14] The line never starts at an abstract and universal god-point to stretch either downwards to illuminate some concrete situation or "sideways" to other equally abstract and universal truths. Very importantly, too, the taking up of any marginal vantage point "experimentally" at which one might linger long enough to gain new insights (and, we should add, new blindnesses) denied by the central conception of the world is, for Hampshire, the best way to cultivate both a philosophical and an imaginative vitality. For Gramsci – and the difference between Hampshire's pluralistic and Gramsci's dialectic notion of contradiction becomes very evident here – the taking up of the emergent and hence still marginal viewpoint in a dominant culture is the only way to shed ideas belonging to a dying age, ideas mystifying real social conditions, and ideas that have been imposed by a fundamental social group with interests antagonistic to the thinker's and the new age's own. The refusal, then, to look at life from a view at the margins, which so often is justified by the charge that marginal ideas are ludicrous, ideological, crazy, or extreme, might be described equally as a psychological resistance to having a familiar notion of the world badly shaken, and as a political resistance to the abandonment of a whole mode of life.

But here we must make a fundamental qualification to the claim that self-consciousness paves the way to the freedom of thought. For the enhancement of vision and imagination that comes from stepping beyond old conceptual boundaries is not, contrary to everything Hampshire suggests, infinitely self-expansive. There is not a release of thought from a cramped, enclosed space to a more and more open and unconfined prospect. The thinker who breaks away from an old mode of thought simultaneously must break into a new one. This is so even if that new mode is, at the very outset, so incoherent and vague as to be better dubbed a structure of feeling than a regime of truth – even, too, if the coherent and precise order into which it one day may gel happens to be that strangely self-corrosive kind in which suspicion, disbelief, and a rejection of truth are a permanent part of the intellectual landscape.

The thinker who moves through criticism and resistance from an old to a new order of thought indeed is no more likely than anyone else to become a resister of *that*, unless she happens to have developed a general taste for criticism along the way, or unless she always has had the temperamental misfortune to seesaw endlessly between a belief in some truth and a disillusionment with it. In every other case, there are all sorts of heavy counter-weights to any thinker's perpetual renewal of the critical stance. Sheer mental fatigue, the comforts of routine, and the seductions of inertia and order must count all together as one. But the counter-weight most pertinent for us is the emergence of a whole culture providing practical support for the new order of thought. To the extent that such an emergent culture survives, thrives, and hardens into a real alternative mode of life, it will elaborate for those thinking and living inside it new classificatory rules, new evaluatory prescriptions, and new norms of conduct.

The critical move made once, in other words, may be the step taking a thinker simultaneously out of one confinement and very happily and permanently into another. Such a step is not merely into a "negative" confinement. It is also into a new, "positive" cultural life. All order is, after all, double edged, at once prohibitive and productive. If a life of permanent criticism and suspicion would be a life of relatively free intelligence *vis à vis* culture in its restrictive and negative sense, it would be a life of impotent intelligence *vis à vis* culture in its fruitful and positive one. Thus, if the history of consciousness is not, after all, the story of a single struggle to move from a limited to a more and more expansive view, but instead the story of multiple moves from orders of "positive" thought to anarchies of criticism to new orders, it is not thereby the story of freedom endlessly snatched at and denied.

How or why does the impulse to self-consciousness emerge? This is a genuine enough question, given the forces lined up against it, running all the way from the sheer weight of any established way of life to dominative power. As we have seen, the impulse in part is a function of the logic of limitation, which slyly intimates the existence of something outside itself. In part, too, the impulse is what all our theorists except Foucault would call very frankly an essential feature or essential potentiality of consciousness. There is a good deal to reflectivity, then, that has to to with an impulse of the intelligence itself to work off its own inner content. But any extraordinary practical circumstance can give a sharp jolt to thought. That circumstance may be some cataclysm internal to a way of life or some juxtaposition of the familiar and the strange: the sudden turning up, perhaps, of one of those traveling ideas to shatter native presumptions, or the catapulting of a native out into a different mode of life where radically different conventions of thought and practice prevail.

However a reflectivity of thought may have been startled into being, afterwards the reverse situation of the one Gramsci described earlier may come to hold true. Thought that is thought may have a greater critical and resistant streak to it than thought that is acted. Williams reminds us of this when he states that there can be public assent to and private dissent from a dominant order – an open affirmation and a hidden negation of official consciousness on the part of practical consciousness. (This is not to say, as Williams already has emphasized to us, that the assent, through being public, is "social," while the dissent, through being private, is "individual," as if something an individual keeps close to her chest must have originated uniquely and singularly there.) The criticism and resistance that are closeted as secret thoughts and perhaps as small secret actions in normal times can burst forth as public speech and great actions in unusual times, so that at all times one must suspect the appearances of conformity, contentment, and complacency inside a hegemonic regime.

It is, by the way, the possibility of criticism and resistance in thought that is thought that normalizing power, as Foucault describes it, directly attacks, by penetrating and reworking the individual's dreams, desires, self-images, and will through therapeutic treatment. Sovereign power, to the contrary, does not have invasive but rather persuasive designs on the dissenting consciousness. It seeks not to rearrange the internal content of that consciousness through the scientific manipulation of it as an object, but rather to wring from it as a subject a recognition of the rightness or truth or absolute power of sovereign law. The interesting point for us is that sovereign power as opposed to normalizing power can inflame the dissenting consciousness precisely by demanding from it that recognition and outward obedience: by imposing its own will on its subjects, and by saying "No" to their own independent ideas, passions, and plans. It is a paradoxical fact but a truism, too, that the spirit of criticism and resistance seems to incubate and mature most successfully not when it is permitted to do "anything it likes," and also not when it is outfitted by normalizing power with likes to which that power is only too happy to say "Yes," but instead when it is subjected to fairly stringent but not thoroughly brutalizing sovereign prohibitions, so that it must smolder, develop and refine itself only, at best, semi-licitly.[15] Two elements seem to be key in making for a vigorous oppositional spirit here. On the one side, there is a power that imposes itself positively as a complex, elaborate, forceful substance (a moral ethos, a set of truths, rules of right conduct, a canon of sanctified texts) and imposes itself negatively as a set of authoritative, prohibitory commands backed up by the threat of punishment. On the other side there is someone subjected to sovereign power who is forced to know its ethos, truths, rules and texts and to bend under its coercive law, but who secretly can and does nourish, as its forced obedience rather than spontaneous consent signifies, a counter-substance of its own. This counter-substance must be only the more complex, elaborate, and forceful for having to withstand sovereign pressure – withstand it at first only in the form of thought that is thought, but possibly, at some unusual time, in the form of thought that also is acted.

The question of what is the end of criticism and resistance when they not only are thought but also acted, and when they are thought and acted to their ultimate extreme, is easy to answer at one level. The end must be to contest the legitimacy of the hegemonic culture; to refuse to remain inside the given limits of everyday life; to question received truths about natural identities and their characteristics, values, and relations; to challenge the dominance of the fundamental social group; to expose the coercive force supporting an order that no longer enjoys the spontaneous consent of at the very least some small knot of critics and rebels, and at the very most of the population as a mass; to launch an assault (which if it is to have any chance of triumph must be launched collectively, not individually) on power as it overshadows and underpins a whole way of life. But this is merely the negative side of the answer, and the moment we consider what is to be put in place of the old order, the difficulties start piling up.

Take, for example, Gramsci's response, which is on one far end of the string of responses to the question that our five theorists give. For Gramsci, the ultimate point of engaging in cultural–political struggle is to replace one fundamental social group, one collective way of life, one cultural–political hegemony with another. Now, when all is said and done, there is an important sense in which Gramsci is simply honest and forthright in his account of what cultural–political struggle is always about. Compare him to those contemporary counter-culturalists who say they are aiming to do away with every kind of hegemonic order so that all individuals would be "empowered" to think and act as they like – as if there would be individuals likes, thoughts and actions outside of any collective order at all. Compare him to those contemporary conservatives[16] who say they are defending "the continuation of our way of life" on the sole grounds that "it is ours" – as if that way had been, or could be, democratically agreed on by "us" from the start.

Against both sorts of pretensions, all our theorists have made it very clear that a mode of social life is something which neither autonomous individuals nor a consensual community have had a great deal to do with bringing into being or reproducing in a self-conscious way. Gramsci does stand out from the rest in not shying queasily away from the goal of supplanting an order that thrives by means of crushing the "simple people," as Gramsci called the peasant population of southern Italy, with an order that would lift the "simples" out of their social subordination, economic misery, and intellectual parochialism to a higher cultural level. By a higher cultural level, incidentally, Gramsci means to signify as much the culture of modernity as the culture of communism. He also is not queasy about advocating the cultivation of an intellectual stratum to spearhead the movement of the subaltern population for social supremacy. Such a stratum would be composed in part of traditional intellectuals won over to the side of progressive historical forces, but in larger part, Gramsci hoped, of organic intellectuals arising out of the subaltern group itself. For in the struggle for power over the determination of the contents of consciousness that every cultural–political struggle is, and despite all banalities to the effect that the consciousness of a culture really is determined equally by everyone, it is the functional intellectuals, Gramsci declares, who will be most centrally placed. By "functional intellectuals" he means to signify not only the theorists, teachers, priests, artists, and journalists but most importantly the political leadership of subaltern formations, whose goal would be to create a new world conception to "fertilise and nourish the culture of an historical epoch"[17] and eventually to initiate a new legal–political regime.

We can only be grateful to Gramsci, I think, for his blunt insistence that cultural life is always collective and always an arena of power. But standing as we do in the debris of the late twentieth century and looking backwards, we cannot be grateful in the same way for his faith in history, which allowed him to anticipate so unhesitatingly the emergence of a new mode of life, the leadership of a new fundamental social group, and the extension of a new moral–intellectual culture into a State in the large, Hegelian sense of the term. We cannot, with Gramsci, speak confidently of the historical function of a dominant group, or of the fact that with its exhaustion, the ideological bloc of intellectuals and great masses supporting that group will collapse, and new social groups and cultures will arise with a progressive ethos and aims, whether or not they will win out against the coercions an old order brandishes when the spontaneous consent for it has run out. Gramsci lived at the very last moment of Western history – really at the moment after the last moment (did his solitary confinement in prison protect him from the truth of history here?) – in which one could be so sanguine about the nature of emergent movements and formations.[18]

It is to find relief, then, from Gramsci's optimism about what the historical entanglement of culture and power can produce – but not from his realism about the fundamental fact of that entanglement –

that we must turn to Foucault. As adamant an advocate of anti-hegemonic politics as Foucault can be,[19] and as scornful a debunker of the liberal romance of a culture without imposition, Foucault's answer to what criticism and resistance should aim at is very far from Gramsci's own. Foucault has, against Gramsci (and against Hegel and Marx before him), no faith in history, no love of modernity, no trust in power emergent that seeks to replace power entrenched. He also has the anarchist's horror of all talk of "collective blocs," "intellectual-moral unities," "counter-hegemonies," "intellectual vanguards," and "the radical seizure of the state." A revolutionary movement that seeks to do battle against and take over the state, Foucault admonishes, must build up equivalent political–military forces to the state's own, organize itself in an equivalently hierarchical and bureaucratic way, and spawn a technical elite capable of running the state apparatus. Thus, what would remain intact after the revolution would be centralized legal–political power along with the intellectual–moral supremacy of some fundamental group, not to speak of the most important "remainder" of all: the "mechanisms of power that function outside, below and alongside the State apparatuses, on a much more minute and everyday level." These are mechanisms that no mere replacement of one top-down leadership with another will do anything to transform, and if they are not transformed, "nothing in society will be changed."[20]

Well, Foucault enjoys over Gramsci the advantages of an historical hindsight making him wary (and appropriately so, to a point) of all attempts to construct an emancipatory cultural–political order. He also enjoys a theoretical sophistication that his temporal, geographical, and institutional location helped ensure him, and a certain contemporary attractiveness through his attention to power as it is wielded from a multiplicity of local sites. But we must be clear on his two great weaknesses, both constitutional weaknesses of anarchism. These are the inability to support any movement that through its massiveness and disciplined unity would be popular and yet powerful enough to undermine an entrenched legal-political regime; and the inability to stand on the side of any positive new cultural–political order at all, such an order's always being at once a new system of imposed prohibitions and permissions, with respect to which opposition properly can respond only negatively. Both inabilities are symptoms of a basic failure of nerve before the whole question of order – which, after all, every tolerable as well as intolerable mode of social life must and will have, and which any serious counter-movement at some juncture will have to develop as well.

Gramsci and Foucault, then, represent the polar positions, each oppositely problematic, on the question of whether an anti-hegemonic movement should have as its end the imposition of a new positive hegemonic culture – including a new system of classification, a new range of sensibilities, new possibilities of action, new norms of conduct, new institutions, canons, and traditions, and even a new legal–political state. To my mind the only unself-deluding answer can be "Yes." It is not sheer absence, after all, that one pits oneself against some cultural–political presence in order to create. But one simultaneously must say yes to the fact that the new positive order will give rise inescapably to new limits and pressures, becoming the new ground for criticism and resistance. The particular content of these new contradictions is entirely unpredictable before their emergence. It is unpredictable, then, from any standpoint inside the life of the old order, including the standpoint of its oppositional groups. Being unpredictable, such new contradictions cannot be prevented in advance.[21]

The point we have left to consider is the strategic question of how an oppositional movement is to proceed in the negative task of challenging an old order and the positive task of creating a new one. And here, I think, Gramsci and Foucault have answers to give that can help not to dissipate but at least to temper the authoritarian element in all social life. Gramsci unintentionally, perhaps, presses us in this direction when he states that the struggle over consciousness – or, as he puts it, the struggle between the traditional socio-cultural content of civil society and a new critical content – must precede the battle for control over the legal–political state. While there is always the impulse to power in any assertion, in civil society, of the truth or cogency or beauty of a particular set of ideas, images, values, styles of thought, and aims of practice, it is an impulse less ruthless (if more ambitious), more easily contested (if less easily recognized), and more stimulating and provocative than the power of centralized state coercion. Then, too, relative to the abruptness of a seizure of state power and the mammoth effects of its exercise, there is in cultural transformation an almost indefinite and leisurely quality that comes from it being made at least at the start of small, dispersed movements and steps, each of which is, in its singularity and initial immateriality as well, able to be reversed or ignored or forgiven. This Gramsci suggests when he describes a new permanent collective will as made of small, individual shifts in thought and action; of diffused and capillary exertions; of "more or less long processes of development." The molecular accumulation of elements by which a permanent new collective will is created requires a correspondingly "extremely minute, molecular process of exhaustive analysis in every detail, the documentation for which is made up of an endless quantity of books, pamphlets, review and newspaper articles, conversations and oral debates repeated countless times . . . which gives birth to a collective will with a certain degree of homogeneity. . . ."[22]

But why does Gramsci press for the forging of a new collective will – so long, arduous, and continuous a process as it evidently is – over the fomenting of political insurrection? Why does he urge the articulation, refinement and gelling of ideas and desires that only gradually will set the stage for a radical redirection of the whole of social life, when revolutionary action would be far more concentrated, instantaneous and cataclysmic? Certainly it is not out of reformist sentiments on his part. Gramsci worries, not hopes, that the cultural–political strategy will bend forever away from a direct assault on the dominant order or the pursuit of truly oppositional ends. It is rather, first of all, that he believes very strongly in the substantive importance of consciousness and culture in social life. To his mind it is always the case that the struggle for power will include a cultural aspect no less than a physical–coercive one; that the effective leadership of a social group will depend on its "moral-intellectual" as well as its material supremacy; and that the wielding of social power will entail the determination of the popular world-conception as centrally as of political and economic affairs. Secondly, Gramsci argues that as much as one must work toward "the moment of struggle," a long preparatory stage must precede "the single moment in which one ethical–political system dissolves and another is formed by fire and steel."[23] For on the one side, the political societies of the industrially and socially advanced West enjoy an overwhelming superiority of coercive force which makes them nearly invincible in those sorts of moments in which a rebellious population would rise up against them from below. On the other side, their civil societies have at their disposal such a great reservoir of popular consent that mass uprisings are quite unlikely to occur. A collective consciousness that is critical and a will that is resisting must be created, nourished, and cultivated first of all.[24]

In a situation in which the rebellious intelligence, desire, and physical capacity are either stunted or stymied as a result of the triumph of hegemonic power, a "war of position" rather than a "war of movement" or "maneuver" becomes the appropriate oppositional tack. This Gramsci calls "seige warfare," where the opposition faces as the "'trenches' and the permanent fortifications of the front," "[t]he massive structures of the modern democracies, both as State organisations, and as complexes of associations in civil society. . . ."[25] Resistance is to be conducted on the margins of such deeply entrenched socio-political wholes. This does not mean that the conductors will be marginal groups. Gramsci's "subaltern population" consisted, after all, of the great masses of peasants and industrial workers. Rather, it means there must be formed conceptions, sensibilities, organizations, and practices outside the ideological–practical bounds of the hegemony but inside its geographical territory. Through their increasing elaboration and expansion, these will provide the ground for a negative critique of the hegemonic order and, at the same time, provide positive ideas and practices at odds with it. The prying away of a whole population from its commitment to the given order of things, to be sure, is only half of the task at hand, although it is intellectually speaking the more painstaking half and morally speaking, the more significant. As for that moment of fire and steel – well, Gramsci leaves us hanging forever precisely at this point, and it is even more certain today that we must leave ourselves hanging there as well. What contemporary critic could look forward to armed revolutionary conflict with any real hope for what would come afterwards, given the colossal capacity for violence and destruction on the part of the contemporary state?

Thus Gramsci makes a general argument on behalf of a cultural–political strategy based on the importance of consciousness and culture, and a historically specific one based on bleak facts about state and society in the contemporary age. It seems to me that a third, substantively specific, argument can be added to these two. A struggle over the control of culture rather than over the control of the legal–political state becomes logically, although not always chronologically, primary, when the identities of dominant and subordinate social groups turn out to be, at bottom, a function of interpretations imposed on the brute human body but represented as if they emanated out of it. Such impositions originally might have been made for the sake of the material interests of specific social groups which they functioned both to serve and to mystify, but they have long since taken on a weighty, effective life of their own. The most prominent examples we have before us today are, as I mentioned earlier, the two systems of social power centered respectively on the skin and on the sites of sexual excitation and organs of reproduction, the essential truths of which these systems claim not to dictate but merely to reflect.[26] In both instances, the dismantling of a detailed classificatory regime is the logical key to transforming a practical way of life. This is not at all to say that mechanisms of interpretive dictation cannot be found inside the legal–political state (the discursive content of the law is quite central here); or that the state may not show the effect of those dictations in its every aspect (in the content and execution/adjudication of the law, in the persons admitted to state office, in the mentalities governing different arms of the state); or that the effects of social domination and subordination do not show up in some of their most punishing forms in the economic life of production and consumption. For such reasons, a confrontation with state and economic power almost certainly will be called for and in fact may break out much earlier than directly cultural tensions and antagonisms. Still, the most crucial and also the longest move of resistance to be made will be to supplant one "moral–intellectual" universe with another, with the conceivable and permissible practices inside that universe changing in tandem.

This counter-hegemonic effort and every other sort, of course, must have aggressive designs on society at large to do the trick. This was an absolutely obvious point to Gramsci, who never dreamed that the goal of transforming a whole society would need to be defended from separatist counter-cultural tendencies. Neither did he wish the cultural struggle to become a means of evading rather than supporting a political one in the broadest sense of the term, or that there should not be, at every non-suicidal point, a challenge to the material domination of the fundamental social group. One should be clear, of course, that the sort of social power preoccupying Gramsci was not one based on human physicality and its brute difference. Class domination and class identity are rather a function of the relations in which people stand to one another in the process of producing their means of existence. With respect to such a system of social power, it is the transformation of those social relations of production, not of discursive elaborations on the body, that will be the all-significant feat. But where power is most fastly fixed in a dictatorial interpretive regime that regulates what is prohibited and encouraged by the political state, where the rewards and injuries of economic power collect and flow, what happens locally in everyday life, and most "capillary" of all, the self-experience and self-presentation of the human body – nothing in society will be changed if that power is attacked legally or economically, but never conceptually and culturally, and only at central, never capillary points.

Now Foucault, of course, is far too suspicious of centralized power to look forward with Gramsci to the creation of a new "intellectual–cultural unity," not to speak of a popular seizure (however distant it might be) of state control. His political sympathies lie on the side of negative, not positive, resistance, and on the micro-level of local resistances rather than the macro-level of a centrally unified oppositional force. Thus if he no less than Gramsci believes that the anti-hegemonic struggle has a molecular character to it, it is not at all because it consists, for him, of the small steps that accumulate to produce, in the end, a new collective cultural formation. Foucault means by "local" or "molecular" resistances, separate and discrete refusals, incursions and subversions that, while at best having a grand cumulative effect, never are to add up to a coherent and co-ordinated unity. In part, this is his prescription for avoiding the authoritarian impositions that he thinks would be sure to come, not merely from an opposition that, by duplicating the coercive power of the hegemonic order, would be the only sort that could force such an order to fall, but from any counter-hegemonic culture asserting a new moral–intellectual truth. But in large part, too, Foucault simply means to describe the way resistance actually works in a situation in which power is not only something centrally wielded, to be counter–centrally challenged and replaced; but also can run through social life in the form of innumerable, separate strands connecting innumerable, different endpoints. The multiplicity of points of power elicits a "multiplicity of points of resistance,"[27] so that there cannot be said to be, in contemporary life, any "single locus of great Refusal," any "soul of revolt," but rather "a plurality of resistances, each of them a special case."[28] We noted before that we need not go so far towards a fragmentary view of power and resistance as this to appreciate the fact that there are multiple axes of power rather than one; that none of these axes need be primary or central; and that, given such multiplicity, there are, more frequently than those "massive binary divisions" cutting a society in two, "cleavages in a society that shift about, fracturing unities and effecting regroupings, furrowing across individuals themselves."[29]

The inappropriate if still magnetic image of power and resistance is, then, that of a unitary resisting self pitted against a unitary power, or that of an oppressed group pitted against an oppressor in a monolithic/reverse–monolithic way. And indeed, that power and resistance play themselves out on the individual and social level as a series of fractured oppositions is a conclusion we might reach by looking over the work of all our theorists. Together they have gone far in introducing complicating (but not fatal) fragmentations into the notions of criticism and resistance, corresponding broadly to their earlier fragmentations of the notion of dominative power. Once again, Foucault's emphasis on local, uncoordinated sites of resistance and on cleavages furrowing across individuals themselves is the most extreme case. The most significant case, I think, is the one we have culled from that: several major systems of power can be operating simultaneously in one society, with any individual implicated in power and resistance in a multiplicity of different ways at once. But we must remember as well all the lines of division internal to any single system of power that Hampshire, Gramsci, Said, and Williams have mentioned: lines separating intentional from unintentional oppositions; thought that is thought from thought that is acted; the impulse to resistance implicit in some situation of subalternity from the impulse implicit in the sheer inchoate promise of a structure of feeling or the infinitude of possibility outside established bounds; the rupture in the native context made by the shock of the strange to the familiar from the rupture generated out of a system of power's internal dynamic.

In closing, we should cast a brief glance over certain last fragmentations of criticism and resistance that Williams has charted out specifically with reference to class society but applicable more generally to any system of social power. These are fragmentations in the sense of irreducible multiplications and variations, as often as in the sense of splinterings and disintegrations. First, Williams refers to the different degrees of pressure by which an hegemony is "continually resisted, limited, altered, challenged."[30] There are initiatives made inside hegemonic bounds that press towards their extension and renovation; initiatives "clearly affected by hegemonic limits and pressures" that still manage to make "significant breaks beyond them";[31] initiatives made outside and in strident opposition to those limits and pressures; and independent initiatives that refer neither positively nor negatively to them. Then there are differences between non-hegemonic experiences, meanings, and values having to do with their relation to history. On the one side, there are "residual" elements, "still active in the cultural process" but "lived and practised on the basis of the residue . . . of some previous social and cultural institution or formation."[32] On the other side, there are "emergent" elements, radically novel cultural forms connected to the appearance of a new social class, or (we might add) the new prominence of some other kind of subaltern population, or the activation of some potentiality of thought and action suppressed by the hegemony but not a function of subalternity at all.

Williams also distinguishes among "incorporated," "alternative," and "oppositional" elements to denote the political relationship between originally non-hegemonic and hegemonic cultural forces. "Incorporated" elements have been diluted, reinterpreted and absorbed by the hegemonic culture. "Alternative" elements are those remaining qualitatively at odds with that culture but having no aggressive designs upon it. "Oppositional" elements, finally, are cultural forces pitted antagonistically against the dominant order that seek to challenge its legitimacy and break its hold over social life. Williams then makes note of authentic breaks with the hegemonic order that, at the one extreme, occur in isolation and are unconnected to anything coming before them or afterwards; and, at the other extreme, are part of a general "pre-revolutionary breakdown" or "actual revolutionary activity."[33] Finally, he refers us back to Gramsci's description of an alternative or oppositional hegemony as composed of many kinds of thought and actions not "easily recognizable as and indeed not primarily 'political' and 'economic'."[34] The sheer structural variety of the political, industrial, cultural, scientific, and community practices that in the very best of circumstances help make up a counter-hegemonic movement, Williams suggests, will be a source of irremediable dissonance and tension for it.

4

Theory's Practical Relation to the World

What is the proper task of a critical theory – a theory, that is, identifying itself not with the preoccupations of a pre-political philosophy of consciousness and culture, and not with the impulses of dominative power, but with the impetus to criticism and resistance? What is its practical purpose, and what are the intellectual steps it must take to produce its understanding of the world?

If we consider the practical side of the question first and ask what difference to the world such a theory should try to make, we will find that Gramsci, for one last time, will be the best help to us. For he does not answer the question quite as others had done before him and would do afterwards again: he does not say that critical theory is to move a subaltern population from false to true consciousness. Instead, it is to transform "common sense" into "good sense." Precisely what he means by this we shall see in a few moments. But it is important to be aware from the start of the handful of thorns he has plucked from the side of critical theory, simply by shifting the terminological field in which its intervention in practical life is understood from "the false and the true," to "the common and the good." First, he puts a stop to critical theory's remnant theological reverberations. There is, in the juxtaposition of "the false and the true", the faintest hint of a universal and cosmic order stretching out beyond the bounds of all transitory and limited social ones – the smallest sense of a difference between things which, in their frailty and error, have their source in the human world, and things which in their constancy and perfection participate in the divine. "The common and the good," on the contrary, evoke the sense of a distinction between things solidly in and of the human world alone. They are what they are – "common" or "good" – within the context of and in reference to some historically specific constellation of ideas and practices, some purely temporal set of interests and concerns. Of course, Gramsci's unwillingness to rely on the terms "true" and "false consciousness" must have been in part the result of a sensitive political organizer's empirical assessment of the thinking of ordinary people. But it is also a manifestation of his general unease with any notion of truth intimating, in however unintended or attenuated a way, the existence of a fixed, extra-human reality.

We must add that one only could be doubly uneasy with such an intimation in those specific kinds of situations in which a regime of truth is at the very rock bottom of a system of social power. Then, proclamations on the identity of things and the nature of their relations will not have their most significant function in obscuring some deeper elements and relations of power; the way, for example, proclamations of equal contractual exchanges between free, independent individuals in bourgeois society obscure the exploitative logic of the wage-labor–capital relation. Instead, proclamations of truth most significantly create the elements and relations of social power in the first place; the way, as I have hinted, the regime of truth of Masculine/feminine creates out of the brute sexed body the realities of masculine and feminine selves, along with the detailed rules governing their interactions. With respect to such a system, the critical-theoretical task at hand is not the penetrating of mystifying appearances to a deeper reality, but the identification of the mechanisms and procedures by which truth and true realities are produced and imposed. Not the assertion, then, of an existing, deeper truth (an assertion that, in *this* kind of situation, always must be suspect) but instead the detonation of truth.

By the same stroke that Gramsci jettisons "the false and the true" for "the common and the good," he does away with the suggestion – which had proved endlessly troublesome both theoretically and politically – of any sharp divorce between the two politically significant forms of subaltern consciousness. "The false" and "the true" ordinarily signify things that are mutually exclusive and antithetical, all dialectical proofs of the interpenetrability of opposites notwithstanding. "The common," on the contrary, does not exclude "the good," and "the good" can be made out of what is "common." It is the porosity of "commonness" and "goodness" on which Gramsci counts when he asserts that the practical task of critical theory is to begin always with common sense and cultivate the elements of good sense studded through it, in order to fashion a new common sense that is altogether good. Will it remain always good? Given Gramsci's general slant on questions like this one, we can assume he would say that the answer entirely depends on whether the new common sense continues to address and sum up the most "modern" – that is, the emergent, vital, frequently iconoclastic – forces and movements in a mode of life, or whether it ends up obscuring or denying them, mechanically reiterating encrusted conceptual conventions and entrenched prejudices and beliefs.

But third, while Gramsci entirely humanizes the distinction between the forms of subaltern consciousness and emphasizes the permeability of the line that divides them, he adamantly retains the capacity and will for critical judgment. There is a distinction between common and good sense to be made, after all, and the distinction as Gramsci makes it is monumentally telling. If he eschews theological absolutism, then, it is not to embrace the relativistic attitude. He never is caught issuing any of those banal pronouncements to the effect that all points of view are equally valid, that no idea or practice is more legitimate than any other, that everything is a matter of subjective perspective, or that everything is a construction with the same value as everything else. I should add that Gramsci does not entirely solve the philosophical problem of how to judge things authoritatively without an absolute schedule of values to prop the judgment up. In defining the criteria of "good sense," he will lean a bit too heavily on the one side towards formal coherence and logical rigor, a bit too heavily on the other towards the substantively modern just because it is modern. But he will still go a good part of the way to grounding a critique of consciousness without reference to an eternal absolute – and who in the history of Western philosophy ever has done better than that?

It is for political reasons that Gramsci provides critical theory with its starting-place in the common sense of the people it is being critical for. Coincidentally, he establishes for theory in general a starting-place in some conception or other of the world that is squarely *in* the world: a conception, that is, that some living population has of its larger social life. He thus enables theory (as Marx did, in a different way, before him[1]) to avoid the pitfalls of what are, for philosophical reasons, two very wrong places for it to try to begin. He saves theory, on the one side, from the contradictions and oversimplifications of empiricism, to which it would succumb the moment it tried to begin its musings with the "pure," "raw," "uninterpreted" facts of the world: an impossible because pre-linguistic beginning. He saves it, on the other side, from the contradictions and inflated pretensions of classical philosophy, in which it would have indulged as soon as it tried to assume an absolute perspective from which the truth beyond mere ephemeral life could be known: an impossible perspective because it lies outside the world at some god-point.

Finally, by declaring that critical theory must find its starting place in the common sense specifically, for Gramsci, of the simple people, but more generally of any relevant subaltern population, Gramsci opens the door to theory taking one next step. It can conceive of beginning with the common sense not of a mass population still spontaneously wedded to the dominant order, but of a perhaps much smaller group that, having already become critical and rebellious, has moved away from the received view of the world and replaced it with an alternative or even oppositional one. Theory can decide to begin at the outermost point of a whole way of life, to see it from the very start as it appears not inside its own regime of truth, but in and to its most radical counter-regime – and see that counter-regime at the same time. With such second sight, theory might just make its way out beyond the limits and pressures on thought and thus action that a dominant order together with its critics and rebels have produced.

Well, this is what Gramsci manages to do by his "common sense/good sense" distinction, but how does he do it? What does he mean exactly by the terms, and what might we want to mean by them?

We have seen how strongly Gramsci emphasizes the fact that all people are philosophically active. "[I]t is not possible to conceive of any man," as he puts it, "who is not also a philosopher,"[2] for every "man" has a "specific conception of the world."[3] A spontaneous philosophy is contained within language itself, religion and folklore, and finally common sense, which, as the traditional popular conception illuminating everyday life for the ordinary person, can be considered "the philosphy of non-philosophers."[4]

While common sense is philosophical, it is, as philosophy, highly problematic, first of all for being "disjointed," "episodic,"[5] "strangely composite."[6] Even "in the brain of one individual," Gramsci declares, the common-sense conception is "fragmentary, incoherent and inconsequential."[7] Gramsci's specific description of common sense as a jumble of religious and philosophical principles, superstitious and scientific beliefs, local and cosmopolitan ideas, most immediately suggests the intellectual contradictions typically bound up with rural disintegration and modern industrialization. But in fact the heterogeneity of common sense has a much more general significance and source, reflecting as it does the helter-skelter absorption of ideas from any larger social environment. The most salient aspect of common sense is thus "the diffuse, uncoordinated features of a generic form of thought common to a particular period and a particular popular environment."[8] The confused abundance of the ideas comprising common sense means that critical philosophy must not look to it to confirm, after the fact, its own assertions – not because there is nothing in it to confirm them, but because there is too much. Common sense is such a "chaotic aggregate of disparate conceptions" that "one can find there anything that one likes."[9]

There is a second failing, this time of deficiency rather than excess, that makes common sense a prohibited proving ground for critical philosophy. Common sense most centrally bases itself on immediate appearances and crude sensation, on the seeming self-evidence of the physically present. Towards immediate presence, critical theory must strike always a posture of suspicion, not of obeisance and repetition. Lastly – shades of Hampshire – common sense is problematic because it is thought that has been "mechanically imposed by the external environment, i.e. by one of the many social groups in which everyone is automatically involved from the moment of his entry into the conscious world."[10] It is thought unreflectively received, "uncritically absorbed by the various social and cultural environments in which the moral individuality of the average man is developed."[11] However unexamined traditional beliefs might be and indeed precisely through their being unexamined, they are tenacious, solid, and have an "imperative character . . . when they produce norms of conduct."[12] Their tight connection to practice, of course, is just the reason why critical theory must begin its work with them rather than with, say, traditional professional philosophy.

What is "good" about common sense? Its intellectuality, yes, and also some and perhaps many of the specific ideas entering into the cacophony of ideas that make it up. Then, too, it is not "rigid and immobile," but vital, "continually transforming itself"[13] by absorbing fragments of new ideas and opinions. Finally, in its directness and simplicity – in its thrust to identify "the exact cause, simple and to hand" – it is inoculated against seduction by "fancy quibbles and pseudo-profound, pseudo-scientific metaphysical mumbo-jumbo."[14]

Of course, as Gramsci is the first to point out, much in life is not a matter of exact and immediate causes at all, so that simplicity is one of the great drawbacks of common sense too. Let us just say that to common sense and metaphysics are attached opposite virtues: the one rarely makes life out to be more complicated than it actually is, the other rarely makes it out to be less.

Counterpoised but not opposed to common sense is "good sense" – thought at the "second level" of criticism and awareness. Good sense is thought that is self-knowing, having come to grips with the whole history of thought and the development of social practice up until its own time. It is self-critical, separating out and rejecting received conceptions of the world that are fossilized, anachronistic, and provincial, and preserving those ideas that are universalistic (in the sense of "non-parochial"), modern (in the sense of "fitting current reality"), and major in historical significance. It is finally, as a corollary, self-active, fashioning its own independent world-view, and working to make that view systematic, unified, and rigorous. In this work it is "exhaustive," neglecting "no argument, positive or negative, of any significance."[15] The cultivation of such self-knowing, self-critical, self-active thought is, according to Gramsci, a preliminary condition for people giving a conscious direction to their own activities and taking "an active part in the creation of world history."[16]

Gramsci very obviously demarcates "common sense" and "good sense" with an eye to describing consciousness in political life – not, of course, in the narrow sense of governmental affairs but in the broad sense of legal–coercive and moral–intellectual struggles to determine a whole society's substance and course. But even thought and action that are broadly political are not coterminous with all thought and action, and we might wonder (even though Gramsci did not) how far the discussion of spontaneous and critical philosophy meaningfully can be extended out into other social dimensions and spheres. Are there contexts in which we need to insist that it does not make sense to make the common sense/good sense distinction? Contexts in which it would be odd to press for supplanting received, or uncoordinated, or parochial thought with thought that is coherent, premeditated, and cognizant of the most recent intellectual developments and widest array of practical social concerns? It seems to me that there are two different domains to which it would be a mistake to suppose Gramsci's distinction applied, but a very tempting mistake, in the one case because he depicts the domain as being full of significance for politics; in the other because he does not depict it at all, so that it might seem not to have its own separate and different conscious life.

Both common sense and good sense, we first should remember, are modes of practical philosophy – tendencies of conception and reflection that manifest themselves as people actively intervene in the world. Gramsci indeed distinguishes between them to articulate the practical problem of how to win over a mass population from intervening in ways that reproduce the dominant social order, to intervening in self-directive, revolutionary ways. The first domain, then, with respect to which such a distinction is inappropriate is that occupied by what I will call "contemplative philosophy." While contemplative philosophy may and, according to Gramsci, must be pursued for the sake of addressing problems generated out of the practical life of the larger population, it has as its most immediate objective the theoretical analysis of that life, not active engagements within it. Marx's *Das Kapital* as opposed to Marx and Engels' *Manifesto of the Communist Party*, and Gramsci's own philosophical writings on common sense and good sense, hegemony, materialism, and culture, are perfect examples of contemplative theoretical works, as is signalled by their expository style, rhetorical devices, and level of abstraction – although not by their general object of thought. This object is still the problems thrown up inside the socio-historical matrix in which political practice takes place. That contemplative philosophy must be distinguished from practical philosophy does not in any way mean, then, that the latter cannot have a steady effect on the former. Nor does it mean that the former cannot have as its ultimate goal the latter's transformation. Between contemplative and practical philosophy, Gramsci hopes, there will be a sympathy of real interest and an interpenetration of intelligence. Contemplative philosophy divorced from practical life can only be mummified overrefined, and irrelevant. Practical life uninformed by the theoretical analysis of it will be condemned to the rule of, at worst, the most unreflective kind of common sense. At its best, it will be ruled by a kind of sense halfway between common and good – reflective and even militantly critical, but lacking the nuance, intricacy, and elaborative detail that a concentrated contemplation of practical life rather than an energetic incision in it best affords.

That contemplative philosophy must be distinguished from practical philosophy is not to say that people who enjoy good sense in practical–political life are incapable of theoretical contemplation, or that people who are professional philosophers do not, in their own practical affairs, think and act with a practical philosophy – although Gramsci does note that the common sense of professional philosophers will tend to be influenced uniquely by whatever philosophical school is current at any given time. Thus, if the line between practical and contemplative philosophy does not divide off different general objects of thought (e.g. socio-historical dilemmas from atemporal, cosmic truths), it also does not divide off different populations of thinkers. Instead, it distinguishes different modes of thinking: questions asked at different pitches, different immediate reasons for asking them, different styles of writing and speaking. It *is* true that while Gramsci is interested in winning all subaltern individuals over to good sense, he hopes to win only a few to contemplative philosophy, so that there will be empirical distinctions between the people who engage from day-to-day in theoretical investigations and those who do not. But this as much bespeaks the key importance, for Gramsci, of practical political activity – with respect to which good sense, not contemplative theory, is the appropriate mentality, and in the service of which contemplative philosophy is to function – as it does his recognition that not all people and indeed not most people will or should want to engage in theoretical activity as a regular occupation. Nor will or should most people want to exercise leadership in mass political organizations – which Gramsci, by the way, and indeed all Marxist revolutionaries up through his time, assumed would be wielded by those as conversant in what I am calling "contemplative philosophy" as they were well-grounded in socio-political realities.

Second, and very differently, there are practical but not political domains of social life where the coherence, reflectivity, and expansiveness of attention characterizing good sense may be fine enough in moderation but would be deadly in too large a dose. What become strengths rather than failings are spontaneity in the sense of the unthinking repetition of the already established, and spontaneity in the very different sense of the impulsive, unpremeditated, instantaneously inspired "rush" of desire, speech, and action that is as little disciplined by habit and routine as it is by reflectivity and logic. For example, with respect to skills and crafts on the one side and organic, cyclical events of birth, growth, decay, and death on the other, the traditionally given, the habitually practiced, and the unselfconsciously affirmed are vitalizing rather than fossilizing conditions.[17] As for spontaneity in the sense of an unpredictability, an absence of calculation, an impulsive rush – isn't this the essential element of erotic passion, sensuous pleasure, and adventures of all sort? Isn't it one essential element, along with reflective thought, in friendship and all creative acts?

Taken discretely, then, the habitual repetition of the given, the unprecedented impulse, and the reflective stance can appear in a variety of domains and contexts. As frequently as not in those contexts, the first two will be as positively central as the last. But when congealed as the twin modalities of common sense and good sense, they must be recognized as characterizing thought in the domain of practice, not in the domain of contemplative theory; of practical thought as it is concerned with or at least significant for political affairs; and of a genre of practical thought for which reflectivity generally is to be looked and hoped for over habit or impulse. I say "generally" because in so far as long-established political institutions have an organic quality to them on the one side and in so far as political transformations have an adventurous and creative dimension to them on the other, tradition and spontaneity will have their special places in political life.

Now, Gramsci's theoretical discussion of common sense and good sense has ultimately a practical point to it – as, he declares, theoretical discussion always does. The point is that critical philosophy's political responsibility is to criticize common sense and help develop a new, popular good sense out of it. This almost certainly will smack of intellectual elitism to radicals and conservatives alike who celebrate the common sense of the ordinary person and denigrate any critical judgment by intellectuals of popular thought. Gramsci, of course, would be shocked at the suggestion that common sense could be altogether worth celebrating under conditions of social domination.

In any case, a more than cursory glance at his argument should reveal how democratic, relatively speaking, his conception of the tie between critical philosophy and ordinary thought really is. For, although critical philosophy is to criticize and transform common sense, it is, before that, to begin with it, neither neglecting nor despising, as traditional contemplative philosophy so typically did, the spontaneous ideas and feelings of the larger population. If critical philosophy is to struggle to make common sense ideologically coherent, to renovate it, to develop the healthy nucleus in it into a form of thought that is superior to it, it is in the interest of raising the way in which the subaltern population reflects on its world to the level of the most advanced thought in the world. The most important conversation in which critical philosophy is to take part is no longer the one joined by Aristotle, Aquinas, and Kant. Only after critical philosophy takes up the thought of ordinary people should it take up the ideas of traditional professional philosophy, which will have helped shaped most directly the common sense of a very limited environment. Still, those ideas will have influenced the culture of society at large in a mediated way, so that they too eventually must become an object of critical attention. Then too, the common sense of intellectuals is not only influenced by but influences their professional philosophical work, and this common sense is likely to have elements in it that have been absorbed unreflectively from ordinary common sense. An additional if lamentable advantage of professional philosophy over spontaneous philosophy is that it has a documented history on which critical theory can draw in its account of the development of the larger culture.

If Gramsci urges critical philosophy to begin first with the "spontaneous philosophy of the multitude" and only second with traditional philosophies in so far as they have left "stratified deposits in popular philosophy,"[18] it is because spontaneous philosophy is the most directly powerful intellectual element in ordinary conduct, which in turn is most powerful in helping to perpetuate a hegemonic cultural regime. It is not at all out of any lack of respect on his part for the intellectual qualities of professional philosophy, which, tuned to the pitch of practical life, are indeed important ends – although not the only ends – of the "cultural battle to transform the popular 'mentality'."[19]

But now we must press our discussion of spontaneous and critical philosophy down a different path. We saw earlier how Gramsci opens the way to critical theory's moving one step further out in the intellectual–cultural landscape to find its starting point not in the spontaneous philosophy of ordinary people but in the counter-hegemonic conceptions of cultural critics and rebels. The whole question of the relation between critical theory and common sense acquires a very different cast as soon as theory takes this step. The common sense of critics and rebels already may be, in Gramsci's meaning of the phrase, altogether good. Indeed, critical philosophy may have developed in symbiosis with that good sense and may continue to work off problems offered up by it for detailed investigation. But the new common sense of cultural critics and rebels alternatively may suffer from the opposite malady of that of ordinary common sense: a hypertrophied rather than underdeveloped reflectivity. The symptoms of this malady include not a passive submergence in the *mélange* of ideas given in the social environment, but a keen self-inspection and self-censoring of thought; not a bizarre heterogeneity of opinion, but an airtight coherence of conviction; not a dull compliance with traditional pressures and limits, but a constant critical interrogation, under the harsh light of new counter-hegemonic principles, of every old desire and intention, and an alert self-urging and self-prohibiting of every action. The result of such hyper-reflectivity, oddly enough, need not be the eradication of the most central of the old conceptual discriminations, the most dubious of inherited premises, the crudest of entrenched convictions, and so the most reactionary of practices. Certain fundamental terms of a dominant order can reappear in absolutely as fundamental a way in a counter-culture, without anyone but a few of its alienated souls taking notice of the reappearance.[20]

Given the characteristic morbidities of an oppositional common sense, the position of critical theory towards it is likely to be almost the reverse of its position towards ordinary popular thought. As we have seen, critical theory must work to make ordinary thought coherent; to force it to come to grips with the logic of what most immediately appears to be a chaotic or free concatenation of events; to paint on a previously *pointillist* canvas the strong, broad strokes depicting massive concentrations of power. On the contrary, critical theory must work to induce in oppositional common sense a mood of hesitation and qualification; to develop in it a taste for subtlety and reversals, a delight in the paradoxical and perverse detail. It must paint over previously strong and broad strokes, short and abrupt ones depicting power exerted from a multiplicity of separate sites and evaded in a multiplicity of ways. Then again, critical theory must seek to inflame in ordinary common sense an anger and indignation against social domination – although, being as enervating to the attempt to understand power as they are stimulating to the struggle against it, these passions must be stilled for the purpose of theoretical contemplation, reanimated for the purpose of political practice. At the same time, theory must seek to interject into counter-hegemonic common sense the attitude of irony, self-deflation, and skepticism, as fortification against any new, self-imposed tyranny of positive truth. Finally, critical theory must strive to generate, in popular common sense, the discipline necessary for the criticism of and resistance against an entrenched hegemonic regime. Very differently, it must do its best to scoff at all dour efforts of self-discipline arising in the counter-cultural context, supporting instead a relaxation of discipline there and a multiplication of occasions for enjoyment, adventure, and experimentation.

5

Theory's Contemplative Relation to the World

We have been discussing the practical difference to the world that critical theory should try to make. But how is it to produce the understanding of the world that is to make the difference? What are the contemplative steps it can be expected to take?

Theory's grandest move, of course, is that of winning a cool distance from the concrete, of epistemologically detaching itself from immediate experience, of acquiring, at the same time, an idiom that jars with the idioms of ordinary life in being less tactile and evocative, more logically rigorous and intellectually exact. This move of abstraction from actually lived and felt life is its hallmark and condition of achievement. It is also what makes theory infamous to all of those contemporary counter-cultural formations that celebrate concrete experience, subjective feelings, and intimate connection. From such quarters, accusations periodically ring forth concerning theory's evasion of emotion, its impersonality, its hyper-rationalism, and its secret penchant for authoritarian control.[1]

It is true enough that theory's refusal to hug the contours of experience makes it vulnerable to a number of weaknesses.[2] It can become self-indulgently pompous and obscure, thereby avoiding the trouble of stating things as sharply and clearly as possible. It can degenerate into a noisy crashing of categories through a disregard for literary grace, an untutored aesthetic, and an impatience with the sensuous form. There can be a faddishness to theory, so that it pursues not the answers to difficult questions but the latest fashionable thinker or thought. It can lose connection altogether with the world and feed like a narcissist off its own concepts and principles. But if it is susceptible to these various faults, it is so in the way that an athlete has certain injuries to which she is especially prone. Certainly its essential impulse is not to look down on concrete experience as limited, subjective, and prejudicial from some putatively universal and objective point of view. It is rather, most generally, to reflect on the causes, significance, and implications of that experience. It is, more specifically, to find secrets in experience that are obscured from ordinary sight: to uncover hidden coherences in what seems to be a mere jumble of unrelated events and details, and incoherences in what appears to be strictly ordered; to make transparent what is opaque, and to expose opacity in what seems transparent.

Theory has an intrinsic passion for the perverse revelation – but then, aren't all revelations perverse? This passion, in turn, is ignited by passions originating in the drama of social life, above all when what is desired to be revealed and known are scenes from that drama itself. Consequently, while there is a detachment of vision intrinsic to theory, there is no corresponding detachment of interest. Its interestedness is only exacerbated by the fact that, although theory certainly can and often does ally itself with dominative power, or alternatively can belong to some camp not classifiable as being either with dominative power or against it, the social interests it most agilely serves are those of criticism and resistance. This is because there is nothing more jumbled and opaque than life's ordinary complexities when they have been compounded by active mystifications, and there is no more fertile source of *those* than dominative orders that are deeply entrenched. Then again, there is nothing seemingly – but only seemingly – more straightforward and clear than the world as dominative power regiments and presents it. Thus the special passion of theory to uncover and unmask, and to unravel and unhinge, coincides with the imperative that a population in the grip of dominative power and lulled in various ways by it, grasp the full significance of its predicament – which means grasping that what seems to be a natural or fated or beneficent order is a predicament, first of all. Social arrangements, of course, are rarely made with the educative needs of subaltern populations in mind, and theoretical education historically has tended to be monopolized by those whose own sympathies lie on the side of domination. Here, perhaps, in the socio-political status of those who have been trained to think in abstractions, lies the key to all those false pretensions generated on theory's behalf. Objectivity, universality, superiority, neutrality –

aren't these they very same pretensions that every "fundamental social group" generates on behalf of itself?

1.

But now we need to consider specifically the sort of ground from which social theory abstracts. We already have seen, on the one hand, the wrongheadedness in assuming that a good social theory always begins with the "raw, empirical facts": facts that are "objective" through subsisting outside any particular interpretation of them. Those sorts of facts social theory never would be able to fathom. One insurmountable obstacle is all the conceptual distinctions and intepretations theory itself is forced to make to identify and describe that which it is seeking to know. The other obstacle is the always partly disharmonious distinctions and interpretations made by the various social participants themselves that at once are about their world and help to constitute it. We also have seen, on the other hand, the difficulties in assuming that a good theory must leave the social world, with its troubling fluidity and transience, to muse on some extra-human, eternal reality behind, above, or beyond it. This is an impossible imperative for any human theory to follow – and a self-defeating one for any theory that has as its purpose the comprehension of social affairs.

The only remaining ground for social theory is some interpretation of the social world that is squarely in it – an interpretation that is at once a reading and a constituent element of social practice. The theory that begins with such an interpretative reading and practical element may refuse to do more than understand it as it understands itself, exploring and affirming it at its own level of sophistication and reflective intelligence. Instead, it may be intent on ferreting out a greater intricacy of conception, a deeper complexity of motivation, and a clearer logic to the details of the interpretive/practical situation than any of the participants directly implicated in it would have the sensibility to grasp or skill to recount – but an intricacy, complexity and logic operating at the level of conscious experience rather than being indicative and descriptive of some more fundamental and determinant force (the structure of the unconscious, perhaps, or the dynamic of a mode of production). Then again, such a theory may search precisely for a deep structure of psychic life or the dynamic of a mode of production that conscious desires, conceptions, and practical purposes at once express and obscure. Or, yet again, theory may suspect there to be, at the rock bottom of conscious life, a regime of truth which is no more a mystified expression of some more fundamental force than it is a natural system of conceptual discrimination, a benign social inheritance of classification and evaluation, or a free intellectual creation of the individual mind – but is, rather, like the perfect police state, primary, dictatorial, punishing, and arbitrary. But whichever of these different senses of interpretation theory happens to make, it will be anti-empiricist through entering social life via some idea of it that is also in it. It will be anti-transcendental through treating that idea not as mere illusion or error blocking, along with the whole imperfect and impermanent social world, the way to a knowledge of truth, but instead as an illumination and aspect of that imperfect and impermanent world – the only sort of world theory could ever really hope to know.

We will be making our own theoretical entrance into social life by way of two different interpretations of it that are also in it: one, a counter-cultural interpretation of an hegemonic order of sex and gender; the other, that hegemonic order's dictations of common-sensical truth. But we should allude in passing to the great range of interpretive material on which theory has seen fit to start its work in different contexts and on different occasions.

What might seem at first glance to be the most obvious sort of starting material for any theory with some serious interpretive dimension to it, but which actually is the empiricist's answer to the question of how to take the desires and beliefs of social participants into account, is "public opinion", as it is tapped and collated (would Foucault be more correct, if he were here, to say "created" and "elicited"?) by social survey research. Such research gathers "Yes–No–Don't Know" responses to preformulated queries, as "attitudinal facts" to be added to the mass of "behavioral facts" about the social world. It assumes a purely discrete, external relationship between "attitudes" and the other elements making up that world; it approaches the conceptualization of its queries as something technically tricky but philosophically straightforward and unproblematic; it presumes it will "get to" habits of thought adequately enough by means of its questionaires and thereby cover the place of ideas in social life. Almost as obvious a starting material for any theory with an interpretive edge are in-depth interviews held with representative members of some target population. Both empiricist and interpretive theory in fact have made use of this material, but differently: the first, as a companion technique to the opinion survey, with basically the same assumptions and ends in mind; the second, as an opposing technique that plumbs the depths of social self-understandings and so of the practice those understandings animate.

But of greater interest for us are theoretical starting-points situated at a further distance from what social science means by "the real empirical world." Let us consider a few starting-places of theories with which we are at least vaguely familiar. There is, first of all, the ground on which professional political theory is so fond of anchoring itself. This is not at all some "real political world" from which theory works out a reading of, say, the meaning of freedom or the logic of the relation between leaders and led. Instead, professional political theory most typically works out that meaning or that logic on the basis of a previously established and more eminent reading that is elaborated and preserved, not to say embalmed, in some canonical political–philosophical text, with a host of commentaries and other secondary readings typically attached to it. We already know what Gramsci would say about *that* particular beginning. But while he would call it the wrong one, it is not because he thinks that theory should start with "reality" instead of with ideas about it. Rather, he thinks it should start with those ideas that have attained a certain popular diffusion and thus have become an element of ordinary conduct, or with professional philosophical ideas that are battling for influence over the popular mentality. Thus Gramsci himself often starts his theoretical discussions by criticizing Catholic theology or mechanistic Marxism.

Then there is the starting-place of a large array of feminist thinkers, the most classic being Simone de Beauvoir and Kate Millett, the most contemporary including academic literary theorists and film critics on the one hand and radical–cultural polemicists and poets on the other.[3] All these thinkers find it appropriate to begin their analyses on the ground of dominant cultural texts, whether written or imagistic, whether "high" or "mass": scientific treatises, theological expositions, novels, movies, advertisements, pornography (a favorite of the polemicists), and the like.[4] Alternately, they begin with the marginal texts of women who created them against the grain (for example, with the work of the isolated artist, unseen, uncelebrated, and ignored); or, once in a great while, with the work of some traitorous man who challenges the hegemonic rule (Genet is a real favorite here); or with texts that can be counted as belonging to a whole alternative cultural formation (for example, with the recorded lyrics and remembered self-presentations of black female blues and jazz singers – lyrics and presentations which, with respect to the dominant dictations of sex and gender, surely must make up one of the most vivid counter-traditions in America[5]).

Then again, there is Said's starting place: the multitudinous monographs, pamphlets, canvases, fabulous tales, letters "from the East" and administrative decrees comprising the discourse of Orientalism, as that discourse was elaborated by European scholars, missionaries, artists, travellers, and imperial bureaucrats. There is that supremely famous starting place in modern Western theory: the opening to *Das Kapital*. Here Marx starts with the categories of bourgeois political economy (the theoretical counterpart of bourgeois common sense), which he reveals to reflect the appearance of the capital/wage labor relation at the level of economic exchange.[6] The other just as famous theoretical starting-point is, of course, Freud's beginning his analysis of the unconscious on the ground of the spoken, misspoken, and silenced words of his patients in the therapeutic session.[7]

One other interpretive ground for theory is curious and suggestive enough to deserve our extended attention. Let us turn for an example of it to Hannah Arendt's *The Origins of Totalitarianism*.[8] In *The Origins*, Arendt is interested neither in exploring sympathetically the self-images of an age nor in searching to find underneath them some hidden structural determinant or dictatorial regime of truth. She is rather, intent on revealing and elaborating, at the highest possible level of complexity and clarity, the covert and overt motivations, conceptions, purposes, actions and large-scale movements, along with all their intended and unintended consequences, that together make up the long, tortuous prelude to European totalitarianism. Arendt's forte in *The Origins* is the making of a wealth of precise distinctions that reveal at once how complex and multiple, and how unmysterious and comprehensible, the history of European anti-semitism has been. But the particular distinction of interest to us here is the one she makes between "political" and "social" anti-semitism: between the prohibitions to which European Jews had been subjected by different states in different historical periods, as well as the privileges those states had granted certain Jews in return for their economic services; and the fantasies, conceptions, and self-presentations of "Jewishness" that surfaced not in the state but in society.[9]

Remarking on the shift in significance from political to social anti-semitism in *fin-de-siècle* Europe, Arendt notes the development of a semi-intimacy between non-Jews who were socially well-placed, culturally sophisticated, and politically alienated, and Jews who were socially ambitious, culturally agile and intellectually enlightened. This intimacy was stimulated by and infused with a magnetic yet antipathetic attraction the Jew held for the high bourgeois and aristocratic non-Jew – an attraction that could and did so rapidly turn into a most dangerous kind of aversion. Arendt notes that when such "internal" aspects of philo- and anti-semitism become pivotal, even the most well-documented economic and political histories of the period cannot provide an adequate ground for theoretical analysis. As Arendt puts it:

> Social factors, unaccounted for in political or economic history, hidden under the surface of events, never perceived by the historian and recorded only by the more penetrating and passionate force of poets or novelists . . . changed the course that mere political anti-semitism would have taken if left to itself, and which might have resulted in anti-Jewish legislation and even mass expulsion but hardly in wholesale extermination.[10]

At this juncture Arendt puts aside the research of historians (on which, to be honest, she never had seemed particularly keen) and picks up the most brilliant fictional account of French high society at the turn of the twentieth century. She fashions her analysis of social anti-semitism directly off the literary transfiguration of the "interior life" of the period and place.

We must not make the mistake of thinking that Arendt takes up *Remembrance of Things Past* in the same way that de Beauvoir did *The Plumed Serpent* or Millett did *The Balcony* – that is, in this instance, as an example of the discursive construction of "Jewishness." She clearly approaches Marcel Proust not as a writer of literary fiction but as an historian – or, more exactly, as a writer of literary fiction who can do what we normally look to the historian to do more perfectly than the historian is able to do it: who can provide us with a direct entrance into the hearts and minds of a class, a people, a milieu, an age. It is, first of all, as a writer of fiction that Proust is able to condense the civil society of an entire epoch and continental region into a concrete portrayal of French salon society; to condense French salon society into a single set of imaginary salons; to condense the complicated motives, passions and ideas animating civil society and social anti-semitism into the motives, passions, and ideas of a single cast of characters. It is, second, as a great writer that Proust can render this with a critical intelligence about social and psychological affairs and with a stylistic virtuosity that surely no other member of salon society would have come close to being able to match, so that no diary or set of letters from the period would have provided a text with anything of the acuity and density of Proust's own.

But third, Proust can provide us with an entrance into the interior of a time and place because it was his time and place. Arendt quite explicitly chooses "the salons of the Faubourg Saint-Germain as an example of the role of Jews in non-Jewish society" because "nowhere else is there an equally grand society or a more truthful record of it."[11] The record *could* be truthful because Proust lived his life "exclusively in society," so that "all events appeared to him as they are reflected in society and reconsidered by the individual."[12] There is "no better witness, indeed, of this period when society had emancipated itself completely from public concerns" – when, through "the victory of bourgeois values over the citizen's sense of responsibility," political issues were "decomposed" into "their dazzling, fascinating reflections in society."[13] Proust was, moreover, a "true exponent of this society, for he was involved in both of its most fashionable 'vices'" – one of which was "the 'vice' of Jewishness."[14] Thus he was perfectly placed to depict the way in which Jewish origin had been transformed by society into "Jewishness," an innate, tainted, secretly exciting psychological quality, which society then eagerly courted for its own titillation to relieve the everyday boredom of a life ruled by bourgeois convention. It welcomed into the semi-intimacy of its salons Jews who "had an unaccountable flair for society and taste in general,"[15] but, even better, Jews who, in the first stages of assimilation, were neither too much like the culturally ghettoized Jewish community to be merely distasteful to non-Jewish society, nor too completely estranged from that community to have nothing mysteriously "Jewish" about them at all. According to Arendt, working off Proust, the great danger to the Jews proved to lie precisely in what seemed to be the condition of their social cachet: the transformation of the political "crime" of Judaism into the fashionable social "vice" of Jewishness. For while "Jews had been able to escape from Judaism into conversion," from Jewishness as an innate psychological quality "there was no escape."[16] This danger materialized "when anti-semitic legislation forced society to oust the Jews" and the "'philosemites' felt as though they had to purge themselves of secret viciousness, to cleanse themselves of a stigma which they had mysteriously and wickedly loved."[17] For Judaism as a crime, punishment was the correlate response. A vice, however, "can only be exterminated."[18]

What can we conclude for our own purposes about Arendt on Proust – more generally, about theory's finding its concrete starting place in literature as history? First, the interior view of social life exposed by the great novelist implicated in that life becomes the more compelling for political theory to enjoy, the more power turns out to have its location not in the legal-coercive state but in civil society; the more power turns out to be, in its operations, not a top-down imposition but movements of "force" from one local, capillary point to another;[19] the more power's function turns out to be not prohibitive and negative but permissive and productive. For it is social intercourse rather than state machinations, the tense interlockings of particular individuals rather than orders issued to anonymous populations from on high, and the forced blooming of various characteristics and propensities of the personality rather than the denial of individual purposes and desires, that fictional literature is so uniquely able to display. At the same time, we should remember that only the theorist with an eye for the complexities of conscious experience would bother to begin with such a ground as this – not the theorist intent only on revealing, as the secret of that experience, something determinant "underneath," whether that be a structure of productive relations or a regime of truth.

Second, the artistic imagination trained specifically on the interior of conscious life and on intimate social connections, as that interior and those connections reflect and refract the pressures and limits of the larger cultural and political world, can provide an historical ground for theoretical analysis, only if theory has already obtained a larger understanding of history from outside the covers of any fictional text. When Arendt went to Proust for a more profound rendering of an historical situation than any historian would have been able to provide, what she was not doing was looking to him for her initial discovery and analysis of European anti-semitism. She moved to his novels not as her original source of information about anti-semitism but rather as a bright illumination of it, and she could judge that it *was* bright because she already knew the real historical phenomenon. The rule that theory must keep in mind the difference between the imaginative portrait of life and life as it is actually lived and felt is all-important here. It will be all-important again when theory approaches the creative work not as historical illumination but as cultural representation. For then, too, it cannot assume a one-to-one correspondence between an imaginative work and actually lived and felt life. The exact relation between representation and life is one of the great puzzles for any cultural–political theory to sort out.

My third and final point has to do with the methodological fruitfulness of what I have called the "concrete condensation." In our discussion of Arendt, the concrete condensation has figured as a particular kind of ground from which theory can abstract. A large historical panorama of social classes, events, geographical regions, social and political institutions, particular kinds of elites, parvenues, adventurers and outcasts is condensed into a scene, or series of scenes, in a novel or series of novels. Theory then works off those scenes. But when we reach the other end of our examination of theory's relation to the world, the "concrete condensation" will fulfill a different function for us. Then it will suggest itself as a solution to the problem of how, once theory has engaged in abstract speculation, it is to make contact with the world once again. This in fact does not become a problem for Arendt in *The Origins of Totalitarianism*, where she never strays far enough away from concrete history to be in need of a way back. It *will* be a problem for any theory breaking more sharply than Arendt does with the world of experience. Then the concrete condensation will have its use in portraying the abstract twists and turns of a theoretical argument in the form a single figure or set of figures. Here a multiplicity of abstract premises, deductions, and conclusions will be concentrated in a form that is relatively palpable, visible, diminutive, and pointed, so that it can be more comfortably seen, more easily assessed – but also so that it can evoke some sense of the world theory has spun its abstractions about.

2.

Before we are ready to consider how theory is to make its way back to the world, we must consider the different steps of abstraction theory can take from it. How far, given its own methodological inclinations and the methodological strategies indicated by the particular situation at hand, is theory able to travel away from immediate experience, felt life and the concrete world, in order to illuminate them? By "felt experience" and "the concrete world" I mean to signify, of course, not life in some raw, brute, and pre-conceptual form, but life as it is felt and understood by people in the middle of living it out – these feelings and understandings, at the same time, helping to make that life what it is.

We already have had a glimpse of the answer to this question. The first and smallest step of abstraction is the one most properly called "hermeneutical." This is the step theory takes when it finds any part of the truth of a situation to be revealed in the self-understandings of its participants. Now it might seem odd to call this a step away from experience at all. Here, if anywhere, theory would appear to be a perfect reflection of how life immediately presents itself to itself. But appearances often deceive, and it does not take much effort to realize that even the strictest hermeneutical theory must have enjoyed a long moment of detachment from the concrete world in order to consider where its truth might be found. The location of that truth, after all, is not, like the key to a map, stamped somewhere on the world's surface. It must be discovered by thought rather than by sensory observation. Moreover, hermeneutics never returns to offer up, in explanation of the world, the self-understandings of participants exactly in the form that it finds them. It never plays back, as if it were a recorder, every declared motivation, intention, and belief it happens to find. Minimally, it relies on its own activity to distinguish the significant from the trivial meaning in any given context, to rescue from oblivion the significant purpose that is inchoate or diffuse, to uncover the reason in what seems to be a confused and haphazard collection of beliefs. Maximally, it acts to lay bare a complexity and clarity to consciously experienced life that its own participants are unable to grasp.

Theory takes a second, longer step away from immediate experience when it breaks with hermeneutics to declare that the truth of experience has been in important respects mystified to its own subjects. To the extent that participants in social life systematically have misconstrued the sources, significance, and implications of their own thought and action, theory cannot trust immediate experience enough to base its claims entirely upon it, although it can work off the misconstructions, as Marx worked off bourgeois political economy, and Freud worked off the spoken words of his patients. Theory must detach itself from the concrete world to determine where the key to that world can be found, and it must sustain the detachment to fathom aspects of the world to which its own participants are blind. This is the step that is taken whenever it is charged that the experience of a subordinate group has been formed, deformed, and obscured in a context of social domination – whether by some self-conscious and manipulative group at the top or by an objective structure of social practice hidden from dominant and subordinate eyes alike.

Now, although theoretical thought is more comprehensive and rigorous than the self's ordinary musings back on itself, the same logic of reflectivity is at work in each case. Yet it is part of the meaning of a system of mystified power that most people in it will not have made ordinary efforts to reflect back on themselves with any great success. The movement of theory towards locating the full truth of their situation in some hidden dimension of it hence will be a movement away from the ordinary view. The cruelest irony that theory has, in this movement, to face is that it will think less and less in line with a subordinate group the more and more energetically it acts in what it sees as that group's interests, to track down the secrets of power and drag them into full light. Its intellectual estrangement from those in whose name it does its work must count as a tragedy for it, although one that is scheduled to come to an end (at least according to an old timetable – Marxism's) when the subordinate group is won over to critical thinking. And indeed, the democratization of critical thought often enough has been theory's fondest hope, to the extent that it has hoped at all.[20] Still, its historical relation to groups it is being theoretical *for* always has been deeply troubled. This is due in part to the fact that the democratization of criticism has taken, in actual life, such an uneven and obstructed path. But it surely also is due to there being something profoundly insolent and offensive – which however is not to say false – in critical theory's characteristic refrain: "You do not understand your own situation; I am here to reveal it to you; it is a situation, as you will see, that anyone – and certainly you and I – would find it humiliating to be in."

But the third and longest step away from immediate experience is taken by "discourse theory" when it claims that the secret basis of a system of power is to be found in the categories of ordinary thought: categories which lock one into the next with merciless exactitude and which, as a configuration, give rise not certainly to the world, but to the world's being of a certain kind, filled with entities of *this* sort and *this* and *this*. Such categories singly and together police the boundaries of what can be imagined, thought, desired, said and so done. This is a more drastic claim about the malignant power of established habits of thought than the claim that those habits appear to reflect the true logic of social life in a straightforward manner, but in fact both express and distort it. For now that true logic is held to owe its original existence to a classificatory scheme, so that the scheme is the bedrock of social domination rather than the other way around. In such a case, a conceptual distinction that merely had seemed to denote the two entities in a practical relation of domination and subordination (a distinction, for example, between "Orient" and "Occident" or "masculine" and "feminine") turns out to exert over those relations its own prior, originative force: releasing into life its own assignments of permissible identities; its own rules for the cultivation of the body; its own dictations of appropriate mannerisms, proclivities, and tastes; its own scripts for the orchestration of social interactions. These assignments, rules, and so on are reproduced and extended through the very course of their being lived out, but also through special instruments and mechanisms of cultural production, and by means of legitimated violence, legal sanctions, and state authority. Together with these instruments, mechanisms, sanctions, authority, and force, they can be said to comprise a single cultural–political formation.

You will remember that the immediate experience of a subordinate group becomes the first object of study for critical theory but not its ultimate source of truth, once a hidden logic is found to govern central aspects of social life. In the same way, the interests of a subordinate group become discourse theory's first but not ultimate obsession, once it finds a regime of truth to underlie an entire system of domination and subordination. Such a theory must make its way from an initial defense of the subordinate population to an attack on the foundational truth of all entities of which the system of power is made up. It must work not towards the celebration of the subordinate identity over the dominant but towards the subversion and explosion of both.

That conventional classifications, while posing as the mirror of some deeper, objective truth, have in fact no bedrock at all beneath them but rather are the deepest bedrock of a system of power, takes theory very far not only from ordinary but from the most characteristic kinds of oppositional interests and views. The separation of theory from actual experience now becomes so acute that even individuals who are able to think theoretically about their mode of life will hardly be able to think theoretically inside it. To inject old, familiar terms of identity with new meanings, and to begin to live those meanings out – that will be, relatively speaking, easy for any critic to try to do. But to think beyond those old terms altogether, to entertain entirely different sets of discriminations and identifications – that will be just barely possible to accomplish in the abstract. How to live it in the concrete? Thus it is that theory's last step away from immediate experience signifies the estrangement not merely of two separate populations – the theoretically minded and everyone else – but of two internal aspects of the self: the self that thinks abstractly and the self that thinks in its practical life. It is almost as if the whole mode of life with which the old distinctions are bound up would have to collapse before there could be such a fusion of theoretical and practical thinking; while that collapse just as surely seems to require that theory and practice be fused together first. But this paradox only points to the fact that when a system of power rests at its deepest base on an interpretive order – which to be sure not every system does – the routing out and dismantling of its few central ideas and its near infinity of little ones becomes the most shattering practical feat. It is as shattering as the overthrow of the state or the undermining of a mode of production would be to other axes of social power. When the force of every entrenched idea has been dissolved, when the dissolution takes place not just in thought that is thought but in thought that is felt and not just in a few isolated corners of a culture but over its entire breadth, then the system of power itself will be close to collapse, and all the worst difficulties of demolition already overcome.

3.

Now that we have gotten a sense of the distance looming inescapably up between felt experience and abstract understanding, we can take the last turn in our discussion. Having hurtled past the limits of the here-and-now in order to make a new sense of it, theory must come part of the way back by introducing a sensuous, palpable element into its arguments and insights. Why it must do so should be obvious enough. However loyally theory works off concrete life as its original material and ground, it has for its own governing principle not life but logic. There is a natural aridity and formality about it as a consequence, with all the advantages (clarity and rigor) and disadvantages (desiccation and abstruseness) that aridity and formality bring in their wake. It is partly, then, in preparation for appearing before and giving pleasure to an audience of readers and listeners that theory ought to cultivate in itself a vivid and sensuous quality. But it is also for the sake of illuminating the world to which it claims to be so deeply and centrally tied that theory should be able to think and speak evocatively as well as abstractly. It would be perhaps too overblown to say that there can be no real insight into social life without a reconciliation of philosophy and poetry, but the basic idea is right.

As to how the connection back to concrete life should be made – the answer that is usually given, when the question is considered at all, is that theoretical arguments should be dotted with historical/empirical examples. This is not, however, always a satisfactory response. One problem with the historical/empirical example is that there can be something overly potent about it, so that it will tempt the reader or listener to equate it with the abstract point it is meant to illustrate. The multiplicity of real instances about which that point may have something to say, consequently, will be in danger of being reduced to only one. "In the year A, region B, C happened to group D" can halt the mind at the boundaries of that year, that region, those people, so that one too easily thinks: "That is what happened *then, there,* to *them,*" or "That may have happened then, there, to them, but it did not happen in some other year and place, to some other group of people I can think of." In such a case, the very actuality of the occurrence keeps the mind from moving back to the theoretical level, so that the theoretical argument collapses into the empirical instance instead of being embellished by it.

Then again, there are important circumstances in which the historical/empirical instance is not potent enough. One such circumstance is that in which no actual instance perfectly illustrates an abstract point, even though that point is the correct one needing to be made. It is correct exactly because it has been generated out of theory's confrontation with all the historical/empirical particulars that originally sparked its interest: particulars which share among themselves but do not exhibit each of them alone the characteristics on which the theoretical argument is built. Another circumstance – so familiar a part of every social scene as to be almost part of the condition of social life – is one in which the particular incidences that actually have occurred are only a subset of all those that quite easily could occur in, broadly speaking, the same situation. Indeed, certain of the incidences that did not occur very well may have a greater logic to them, given the general lines of that situation, than the incidents that did. All of this is only to say, first, that the details of a situation never are entirely determined by its overall logic (or logics), if it is a developed enough situation to have one. They are partly a function of what in the particular context of that situation must count as accident and chance. It is to say, second, that the logical potentialities in any situation are typically more numerous than actual time and space ever can accommodate: there are many more things that quite "naturally" could happen than there is room in lived life for them. As a consequence, there is something semi-fortuitous about incidences that do occur – not this time because they fall into the category of sheer accident or chance, but, to the contrary, because they add up to only a fractional proportion of all the incidences that are highly conceivable and strongly warranted in a given set of larger circumstances.

Both the historian and the historical example are made and confined by accidental facts and actual occurrences, which in every real situation compose, paradoxically, at once a more chaotic and a more threadbare collection than the array of logical potentialities that the situation holds in store.[21] The theorist is not so made, and the theoretical illustration must not be so confined. It is theory's special task to reveal the inner logic of a situation (which may be a logic of coherence or dissolution), not to record – to use Hegel's words – the "mere chance" in it, nor to humble itself absolutely before the concrete particulars that logically belong to that situation but which still have something semi-fortuitous about them. Two cardinal rules for theory, then, are that it should not overly defer to the semi-fortuitous, and it must not touch the sheerly accidental at all, except when the place of the fortuitous and the accidental in human life are the abstract questions it has set out to explore.

A different kind of point is that the jealous demands of specialization can weigh against theory's good use of the historical example. That good use may require the theorist to become an historian in order to draw on episodes and figures from the past in a sure and illuminative way. But as an historian, the theorist would be pressed in her interests away from some abstract logic of practice for which concrete particulars serve as source material at the start and illustrative material at the finish, to concrete particulars to be savored for their own sake and not as they serve anything else. The logic of intellectual activity itself is at the root of this predicament. To think seriously and systematically is to refuse to think seriously and systematically in almost every vein but one – to block out, therefore, whole lines of inquiry which are quite clearly important or promising. To open up one of those lines as an auxiliary route and to take that route for any meaningful length of time is inevitably to leave the main route behind. Different dimensions of social life come to be seen as central (the concrete detail, not the inner structure or disintegration of structure); different analytic methods come to be favored (the historical/narrative, not the theoretical/deductive); different criteria come to be established for marking off the primary inquiry from the auxiliary one.

Does theory itself suggest a specific strategy of return to the palpable and concrete? I think that it does. For if in its almost mathematical formality it is so little sensuously satisfying that it begs for concrete illustration, it also may beg for an illustration that is ice-clear: one that dovetails, as actual historical examples may not, with its own abstract twists and turns. Under particular circumstances, it may call for the conjuring up of an imaginary figure or scene that is its own concrete condensation.[22] This conjuring-up process is unlike the process of creating a purely literary fiction in a number of ways. The theoretically imagined figure or scene cannot be allowed to fly away on its own independent wings. It must not be embellished by any colorful but accidental detail or developed along lines betraying the spirit of the theoretical argument for the sake of aesthetic effect. That it must be tailored to theoretical specifications is not to say it has no distinctive power to wield of its own. It has the positive power of creating atmosphere, image and mood – which may be spartan by the standards of literary fiction but will be vivid enough when compared with the barrenness of an abstract theory left to itself. It has the negative power of exposing a theory entirely at odds with life – for what is more telling of a theory that fails substantively, than an illustration perfectly cut and fitted to it that cannot be gotten to ring true?

If the theoretically drawn figure or scene is more tightly reined in than the literary fiction, it still can be more suggestive and generous than the historical/empirical case. It is not able to puff itself up, through having actually occurred, into something grander than the theoretical abstraction. It does not work to shrink that abstraction to dimensions as small and specific as its own, halting the mind at the boundaries of *this* year, *this* region, *this* group. It can allude to a whole array of actual historical characters or events, not one of which alone would have precisely illustrated the abstract point. It can illustrate the logic of a situation that through a chance combination of circumstances had been stymied or only partly played out in actual life, with the result that it has no historical examples to show for itself. The most meaningless real event – Napoleon's catching a cold – may have been all that queered the works, and while such a triviality could be used to illustrate the operation of chance in human affairs, it hardly could illustrate anything else. Finally, it can suggest figures and scenes that might possibly have a real existence, but one too secretive or subtle to catch the empirical researcher's eye.

For its evocative quality on the one side and submissiveness to logic on the other, the concrete condensation of the abstract idea is suited to various kinds of theoretical adventures. Thus it was that Marx, to take the simplest kind of example, breathed life into the structural logic of the wage-labor–capital relation in the pages of *Das Kapital*, by referring to the doings of "Mr Moneybags," "our capitalist," "our friend" – all concrete representations of the abstraction "capital" rather than actual historical men.[23] But for an additional reason the device of, to use an abbreviated phrase, the "concrete type" is uniquely suited to the purposes of discourse theory. It is this sort of theory, you will remember, that finds the bedrock of a system of social power to be a conceptual regime dictating what kinds of entities there are in the world and policing the boundaries of what can be thought, imagined, desired, said and so done. Now, the problem that automatically arises is how theory is to make its way out of a system of classifications it declares is entrenched, hegemonic, over-weening – but, for all that, fundamentally contingent, with no privileged relation to a true order of things. What route is more promising than an elaboration of concrete types that are at once intimated in and at odds with hegemonic classifications? What more promising route to challenge the power of, for example, the masculine and the feminine (abstract ideas about the meaning of the body that have fortified themselves in every imaginable cultural and political way, that show up in a thousand different concrete guises, and that exert constitutive power over "the normal," "the good," and "the real") than to see whether a greater profusion of subjective types can subsist side by side with these two, overshadowed and obscured by them but intimated in the very fact of their distinction? Such a way will seem overly oblique only to those insisting that authoritative and constitutive ideas must be refuted by something called "facts" in "the real, empirical world."

The very simultaneity of the concrete type's being at once arid and vivid, abstract and concrete, suggestive of objective determination and subjective agency, has a drawback to it. As with any double-edged thing, it is easy for one of its edges to fade away from view. Most typically, the whole meaning of the concrete type is pinned on its concrete, subjective side, and it is taken as a very poor portrait of an actual living being. The same mistake of taking the type as a direct semblance of something in lived life will prompt the reader to suspect that the author sees all of lived life in terms of types and so even the reader as a mere instance of one type or another. And this is an agitating thought – for aren't all readers (and all writers, too) convinced of their personal uniqueness and originality?

The device of the concrete condensation or type, however, is meant not to reduce the complexity of lived life but to expand the complexity of theory, by multiplying the different kinds of subjects of theoretical sentences and specifying them with some vitality. The goal is to elaborate a vocabulary of the subject less destitute, more finely discriminating, and so more in keeping with the over-abundance of actual life than the vocabulary of traditional theory – without succumbing so completely to the charm of the particular and unique that the ability to use general categories or make large distinctions is entirely lost. The goal, that is, is to create a variegated vocabulary of the subject without forsaking the theoretical stance and being left with only an infinite number of names to denote an infinite number of individual qualities and things. Here I should add two important asides. First, the wish to create such a vocabulary does not signal a belief in the coherence, logical priority or autonomy of the subject. That subjectivity is worthy of a theoretical attention to detail does not mean that it is a whole and uncontradictory "thing," that it is the foundation of everything else, or that it is self-positing and self-determining. Second, the creation of such a vocabulary is likely to have more than theoretical implications. For the homely discourses of the everyday world, no less than the rarified discourses of traditional theory, present constricted ranges of approved and legitimate types. Outside live the illicit possibilities of subjectivity, sometimes listed in a companion set of classifications, sometimes conceptually suppressed. Such homely discourses, then, are systems of authorization and prohibition for practical life. If this is strongly true of the discourses of the dominant culture, it is true in a weaker way of those discourses confined within the bounds of an alternative or marginal community. It will be, then, a political as well as philosophical act to pry open and cut across dominant or counter-cultural authorizations and prohibitions – not to speak in fantastical, utopian terms but to announce secret actualities and potentialities outloud.

In conclusion to our considerations on theory and method, and in anticipation of our considerations on Masculine/feminine, we should review very roughly the classificatory schemes of sex and gender already in place, against which acts of political–philosophical disobedience might be committed. There is, at the least differentiated, least nuanced end of the spectrum (a spectrum that does not, however, stretch very far in the other direction) the discourse of pure abstract philosophy. Its categories of "man," "mind," "the individual," and "one" repress the world of power, sex, and gender altogether – or almost altogether. The obsessive use of "man" to stand for the universal subject must count as being an escaped symptom of that world. There are, next, most of the discourses of ordinary life, that include everything from pedestrian idioms to the conversational phrases of high literate culture. Here we find the binary, complementary, asymmetrical, and phallocentric categories of "man" and "woman," "masculine" and "feminine," and hundreds of more minor and more graphic versions of these. Finally, there are the discourses of outlawed sexual subcultures and of the gay and feminist formations that surfaced into public view, it seems, only yesterday. Of these, the discourse of radical feminism pits itself most militantly and self-consciously against the dominant conceptual scheme. Its categories – alien to the larger society but common coin in feminist enclaves and women's communities – cover almost the same narrow range as their phallocentric counterparts, the two solitary points on that range, however, having their values reversed, their significances transformed, and their complementarity obliterated.[24]

The schedules of concrete types in the chapters to follow do no more than begin to break open the entrenched schemes of sex and gender by just a hair's breadth. If they are modestly richer than those entrenched schemes, they are poorer than the actual realities of life, as all classificatory systems must always be. The parsimoniousness of my classifications will be especially evident with respect to my discussion of erotic desire. First, I will be elaborating only three or four more types of desire than the established schemes allow – hardly any more at all, and, moreover, types that for strategic reasons will be conservatively close to rather than adventurously far from the ones that are already given. Second, the very idea of "types" where eroticism is concerned offends against most people's conviction that their own experience of sexual passion is something individual and exceptional. Unfortunately, that conviction rarely has stopped anyone from falling back, in their everyday depiction of desire, on the crude typology of "masculine" and "feminine" eroticisms. Finally, concrete types of erotic desire, which are necessarily as deductive as they are expressive, will appear almost sacrilegiously mathematical when juxtaposed to the profuse, undisciplined erotic experience recalled in memory and brought to life again in literary writing. At this point, it is important to keep in mind that the purpose of the concrete type is to be highly cryptic, to make concrete only the logic of a position or relation, not to conjure up the whole thing or lavish attention on whatever aspect of it happens to catch an author's inner eye. Equally, it is not meant to reproduce the plenitude of actual life, the infinite ways in which life is more than logic, the sheer detail of what is present to the senses, the pure chance, the idiosyncrasy of character, the action taken for no reason. A schedule of concrete types of erotic desire, consequently, will be meant not to simulate types of experience, but on the one side to suggest the physical/emotional atmosphere of the erotic encounter, and on the other to launch an assault on conceptual rules for which sorts of bodies can desire which sorts of things.

One must keep in mind, too, that the static, frozen quality of the concrete condensation does not signify any absence of dynamism in actual life or any absence of movement on any living individual's part from one concrete stance to another. Nor does the individuality and unity of the condensation signify that its nearest correlate in actual life must be a whole individual self, instead of – smaller than a self – a fleeting mood, a single facet of the personality, a biographical phase; or – larger than a self – a subculture, a political formation, a social domain, an historical epoch.

Are concrete condensations meant to have some universal significance to them? The answer to this question is largely no, in that particular types have their relevance within a historically and culturally limited mode of life and often within a single aspect of that mode. When a whole way of life changes drastically enough, or when we shift our sights from one aspect of it to another, the types that illuminate it change as well. But there is a guarded sense in which the answer to the question may also be yes. For there are certain schedules of types that seem to be intimated by features of social life so recurrent as to be, at the least, characteristic of all ways of life that are conceivable to us, and, at the most, characteristic of the human condition. Now, it seems to me that the schedule of concrete types of erotic desire I will present to you here pertains to only one dimension of social life, and to only one cultural and historical moment. But the same does not strike me as being so obviously true of my second schedule. That one will mark the postures it is possible to assume towards the regime of Masculine/feminine as a whole: those of the naive loyalist, the self-conscious loyalist, the eccentric, the critic, the traitor, the rebel. In their particular details, such postures will refer to a contemporary order of sex and gender. But in their broadest lines, are they not relevant to times and places different from our own, and to other centers than that inscribed by the sex/gender system? Might they not make some distant kind of sense when and wherever there is social order at all?

Part Two

On Masculine/feminine

The questions about culture, power, and resistance that we considered in the abstract in Part One we now are ready to consider again with our sights set on the domain of sex and gender. Specifically, we will investigate Masculine/feminine as a cultural–political regime and radical feminism as a formation in antithesis to it. We will pose our questions about opposites of style and of substance in the following way. Can a theoretical language of the life of the sexed body be designed to evoke the sensuous experience of that life? And can there be sealed to the notion of a rule that is hegemonic, phallocentric, and effective, a notion of figures and episodes that negate that rule?

6

Point and Counterpoint

1.

The novelist delights in the ambiguities of character and the intricacies of social life. The lover thrives on them, the liar enhances them, and the naif must learn to take them into account. But for the political actor deliberating on what commitments to make or the political theorist attempting to comprehend the causes and consequences of the commitments of others, such ambiguities and intricacies are the source of frustration rather than of artistic pleasure, erotic desire, or the necessary pains of a social education. Thus the person who must decide to act in one way or another in the political world, and the person who must fix on an explanation of why things in that world happened as they did, are especially prey to the temptation to act or explain not in the face of great complexity but as if that complexity did not exist. Those who fall to the temptation do so not, like the naif, out of innocence, but out of a tacit knowledge of how difficult things would become for them were they to acknowledge an opacity and indefiniteness in human affairs.

It is possible that in the course of one's political adventures or theoretical research, one might come upon an individual who seems the pure incarnation of some good or evil, an action which has one clear meaning to it, or an entire mode of life which in all its dimensions shows essentially the same smooth surface, so that a single description would suffice to capture its truth. But such an absence of complication in the human realm is exceedingly rare. Most often individual persons are domineering and manipulative but also generous and self-sacrificing, or they are austere and remote but secretly sensitive, or they are warm and kind-hearted but superficial in their attentions and promiscuous in their affections. Certainly it is by no means the case that all people are an equal mixture of virtue and vice, and there is the most important difference in the world between those in whom a virtue and those in whom a vice turns out to be the surprise. But almost all people are a contradictory mixture of some sort.

Every action in its turn is like to carry with it the contradictions of its individual author, so that the manipulative tactic may be softened by the generous end for which it was devised, the warm gesture diminished by the shallowness behind it. But action is complicated further in that it is never simply the expression of the individual's own character and intentions. It also refers to a wider set of social practices which fixes the boundaries within which the individual usually thinks to move.[1] Even the action which breaks out of those boundaries makes a negative reference to them, either implicitly (as, for example, bohemianism makes a tacit reference to the propriety of bourgeois culture) or explicitly (as atheism makes an aggressive reference to religious faith). The double situation of every action – located at once within the individual's unique biography and the shared practices of a social whole – is a fresh source of contradiction in, first of all, ordinary human affairs, because there is never an assured identity between the broad substance of conventions and the sensibilities of the person who acts conventionally. Social arrangements may encourage among participants co-operation or self-absorption, sympathy or brutality. But the general tenor of those arrangements may be pernicious while the individual's own beliefs and purposes are the most humane ones that could be expected to arise under the circumstances; or, on the contrary, social arrangements may be conducive to comradery and fairness, while the individual's purposes are spiteful and self-serving. It is always possible, then, that a single action may reflect perniciousness and humanity, or fairness and spitefulness, at one and the same time. Thus too it is always possible for there to be admirable and not so admirable individuals acting according to more or less the same set of conventional rules. These possibilities do not mean that action is too diffuse for any rigorous analysis to be made of it or any stringent posture to be assumed towards it, but it does mean that theory and practice will miss the mark if they treat action as a flat and monotonic thing.

Second, conversely, there is never an assured disjuncture between shared conventions and the sensibilities of persons rebelling against them. Here human affairs are contradictory precisely because there is not the sharp contradiction where one expects to find it. The rebellious act in its essence stands in a highly ambivalent relation to established social practice. It declares itself the very negation of that practice, but as such it is bound up with it in a way in which acts of passive compliance or of merely eccentric deviation are not. It is the rebel rather than the ordinary or idiosyncratic actor who is passionately attentive to the given order of things; who thinks, writes, and talks of little else; who determinedly ferrets out every secret strength and weakness of that order; who searches for the explanation of how it came and continues to be; and who out of the greatest intimacy with it and in the greatest deference to it, understands herself as *its* critic, *its* judge, *its* enemy. Meanwhile, in all the qualities and habits "accidental" to her political position, the rebel may duplicate conventional actors. She may share with them any or almost all of their talents, limitations of thought, sensuous tastes, exaggerations of character, their kindnesses and faults – with the sole exception that she must reject and then accept some condition central to the given organization of social life.[2] The possibility of a multiplicity of resemblances between rebel and loyalist does not mean that there is not an all-important difference between opposing and defending an established order, or that this difference has no implications for the way rebels and loyalists live out their lives, or that there are not distinctive values and traditions which separate groups and individuals with antagonistic allegiances. It also does not mean, to make an opposite point, that the dominant order is responsible for the rebel's flaws. But it does mean that, just as no simple statement of identity can be made about the conventional order and the conventional individual, no simple statement of opposition can be made about those who act in accordance with that order and those who act against it.

In its consequences no less than its underpinnings, action is complicated by its double situation. The single act inserts itself in a collective web of actions extending far beyond its own author's range of vision, and hence it is bound to have a signficance and influence somewhat at odds and sometimes in utter conflict with what that author had meant to accomplish by it.[3] The potential for contradiction between the intended and actual consequences of action is greatest when the entire web of action becomes, so to speak, unstuck, so that actions are cut adrift from past conventions; or when, because the principles governing a society dictate it, the rule of convention is relatively slack; or when hidden dimensions of familiar practices subvert the purposes of their participants. But the potential is present, if in a more muted form, also when detailed social rules strictly regulate the appropriate responses for participants to make to different types of actions on one another's parts. For even in a highly structured social life, rules cannot anticipate every possible variation in how an appropriate action may be performed, or every kind of action participants might conceive of taking, to say nothing of every abstract possibility of action inconceivable only because no one has taken it yet. And of course no rule can ensure that it will not be perverted or broken.

The social order's being, as it is, the entire maze of ambiguous and contradictory characters, single actions, and shared practices, it is rarely clear or simple enough to be reprehensible in some total, unredeeming way and is never, unfortunately, so clear and simple as to be totally good. Often, very often, its most appealing features bear an unseverable connection to its most contemptible ones. A society which rests on the unrelieved physical toil of its masses, enforces the erotic, domestic, and public subservience of one sex to the other, and explains the misery of its population by reference to fate, lowly birth, or wrongdoing in a previous life, may be also uniquely appreciative of the human need for sociability, security, and minute rather than massive variation in physical surroundings. This appreciation may be expressed in its norms of mutual obligation and the observance of custom, and also in the external shape of its open-air markets, public squares, winding streets, houses built to mirror rather than dwarf the size of human bodies, and in the physical grandeur of its churches or temples as the embodiments of reassuring authority. Thus, too, a society which glorifies the endless production and consumption of material goods, pits its members one against the other in a competitive struggle to survive and succeed, and brutalizes a variety of different colonized populations – this same society may undermine traditional restrictions on specially delineated groups, and it may create the principles, sensibility, and material conditions by which individuals can exert and defend their autonomy as equal human beings. That egoism and atomism are exacerbated at the same time only underscores the rule that one must be delicate – which is not to say over-generous – in one's depiction of every social whole.

To underestimate these paradoxes and convolutions threading their way through the human condition invites, for the political theorist and political actor, the twin dangers of misunderstanding human character, action, and society; and of making too easy distinctions between friends and enemies, good deeds and bad, praiseworthy and contemptible modes of life. There is, of course, the opposite set of dangers. The political theorist may become so infatuated with the complexities of her subject-matter that she works to cloud rather than clarify circumstances already less than plain but not as obscure as a baroque theoretical aesthetic would have one believe. The political actor may be so impressed by the complexity of a situation that she cannot make her own move in it and so by default lends her weight to whatever happens to be the strongest current in the general flow of events.

2.

Neither intellectual super-refinement nor practical paralysis are the characteristic weaknesses of radical feminism at the present moment. Instead, it has been drawn further and further into that cold, clear region of thought in which a clean line separates good forces from evil. This is the region where it is believed that quiescent members of the oppressed sex are powerless, innocent, and blind, and their oppressors wield power self-consciously and with malignant intent; where it is admitted only that members of the oppressed sex may be manipulated to do harm to one another but of their own free accord would act always lovingly, nurturantly, harmoniously; and where it is asserted that the good principle embodied in the subordinate sex must be precipitated out from a history and civilization created and dominated by the bad. Joining the radical feminists in such declarations but understandably kept at a distance by them are many other women who flirt with notions of a sexualized moral dualism but continue to indulge in and presumably enjoy heterosexual connections in the so-called man-made world.[4]

In its most militant mood and sometimes in its most ambivalent one, feminism thus has moved surely and steadily towards a theoretical manichaeism. But although no one may be eager to ask them, three questions wait patiently to greet its arrival. The first question has to do with how radical feminism came to *this* particular theoretical territory. Why has it been attracted by a drastically simplified version of human affairs rather than, say, by the ultra-ornate theoreticizing so in vogue with the non-feminist intellectual avant-garde? The second question concerns the particular inadequacies of what in another tradition is called an instrumentalist analysis. How, specifically, does the idea of a society divided into manipulated victims and knowing victimizers evade the full truth of the sex/gender system, and what kind of methodological revisions would feminism have to make in order to grasp that system at its most rather than least complicated points? The third question becomes pressing precisely to the extent that the critics and not the proponents of a feminist manichaeism prove to win the day. Can a theory that keeps at the very forefront of its consciousness a sensitivity to the complexity, opacity, and contradictions of gender relations at the same time preserve an unqualified commitment to challenge those relations?

This third question must be met head on by all those who stress the intricacy of social life. For, in the past, such an emphasis has gone hand in hand with a compulsion to excuse the most deplorable actions and cultural forms, on the grounds that complicated forces were at work beyond the actor's or the epoch's knowledge and control, or beyond the observer's own capacities of empathetic understanding. It has fed a proclivity for a mild conservatism in politics, which does not require that one make active judgments and take oppositional stands in the inevitably hazy circumstances of social life, but instead allows one simply to drift on in the same direction as before. Finally, an emphasis on the intricacy of human affairs can lead to an abandonment of political questions altogether, as a way of avoiding the whole uncomfortable problem of how to assign responsibility for the actions of others and how to make one's own incision in what often seems an impossibly twisted tangle of events. At this extreme point, the appreciation of an essential ambiguity in life gives way to a disdain not only for radical political theory, but for political theory *per se*. However delicately it prepares the way, political theory must make, in the end, definitive statements about the given distribution of social power, the legitimacy of that distribution, and theory's appropriate role with respect to political practice. The tendency towards a depoliticization of interests on the part of thought which becomes preoccupied with the shades of grey in the social world, forces us to consider whether an adequately complex political theory may be only a chimera, a pipe dream for intellectuals, a contradiction in terms.

But I had said we would start out from the opposite direction. How did the most militant segment of feminism come to be enchanted by the eminently simple notions of a wholly victimized and innocent sex, and a wholly victimizing and responsible one?

Certainly this segment must have been drawn to the idea that power and evil are aligned on the one side and powerlessness and goodness on the other, partly out of shock. That the imperatives to do with sex and gender, which had seemed as fixed in nature and as inevitably fused with suffering as birth and death, were in fact the exigencies of a social system of power was a cruel if ultimately heartening discovery to make. Drastic explanations for the asymmetrical ties between women and men were bound to follow from it. This social system of power, moreover, seemed to swell in magnitude under the investigating eye. It proved to regulate relatively external features of social life such as the organization of reproduction, the division of labor, and the boundaries between public and private realms. It pressed in on the intimate meetings of bodies; and more inward still, it dictated erotic desire and the self's fundamental understanding of itself. Then too, the mystification of everything touched by sex and gender, whose myriad cultural forms radical feminism undertook to penetrate and expose, was of truly impressive proportions. It was dense with accretions from the past and with newly sprouted prejudices, pretensions, distortions, and delusions. In religious accounts of the spiritual and mundane, in philosphical reflections on the infinite and the limited, in scientific theories of male and female biologies, psychologies and sexualities; in the multiplicity of essays, novels, commentaries, and poems flowing from the pens of those who wrote down their thoughts at the refined edges of public culture; in the films, magazines, and advertisements concocted for mass consumption; and finally in the very categories of language itself, the notions of a natural masculinity and a natural femininity were endlessly generated and regenerated. Everywhere the self-affirming, positive, active, dominant, aggressive value-in-itself did its macabre symbolic dance with the self-denying, negative, passive, subordinate, submissive value-in-relation-to-another. The vigor of the entire ideological formation, its monstrous size and creativity, and its triumph over other possibilities of self-interpretation led to suspicions that it must have as its authors malevolent, self-conscious, and masterful men.

These suspicions, which duly haunted women as they tracked down the secrets of the sex/gender system, were not allayed by the dominant culture's responses to their revelations. True, the posture of state institutions and the communications industry, which together reduced feminist charges to complaints about individual rights and unequal opportunities, scarcely could be credited with a special phallocentric intent. Political liberalism worked to absorb feminism in a way which only replicated its absorption of every previous oppositional movement. Reactions in the academy, on the contrary, easily could be read as further evidence of the masculine will to power women were unmasking as the guiding principle of the world at large. Conservative academics greeted feminist critique with attentive counter-attacks, defending on biological, historical or psychological grounds male domination and female subordination. Other less forthright scholars fell back on ridicule and willful ignorance of feminist literature, buttressing their posture with the claim that questions to do with a sex/gender system were inappropriate to the pursuit of knowledge and truth. But the most telling refusal to engage with feminist critique occurred on the part of avant-garde social, political and literary theory, usually so open to seduction by iconoclasms of every sort. At the same moment that theory, having freed itself from the stolidity of Marxist discourse, acquired a fresh appetite for the imaginative and anti-traditional, it actively neglected radical feminism, which had made itself the living embodiment of the imaginative and anti-traditional both as thought and as cultural practice. At this point, instead, the theoretical avant-garde began to condemn as repressive the application of egalitarian and cooperative public ideals to the self's private proclivities. It developed a fascination for Nietzsche, who saw morality *per se* as a mere cover for the resentments of the lowly, the miserable, the "botched at birth." Hence there threatened to emerge what could only be, for feminism, a dangerous new standpoint: an anarchistic rather than reactionary prohibition against any political critique of sexuality made in the name of an emancipatory moral ethos, and/or on behalf of a sex that, historically accused of being "botched at birth," had been said to be outside of ordinary moral bonds between men to begin with.

Ultimately, however, it was the newly virulent misogyny in "popular" culture, and additionally the literati's attraction to its most bizarre forms, that confirmed radical feminism's nightmarish fears and convinced it to take its nightmares as reflections of waking life. A sadistic masculinity and masochistic femininity paraded as truth in "entertainment" movies, in the lyrics of popular music, on album covers and fashion magazines, in self-confessed pornography, and only somewhat more covertly in a cult of criminality among progressive writers who gravitated to male torturers, rapists, murderers, and child molesters as liberation heroes flaunting the authoritarianism and puritanicalism of moral convention and legal right.[5] Every rhetorical flourish radical feminism used to emphasize that men lived off the brutalization of women found its correlative in some graphic depiction of male brutality in "popular" culture, to which no member of the established intelligentsia seemed to object, and on which some member was sure to add an appreciative gloss. Radical feminism declared that "we live in a profoundly anti-female society, a misogynist 'civilization' in which men collectively victimize women," that "a woman's erotic femininity is measured by the degree to which she needs to be hurt, needs to be possessed, needs to be abused," that "the basic elements of rape are involved in all heterosexual relationships."[6] How could one possibly take issue with it on this score, when the culture produced for popular enjoyment, and the commentary produced on that culture by critics and men of letters, nodded its many heads in avid agreement? The portraits that phallocentricism and radical feminism painted of how the world worked were in fact in such perfect correspondence, that if one looked to one to test the likeness of the other, one would be convinced that the world spun on an axis of male power and female powerlessness, eroticized as sexual violation and humiliation.

Given the imaginary state of affairs in contemporary Western culture, it was hardly surprising that radical feminism saw real relations between women and men in an extremely stark light. The misogyny of cultural artifacts, however, while helping to account for why radical feminism believed women to be victims, did not account for why it believed them to be inherently good. How did it come to claim a natural female inclination to virtue, which meant, in the feminist context, an inclination to empathy, cooperation, nurturance, harmony, and peace? One answer, obviously enough, lay in the equation of masculinity with the schedule of true virtues (a different schedule, to be sure) that was such a constant feature of society at large. The celebration of masculine violence, after all, was only one limited and especially nasty instance of a long-lived and variegated tradition valorizing whatever qualities happened to be associated with the phallus. When feminism began to expose the secret vices of a sex which had proclaimed itself the epitome of virtue, it was a natural next move to expose the secret virtues of the sex which men would have proclaimed the epitome of vice had they not held the feminine in too much contempt to use the term "vicious" about it. Unfortunately, it has always been a very short step from pointing out the virtues of a group historically maligned, to pointing out that group as the very synonym of virtue. Feminism found this step too irresistible not to take. And so it indulged in the temptation, reifying the feminine at the very moment that it revealed the underside of the masculine delusion of grandeur to be egoism, officiousness, pomposity, fear of the body, denial of the mundane, worship of authority, and obsession with power and force.

Resembling hegemonic images of masculine and feminine in this sometimes direct and sometimes inverted way, the ideas of an evil male agency and a defenseless female goodness thus turn out to be more familiar than they first might have appeared. But these ideas have another genealogical connection altogether with traditional habits of thought. They are bound by a long thin strand to given rules governing the appropriate method of explaining thought and action, whether thought and action have to do with sex and gender or not. The line from the staid prejudices of methodological individualism to the conspiratorial predilections of radical feminism is not a straightforward one. It was, after all, in its strenuous efforts to extricate itself from the premise that the individual is the fount of its own beliefs and practices, and in its subsequent journey away from a liberal analysis of social life, that feminism found its way to the idea of a victimized and victimizing sex. But it was precisely here that the old premise and analysis left their secret stamp. Surely if stealthily, they had marked out a meta-theoretical path that feminism in its most adventurous mood set out on and faithfully followed.

Feminism's original point of departure, the spot from which it had to make its first escape, was defined by these two explanatory principles: that the primary unit of society is the individual, abstracted from any structural position he might occupy or social group to which he might belong; and that the adult individual is the sole author of his own beliefs and actions, unless he has fallen under the sway of irrational custom or religious or political dogma, and/or unless external obstacles prevent him from executing his plans. An organic individualism which represented the subject's ideas and actions as expressions of his uniquely flowering self had long since given way to a mechanistic individualism which showed the subject to be a summation of environmental pressures, of which "the socialization process" was the most central. But a person's having been conditioned by environmental stimuli in no way distinguished him from any other person. He still was an individual like every other, no more or less the product of objective conditions, so that theory could continue to treat him as if he were his own author as long as it remembered that ontologically he had more in common with a thermostat than with a wild rose. His agency in this modified sense was diminished only if he had been socialized into a traditional or a totalitarian culture rather than into a liberal one – in which case, he had been not simply socialized but imprisoned by custom in the first instance, and brainwashed by a government in the second – or, once again, if external obstacles stymied his projects.

An immeasurable distance separates the idea of "an individual like every other individual" from the idea of an engendered self, and liberalism, the socio-political theory most closely aligned to methodological individualism, negotiated this distance very clumsily. Without any pause to wonder why, it used the masculine pronoun to signify the theoretically genderless subject and gave the generic "he" a masculine referent whenever it analyzed a concrete situation or used a concrete case to illuminate an abstract point. These formal gaffes were signs of a deep-seated contradiction on its part. Liberalism declared as its most precious principle that all individuals, by nature and, when properly organized, in society, are free to try to make of themselves what they will, are equal in their humanity and independent in their relations with others. It also insisted that natural differences between the sexes dictated for them different proclivities, desires, talents, behaviors, and social opportunities – a dictation which until very recently it thought should be reinforced by religious strictures, moral sanctions, and the law. Female nature was believed to bend away from the virtues of autonomy, rationality, impartiality, as well as from what deceptively were called "necessary vices" but in fact were treated as warrants for praise: self-interestedness, aggression, competitiveness, and impersonality. Hence neither relations between women and men nor relations among women could be governed by the liberal ideal.[7]

Its detachment from what it believed to be things to do with women allowed liberal theory to dismiss these contradictions as of no real importance and to turn a blind eye to all the curiosities of its position. Its refusal to reflect on a knot of gender-related hesitations and confusions was an arch-instance of theoretical self-protection, for such persistent and pervasive muddles could hardly be counted as quirks of thought to which liberals as mere individuals were prone. Their explanation required a move liberal theory had not the competence to make, one which its entire methodological apparatus was designed to forbid: a reference to relations between social collectivities irreducible to relations between individuals as the sole authors of their own thought and action. More specifically, it required an investigation of how a social order of sex and gender infused the self-understandings of all its members and ensured an asymmetrical set of experiences for women and men. There was, moreover, no reason to assume that the self-understandings and experiences were enforced only by means of discrete external obstacles to the actions of one sex or the other – the only kind of constraint on free agency liberalism normally was willing to acknowledge. Legal prohibitions, physical punishments, financial liabilities, and so on did play their part in the sex/gender order. But the engenderment of personality, the creation of heterosexual desire, the aspects of sexual power that operated under the rule of affection and love, the sexual division of labor, the public cultural representations of masculinity and femininity – all were forces of a far more systematic and tenacious sort. Such forces very often were present as internal constituents of consciousness, very often were "absent" as internal constituents of the unconscious, so that even the most sharp-witted of individuals were likely to be blind to them. Whether or not they felt themselves to be self-determining, whether or not they were aware of only the most obvious restrictions upon them, all individuals were etched by the demands of a social system of sex and gender much larger and more powerful than themselves.

It was not, then, that liberal analysis was simply the wrong way to come to grips with one of the most fundamental facts of social life. It actively seemed to obscure that facet under the veil of methodological individualism and by means of a social theory that, sliding back and forth between the generic and the masculine subject, ignored the existence of an order of sex and gender while remaining loyal to its every principle. But perhaps it is unfair to say that liberalism could produce no answer of its own to the questions of why it stumbled so awkwardly over the conceptual terrain occupied by "women" and "men." Did it not have a means of explaining its own theoretical lapses where women were concerned? In the nineteenth century, a few liberals found it congenial to consider the subjection of women to be the last irrational custom modernity had inherited from the past, the remains of the superstition and narrow-mindedness endemic to the traditional world. If the root of the problem was ignorance born out of the tyranny of custom, the solution was the greater expansion of individual autonomy, the more thorough triumph of reason, very happily the extension of liberalism itself.[8] In the twentieth century, others have traced sexual inquality to a socialization process which conditions individuals to glorify masculinity, scorn femininity, and collaborate in reproducing both. The proposed solution to it has shifted accordingly from the forward march of knowledge and its defeat of prejudice, to the project of revising the ideas of masculine and feminine with which persons are inculcated as children.

Despite the surface explanatory appeal of blind tradition and specific socialization patterns, explanation by "custom" or "socialization" always has substituted the pretense of analysis for analysis itself. It dissolves history into a series of meaningless accidents and turns attempts at comprehension into laments against the efficacy of comprehension: "That was just the way people did things when they acted habitually"; "That was simply what we all were brought up to believe." Certainly in its account of its own stance towards women, liberalism has evaded every crucial question it should have asked itself, but which it could not ask as long as it clung to a vocabulary too bare to capture the collective dimensions of power, its systematic forms, and the subtle ways in which it shows its face. Neither has liberalism been able to make up for its past inadequacies by doing anything more than scrupulously obliterating the categories "male" and "female" from its theoretical musings and the rules governing its practical social life. The advantage in treating women unequivocally as persons is that liberalism can savor the pleasure of meaning what it says, when it says that all individuals incline naturally to independence, rationality, and self-determination. The price of the pleasure is a final renunciation of sex and gender as matters for investigation, significant in their own right rather than as mere landmines to be more carefully avoided.

And yet, as we follow in radical feminism's tracks to a new territory, let us not too quickly leave the old one behind. We should linger long enough to note that liberal individualism harbors one other approach to sex, gender, and power than simply erasing the words for them from its vocabulary. At its outer edge, just where it meets up with anarchism, it charges that the engenderment of personality is the most inward, recalcitrant social constraint on human freedom. It denounces that constraint for forcing all individuals into one of two tight psychological and physical spaces on the arbitrary basis of their genitalia, and for dictating the paths self-expression must and must not take. The authoritarian rule evidenced in the very normality of masculine and feminine selves is only doubly severe for punishing twice instead of once the persons it forces to be feminine.[9]

Nevertheless, the outer region of liberalism is, in the end, only that – a marginal preserve for minor tendencies of thought, eccentric concerns and perverse political sympathies banished from the center and unable to make a dent on it. And indeed, were it not for its line of intellectual descent, the standpoint which describes gender as tyranny over individuality would belong to some other camp altogether than that of an individualism that, when it thinks about gender distinctions at all, guards them jealously as if they were the very heart of distinctiveness in human affairs.

In any case, it was not an anarchistic liberalism but the far more conventional sort that determined the flight-path radical feminism took in search for a new mode of analysis. It was conventional liberalism that radical feminism had to refute by claiming that women were not the original authors of their thought and action; that the restrictions upon them came only secondarily, if still importantly, in the form of external barriers in front of what they wanted to do; and that explanations of sexual inequality based on custom or socialization were insufficient to capture the truth of the system of power in which masculinity and femininity were produced and preserved. But conventional liberalism also supplied radical feminism with the positive conviction, to which radical feminism has clung faithfully if sometimes ambiguously until this very day, that the origins of thought and action always can be traced back to self-conscious human authorship and clear-sighted human agency. For liberal theory, this tracing back normally stopped short at the particular individual doing the thinking and acting. Radical feminism, on the contrary, was pressed to look beyond that particular individual at least where women were concerned, because of its claim that women typically did not understand their situation or determine even "their own" contribution to it. But it continued to presume that someone was responsible for what was thought and done in the world: that the meaning of a situation was to be found in some human author's understanding of it, that the explanation of what had been done was to be found in some human agent's intentions and plans.

Thus radical feminism lifted the veil of women's thought and action to expose other thinkers and actors hidden behind them. It uncovered men as the ghost writers and secret agents of social life. If women were blind to the ramifications of their ideas and practices, it must be men who had clear vision; if women did not shape what they thought and did, it must be men who manipulated them; if women passively suffered under an infinity of burdens, it must be men who actively concocted those burdens and conditioned women to accept them without complaint. Radical feminism gave this kind of account of how things went on in every arena of the sex/gender system, although it did not give only this account.[10] More striking still, it attributed to male authorship and agency the petty faults and serious failings of women in contexts where something other than sex and gender struck the major chord.

These instrumentalist assumptions about gender and power, which pervaded feminist discourse at its own margins, insured that the radical insight into sex/gender relations would remain trapped at a simple level of social critique. Nevertheless, the principle that men control women did usher feminism into the domain of critical social theory in the first place, and here it was able to draw on concepts of ideology, mystification, administered desire, and social domination that liberal theory absolutely ruled out. Its embrace of this same principle led radical feminism to two distinct conclusions it could not have reached under the established conceptual order: first, that there is such a thing as a sex/gender system, saturated with power and with its cruelest consequences reserved for women; and second, that the power saturating this sytem flows out of one source, flows out in one direction, and is utterly simple in its cause and effects. In asserting that men wield power as a monolithic bloc, radical feminism denied the only source of complexity in social life for which liberalism has had any special affection: the fact of a vast plurality of authors and agents in the world. Condensing human authorship and agency not merely into members of a single sex (for wasn't this condensation already implicit in the conventional view?), but into members of a single sex thinking and acting as a single author and agent with a single purpose in mind, radical feminism substituted for an immense field of particularities, contradictions, hesitations, and ambivalences a uniformity of thoughts, and actions which, while they may have appeared in an infinity of forms and occurred in a multiplicity of times and places, were infused with a single sensibility and interest.

In shifting the locus of knowledge and self-determination from the individual to an all-powerful sex, feminism at once was faced with the task of devising a new set of concepts to capture the condition of the powerless. It had to find words for the process by which women were stripped continuously of their capacities for critical reflection, blinded to the origins and often the very fact of the limitations upon them, and habituated to their subordinate status. A language of passivity and pure receptivity in the determination of consciousness again lay close at hand in the established discourse, this time in the stock-in-trade terminology of mechanistic individualism and technocratic theory. Words like "conditioning" and "socialization," used by behavioral scientists to describe the process by which individuals were inculcated with beliefs and values in any society, and words like "brainwashing" and "indoctrination," specially devised to evoke the making of the communist consciousness, were taken up more or less as synonyms by radical feminism in order to characterize the derivative mind of the victim as opposed to the originative mind of the victimizer, the mental servitude of the controlled as opposed to the mental freedom of the controller.[11] That the mechanistic imagery radical feminism imported to depict female consciousness in a male-dominated world conflicted with its own organic sensibilities was evident in its ambivalent account of "women's experience," which it alternately condemned as "man-made" and celebrated as if it flowed directly from some privileged, essentially female inner source. Its explanation of how the contents of women's consciousness typically came to be there – through "implantation," "instillation," "manipulation," and so on – was also at odds with its belief that, once freed from the prison of patriarchy, women's consciousness would flower like a wild rose, not register like a thermostat.

The contradiction between its mechanistic understanding of consciousness in the present and organic vision of consciousness in the future was very much the romantic analogue of the contradiction in orthodox Marxist theory, between the ideas of a proletariat thoroughly blinded and manipulated by the bourgeoisie and a revolutionary class thoroughly self-conscious and self-determining. Indeed, that analogue should have served as a reminder to radical feminism, if it had not believed itself utterly without precedent in human history, that the path from individualism to instrumentalism to utopianism to, inevitably, disillusionment has been traveled before. Located along its trajectory are two tendencies radical feminism always has found loathsome: reductionist Marxism and the hyper-theoreticism of Marxists and post-Marxists in revolt against it. What that feminism did not see was that the flight of the left from a theoretical millenarianism to a more subtle and wary analysis came partly on the heels of the suspicion that the oppressed class would not be as thoroughly self-reflective or good as it had been expected to be, once it was able to think and act of its own free accord. That older expectation, in turn, frequently had hinged on an attribution of full self-consciousness, total power, and evil intent to the oppressor class, so that it became responsible for every distortion of thought and failure of action on the part of the oppressed. Finally, the belief that the conspiratorial machinations of the oppressor lay at the bottom of what was thought and done in the world bore a strong family resemblance to the apparently opposite premise: that the source of whatever was thought and done in the world lay transparently with the individuals who thought and acted, that there was no "at bottom," no hidden self-conscious authors and agents – only a plentitude of undisguised ones.

7

Impositions and Evasions

1.

These, I want to argue, were the errors – derivative of privileged ideas in the dominant order and yet also uniquely its own – that radical feminism made as it struggled towards a critical understanding of sex and gender. First, it took the ugly word of phallocentric culture for the truth of the world. It accepted the key conceptual distinctions of Masculine/feminine, and the point of them, that helped make up the established language: the distinctions between "man" and "woman," "activity" and "passivity," "dominance" and "submission," and their underworld cognates, "sadism" and "masochism." It trusted the images of male/female relations it found in films, magazines, and novels. It interpreted as strict reflections of heterosexual reality the everyday remarks men made about that reality at work, on the street, in the lecture hall, and in social conversations. Second, radical feminism held to the reverse conceit of its enemy. It declared power to be allied with vice (except for that harmless and therefore admirable hybrid it called "self-empowerment") and powerlessness to be allied with virtue. To have power was in itself a vice, and to have none a virtue. To be oppressed, while not a virtue, was a sign of one's virtuousness. To be oppressed by others was to bear no responsibility for one's failings. To oppress others was to bear responsibility for their failings as well as one's own, because it automatically was to have authored all the vicious things those others thought and did, and to have acted in full knowledge of all the vicious things one did to them. Third, radical feminism was convinced that at the core of every social situation and of phallocentric culture as a whole was a clear understanding of it, a straightforward intention to bring it about, and an undivided will to carry that intention through. In the case of the established sex/gender system, moreover, it believed in the essential sameness of all situations – the sameness of their meanings, their consequences, and their animating geniuses.

All of these convictions and conceits, which at their heart had to do with the nature of power, were significant far less as instances of radical feminism's having, intellectually speaking, gone wrong than as symptoms of more general difficulties in feminist discourse. If radical feminism was pitched into the center of the storm of that discourse, it was only because it spoke its mind sharply and without vacillation.

Let us begin with the first, and, I think, most tantalizing conviction of the three. What *is* the error in presuming that shared concepts, images, artifacts, and the idioms of ordinary speech are the distillation of sex/gender relations as those relations are actually and normally lived out? Certainly it would not be hideously far from the truth to say that there can be little more to any established social relations than this – little more, that is, except the body in its pure, uninterpreted state. (But here at least the body seems to underwrite culture's main thrust: that masculinity is the cunning bird of domination and femininity is its vulnerable prey.) An identity between a received language, images, artifacts, and idioms of speech on the one hand and the actual experience of sex and gender on the other may not be hideously far from the truth – it indeed may be close to it – but I want to argue that it is not quite *it*. And I want to make my argument precisely with respect to that arena in which, above all others, radical feminism has declared the identity supreme: the arena of heterosexual eroticism and desire.

In our own "unrepressed" era, the dominant culture has been extraordinarily loquacious about erotic desire, and radical feminism as its hostile critic has had to be equally loquacious in return. All this talk on both their parts has done much to fix the idea of a male eroticism as aggressive subject, driven by the lust to conquer and subdue; and of a female eroticism which when joined to it either by force or by willing compliance is a mere submissive object, overcome by the wish to be taken and controlled.[1] The fantastical dimensions of this idea demand that we indulge in yet a little more talk of our own. But while we must conclude, I think, by showing how the critic's portrait of desire has been painted under the dubious artistic tutelage of its cultural opponent, we surely must begin on a more appreciative note. We must recognize the arduous task radical feminism took upon itself when it chose to criticize the thought and practice of heterosexuality, the painful discoveries it made, and the thanklessness of its efforts, given the unreflective loyalties of so many people in the other direction. We also must acknowledge the truths it has to tell. It has, after all, been relentless in digging out all the deeply rooted notions of eroticism centered on the premise of women as passive receptacles for men's active desire, or, if not passive in their sexuality, than all the more basely the receptacles for men to use and abuse. These notions were scattered throughout ideological life like fragments, appearing in a thousand different shapes and places – as an image in a photograph, a sentence on a page, a joke in a conversation, an aside in a scholarly text. They surfaced in more fleshly form as the living passions of men in everyday situations (without this vitality, they would have been as barren as a language written and spoken but not thought or felt): in marriage, as the demand for the virgin; in the family, as the yearning suspicion that the molested child was seducer of the adult; in the brothel, as the use of and contempt for the prostitute; in the street and the courtroom, as the hatred and scorn for the woman raped; and finally, transmuted in the different context of the prison and the military training camp, as the taunting provocation and humiliation of the woman believed to be secreted in the man.

Radical feminism pressed women to study each fragmented notion it collected and heaped up, to face their ceaseless replications, to measure their magnitude, and finally to see them as aspects of what in another discourse would have been called a hegemonic order. This order dictated the body's experience of itself and its gravitation to other bodies. It marked out, for females and males, diametrically opposed erotic self-images and contrary but "complementary" occasions for excitation. To the phallus was assigned the position of the active force: its pleasures and passions determined what was to count as pleasure and passion, and what was to count as objects for their release, in the common world. The revelation of the phallus as ideological center of that world was one that men always had known and taken for granted, but that women, who were centers for themselves if peripheries in the world they shared with men, had only partly understood.

Radical feminism was astute in all these acts of ideological demystification and critique. It was also courageous in its refusal to honor hegemonic demands. It would not worship the phallus, be the passive object of its gaze, the willing target of its forays after pleasure. It built defensive shelters against its force, waged offensive battles against its attempts at self-aggrandizement, and generated counter-hegemonic discourses and practices. And yet it took two false theoretical steps at this same point, with inevitable repercussions for its practical life. The first step, to which we will not return until later, was its tracing of phallocentric culture to the knowing, ill-intentioned machinations of men. The second was its move from the discovery of a phallocentric hegemony (which it called "patriarchal" or "phallocentric" society) to the belief that the hegemony must have a reach so extensive and complete that only a total alienation from heterosexual encounters, or a total rebellion against them, could safeguard women from its power effects.

Now it is possible to speak the sentence, although it is not really possible to think the thought, that a hegemony can achieve total closure over the experience of its members, its outright revolutionaries and fully alienated souls aside. In the case of a phallocentric hegemony's relation to erotic experience, such a closure would mean that the projections of Masculine/feminine pre-eminent in language, artifacts, and speech would determine strictly and fully the lived life of heterosexual desire. The idea of an air-tight connection between dominant culture and felt eroticism does seem to me to be closer to the truth than the opposite view: that the culture has no compelling effect on the individual's felt life at all. This is the more commonplace approach where the cultural fetishization of the phallus is concerned. That fetishization normally is considered, when it is considered at all, to be either secondary or weak in its effects on sexual passion. It is considered secondary in its effects when it is believed to be the honest reflection of a natural sexuality, the manifestation rather than the regimentation of the pure body. The impulses of the body here are taken as the fundamental fact, and while culture may discipline and censor those impulses, or liberate and indulge them, it is never seen as enforcing in an originative way the power of one kind of body over another. Phallocentrism is considered weak in its effects when it is believed to be unfounded in nature, accidental to the larger scheme of things, and only incidentally related to autonomously chosen desires and discretions. With no pressing connection in one way or the other to received notions of Masculine/feminine, the demand for the virgin, contempt for the prostitute, and humiliation of the woman in the man become odd recurrences in the individual's life and mysterious repetitions in society at large.[2]

But must we attach ourselves to one theory of culture simply for its being somewhat less bizarre than the other two? Are we forced to say that culture has a totalitarian grip on erotic desire, in order to avoid saying that it is expressive of bodily impulse, or inconsequential and fortuitous wherever desire and impulse come into play? Surely we can think up yet one more possibility: that culture is phallocentric, hegemonic, and effective, but that its grip on individuals is less than fully secure. In this case the fit between the public screen of sexuality on the one hand and actual erotic experience on the other becomes imperfect and inexact. Between the rule of Masculine/feminine and the triumph of the rule, perversities, insurgencies, and overturnings always are able and likely to occur – not merely for those who break with heterosexual desire but for those who receive pleasures from it.

A culture that is hegemonic in this modified sense is not a fully determining system but a constraining and enabling one. It exerts its power by giving authoritative consent in language, artifact, and speech to the eroticism of male dominance and female submission. It actively encourages that eroticism and rewards the men and women loyal to it with public admiration, customary approval, and the self-assuagement that comes from seeing one's personal proclivities mirrored on a public screen. These are different rewards, to be sure, from the advantages promised to men alone through their position as erotic subject and active force. It permits those who try to break with the received eroticism to be punished by those who do not. Such punishment typically is levelled in the form of public ridicule and the private withdrawal of desire for the renegade on the loyalist's part, but it occurs as well in the form of brute violence and sexual force. Finally, this hegemony works to suppress, in the female and the male, modes of desire assigned to the opposite sex; and it consigns to cultural marginality those whose pleasures bear no correspondence with the pleasures dictated to them. But for all its immense strength and weight, it does not stand in a one-to-one relation of identity with felt life, and the ways that life deviates from its rules and evades its grip are as real and telling as the rules and the grip themselves. As for the experience of bodily impulse and the "pure flesh": for all that it might seem to underwrite hegemonic pressures, or on the contrary to favor the subversion of them, it is elaborated out of those pressures and subversions rather than the other way around.

I want to argue, against both radical feminism and traditional view, that the bond between established culture and desire is exactly a bond of this sort: constricting but not choking. Such an argument, however, requires as its prelude a solution to the delicate problem of how to conduct a search for evidence. This search would not be a problem, or at least not a delicate problem, were one investigating the power of, say, bourgeois culture over the actual experience of everyday life. The power of bourgeois culture is exerted and evaded primarily in settings open to general view: in offices, shopping malls, churches, playing fields, schools and clubs. Phallocentric culture and the felt pangs of desire, of course, also have their public meeting places, as well as places where they openly clash and collide. But it is only by mistake or in calculated error that one could take the episodes of sexual provocation and arousal in cafes, bar-rooms, dance-halls, beaches, and the street either for a miniature sample of erotic experience or for its most important part. To conflate the publicly visible world with the entire world of erotic pleasure is to blind oneself to the very real possibility that the valorization of the phallus leaves its sharpest stamp precisely on public interactions. Here all the signals of predator and lure are sold, bought, adorned, and displayed, and the pressures to conform to the dictates of Masculine/feminine come from not one but one hundred directions. The most serious erotic encounters, meanwhile, do not happen in public at all.[3]

This is theory's acute dilemma: that desire expresses itself most fully where only those absorbed in its delights and torments are present, that it triumphs most completely over other human preoccupations in places sheltered from view. Thus it is paradoxically in hiding that the secrets of desire come to light; that hegemonic impositions and their reversals, evasions, and subversions are at their most honest and active; and that the identities and disjunctures between felt passion and established culture place themselves on most vivid display. The theorist is stopped in her tracks before the intimate domain, to which none but the intimate are admitted, and where the filaments of experience are so fragile that any outside intrusion would shatter them or transform them into something very different from what they were before. To trespass on eroticism's favorite and most protected milieu would be to corrupt its internal aesthetic. To expose it to the investigating eye would be to corrupt the investigation as well. To stare in directly at the intimate encounter or to question its participants in retrospect would encourage all the hegemonic aspects of desire to step forward and speak up for desire as a whole, to testify that the felt passion was identical with the received idea of felt passion: "I made love to her," "I took her," "I laid her," "I fucked her," and the unfathomable "I shot her."

2.

Are we then condemned to choose either to make a corrosive journey, in the company of the sexologists and psychoanalysts, through millions of real bedrooms; or to maintain a stony silence about sexual intimacy? But surely the dominant culture and radical feminism, those two great chatterers on the subject of erotic desire, have labored under these very same constraints: unwelcome as observers in the intimate domain and unable to intrude there without subverting the discovery of what that domain is really like.

Consider the established writers of novels, directors of films, makers of advertisements. All of these professional publicists who create with such abandon the artifactual images of sexual passion have no privileged access to any bedrooms but their own. The same must be said of the ordinary men who speak these images as sentences in everyday conversation. As for the people who think their thoughts in a language in which Masculine/feminine, activity/passivity, taking/yielding are central and essentially connected conceptual distinctions – well, this category embraces multitudes in contemporary social life, and the intimate moment is intimate precisely for keeping these multitudes *out*. In short, the individuals who produce and reproduce shared interpretations of desire do not do so on the basis of authoritative knowledge of heterosexual desire in general. Can we admit at least that they do so on the basis of their merely personal experience? But this is to beg the question with which we began our discussion: whether the culture of Masculine/feminine in which individuals take part is identical with their felt erotic experience or not. And even if men, as members of the more publicly vocal gender on the subject of sexual desire, were to give their heartiest assent to the accuracy of Masculine/feminine where their private sexuality was concerned, this would not guarantee either that they were telling the truth in public about their private moments with women, or that they had interpreted the gist of those moments correctly. The chance of quite crass misinterpretations occurring on men's part is as great as their tendency to presume that women see sexual encounters as adventures starring the phallic subject and made essentially of *its* excitements, *its* pleasures, *its* rages, *its* disillusionments.

If received notions of desire turn out not to be based on an investigation of desire in general, and if they also cannot be taken as straightforward replicas of the individual's erotic life, where do we look to find their original source? There is, after all, only one other possibility: that the phallocentric concept, or comment, or image, refers back narcissistically to other concepts or comments or images that are themselves phallocentric; that these other notions have the same narcissistic point of reference; and that, supporting and supported by like-minded representations, each notion has a solidity and persuasiveness about it for this reason above any other.

What about radical feminism? It too has been barred from sweeping its glance across the entire breadth of the intimate domain, and its descriptions of sexual desire for that reason have had a brittle link to actual life. The individual radical feminist almost certainly will have drawn on her autobiography in constructing her general claims about heterosexual eroticism. Her readings of her own intimate moments, at least, are bound to be more inclusive in their sensibility than the readings of the self-centered men. A lifetime in the larger society would have made her well aware that men did not share *her* perspective in desire, so that she would never be in danger of confusing their point of view with her own: of thinking that men experienced eroticism as if it were constituted primarily by the adventures of the clitoral, full-breasted subject. But personal testimony can bear witness only to particular episodes in one particular life; this is true of the unassuming testimony no less than of the arrogant and self-inflated one.[4]

Once we put its members' testimonies of their erotic experience aside, radical feminism's account of heterosexual desire turns out to have had both a surer and a shakier footing in actual life than its hegemonic counterpart. It has had a surer footing because feminism has chosen to trespass restrospectively on sexual intimacy in two kinds of situations where the normal rules against trespassing hardly can be said to apply. The first kind of situation is that of the intimate encounter so emotionally and/or physically brutal for the woman involved that she was driven afterwards to speak publicly about it, once a political movement had emerged that cared deeply enough about women to listen to her. The second kind of situation is that in which whatever willful passion was felt was felt only by men, and in which the objective conditions in plain view were so explicitly and unrelentingly oppressive to women that they could be counted as proof of their subjugation, whether individual women were willing or able to speak of their injuries or not, and to a great extent regardless of what they happened to say. In these instances, the solipsism of masculine passion and the organized force behind its enjoyment make the very term "intimacy" a necessary but very ugly misnomer. Their most extreme examples include all rapes, but above all, rapes that end in murder, gang rapes, mass rapes; child prostitution and sexual abuse; prostitution organized on a collective scale by a centralized power and/or occurring along racial, ethnic, class or national lines.

It was when radical feminism leapt very casually and quickly from these living nightmares of sexual violence to a summary of heterosexual eroticism as a whole that it left behind empirical revelation for the fanciful realm of imaginative construction. Adrienne Rich's famous, perhaps infamous essay "Compulsory heterosexuality and lesbian existence" was prototypical of the genre, setting its general proposition that violence against women lay at the heart of "ordinary heterosexual intercourse" against a backdrop of empirical harassments, rapes, and dominations, all the real "enforced conditions under which women live subject to men: prostitution, marital rape, father–daughter and brother–sister incest, wife-beating, pornography, bride-price, the selling of daughters, purdah, and genital mutilation."[5] A line of identity runs through Rich's critique of heterosexuality from the organizers of world-wide prostitution rings, to the operators of "entertainment facilities," to the owners of brothels, to the procurer and the pimp, to the purveyors of pornography, to the men buying the pornography and frequenting the brothels and being entertained, to the wife-beater, to the child-molester, to the rapist, to the male employer, to the male professor, to the male lover, to the husband, to the brother, to the son – that is, to all men, united, according to Rich, through their claim to a universal sex-right to women, on the grounds of a putative "primacy and uncontrollability of the male sexual drive."[6]

But more drastic in significance than radical feminism's emphasis on the ugliest real incidences of phallocentric sexuality has been its steady reliance on the hegemonic images of Masculine/feminine in its own depiction of erotic life. Its representations of heterosexual desire have been highly parasitical on received representations in the shared language, cultural artifacts and ordinary speech and as such have been one step further removed from felt life than they. Very frequently, for example, radical feminism painted its terrible pictures of desire directly after immersing itself in the world of pornography, which admittedly fast was becoming the same world as "popular" culture. Thus Andrea Dworkin, one of the most persistent and powerful critics of the established eroticism, introduces her impassioned attacks on it with recitations of pornographic scenarios and immediately moves from them to her portrait of sexual relations between women and men. Literary pornography is "a distillation of life as we know it,"[7] she says, but at least where her own method is concerned she has not quite put it right. It is rather that she knows and shows life through its pornographic representations:

> In pornography . . . [l]ove *is* the erotic masochistic drive . . . love *is* the consuming sexual impulse toward degradation and abuse. The woman does literally *give* herself to the man; he does literally take and *possess* her . . . The primary transaction which expresses this female submission and this male possession, *in pornography as in life*, is the act of fucking.[8] (Last phrase my emphasis)

> The sexual sadism of males rendered so vividly in pornography is real . . . male domination over and against female flesh is real . . . The brutal uses to which female bodies are put in pornography are real . . .[9]

> Pornography reveals that male pleasure is inextricably tied to victimizing, hurting, exploiting; that sexual fun and sexual passion in the privacy of the male imagination are inseparable from the brutality of male history.[10]

Pornography becomes the looking-glass into the real world, which it distorts only in reflecting penile penetration as "the ultimate pleasure . . . a natural and easy act" for men, and of sexual abuse as an instinctual, ecstatic pleasure for women.[11] Dworkin's use of pornography as a glass or keyhole through which one might peer into the room of heterosexual desire has been characteristic of radical feminism at large. And after all, how easy would it be to renounce such a use, to shut one's eyes to all the women who, "bound, stripped, gagged, whipped and cut, and usually enjoying it, stare at us from billboards, record album covers, newspapers and magazines," to refuse to form one's conception of actual heterosexual eroticism on the basis of their silent testimony, to resist concluding that "[f]or women, sex is structured as masochism"?[12]

> . . . the very existence of the inner productive space exposes women early to a specific sense of loneliness, to a fear of being left

empty . . . of remaining unfulfilled and drying up . . . Emptiness is the female form of perdition . . . [it is] standard experience for all women." (Erik Erikson, quoted by Andrea Dworkin.)[13]

. . . orgasm cannot be taken as the sole criterion for determining the degree of satisfaction which a female may derive from sexual activity . . . Whether or not she herself reaches orgasm, many a female finds satisfaction in knowing that her husband or other sexual partner has enjoyed the contact, and in realizing that she has contributed to the male's pleasure. (Kinsey, quoted by Andrea Dworkin.)[14]

Almost as rich a source of images for radical feminism as pornography has been the literature on sexuality which speaks in a scientific tongue. If it would take a steely effort of will not to be swayed by representations of heterosexual desire in illicit and popular culture, it would be even more of a strain to stand firm against the learned declarations of eminent scholars and researchers. Is it really so odd that radical feminism took science at its word – so authoritative *is* that word – when psychoanalysts and sexologists depicted ordinary eroticism as the charge between a positive, active, desirous subject and an object that is empty, passive, waiting to satisfy the subject's desire? That the dynamic between subject and object is not based on an original absence of autonomous passion on the part of the female, but rather undermines her autonomous passion with its every pulsation, was the point that turned a pleasant dream for phallocentric science into a nightmare for radical feminism. The dream and the nightmare were identical in almost every other respect.

Thus, ironically, on the real character of heterosexual eroticism, radical feminism and the dominant culture have been in fairly good agreement. Both represent sexual relations between male and female as relations between master and mastered, predator and prey, and, in the bluntest of representations, sadist and masochist. Both portray man's eroticism as bound up with aggression and conquest, and women's eroticism with a passive yielding in front of man's desire. Both depict the penis as an instrument of power, and the erect penis as so directly evocative of violence and domination that the very movements by which one body enters, and one takes in, the other become the movements of invasion. The dominant culture, of course, usually (but not always) coats its images of heterosexual sex with a romantic veneer, while radical feminism always portrays that sex in its starkest, least decorated form. The dominant culture shows woman as finding her most ecstatic delights in submitting to man's power and in becoming the object of his pleasure. Radical feminism, to the contrary, shows woman either as compelled to submit to man's desire against her will, or as, in the masochistic content of her will, already the victim of a prior, psychological compulsion. Thus the dominant culture celebrates heterosexual desire as the magnetic attraction of two opposite but complementary types, while radical feminism denounces it for being a compulsory system of desire imposed on woman for man's sake.

The tangle of actual practices centering on the sexual exploitation of women, and the sexual images of male aggression and female abasement permeating the dominant culture, provided radical feminism with more than enough mental stimulation. But in addition it accumulated a growing hoard of its own essays and texts to be drawn on as further food for thought. In other words, like every other point of view that solidifies into a general school or tradition, radical feminism has become to a certain extent self-generative and self-validating, so that a sympathizer like John Stoltenberg now can model his miniature sketch of the heterosexual bedroom after Dworkin's grand study: "For most women in this male-supremacist culture, as Andrea Dworkin has written, sexual masochism makes sensate the cultural judgements of female inferiority and female malignity."[15]

What, then, do these twin portraits of heterosexual eroticism – the one painted by the dominant culture, the other by feminist critics – really expose to view? It seems to me that they show us nothing so much as imaginary dramas of sexual desire: dreams and nightmares of a scene in which the phallus is subject and active force, and femininity its erotic object. These dreams and nightmares have their origin in an ideological system so vigorous that its very enemies have taken its fantasies for facts, but hardly so vigorous that it has been able to turn its fantasies into facts in some magical and automatic way. The sheer massiveness of the system is proof of its vitality, but it is not proof of its veracity.

We are, in short, confronted on the most fundamental level by an *idea*: a monumental idea, supported and maintained by a near infinity of its own ideological expressions. Against its claims to truth, two strategies of war are open to us. We can carry out the invasion of millions of real bedrooms in the hope of uncovering empirical evidence of the distortions and delusions of the phallocentric imagination. Or we can remain on ideological territory but take a different flight of the imagination than the one dictated to us. We can conjure up possibilities for eroticism not when the phallus is subject and force, but "merely" when the phallus is assigned by a hegemonic culture to the position of subject and force. Given the veil of secrecy over the actual bedroom, this is surely the more sympathetic course, and it is the one I mean to follow here. It *does* require that we exchange an empirical method for one that is partly literary. We cannot behave as if we were searching for facts when we really are looking for plots that are persuasive and characters that ring true. Yet neither are we free to fix on any erotic possibility that happens to please us. Instead, we must confine our imaginations within narrow, deductive bounds. We must look for plots and characters that are logically possible – given, first of all, the existence of a hegemonic culture of Masculine/feminine; given, second, our rejection of the idea that such a culture is totalitarian in its wielding of control or that it has a one-to-one correspondence to actually lived and felt life; and given, third, our refusal to presume at the start any essential significances to the male and female bodies.

An intimate eroticism, disciplined but not necessarily determined by the hegemonic rule, very likely can take a great many different shapes. In a more adventurous kind of discussion, we would seek that multiplicity out. But here, where we have time and space only to move the slightest distance from singularity to variation, I want to focus on a few variations of heterosexual eroticism – heterosexuality's being the truly problematic kind of eroticism, once one takes up in any serious way the feminist point of view. We will ignore altogether many other sorts of significant dramas: those of erotic celibacy, those of erotic solitude, those of collective erotic ritual, those in which erotic passion becomes ecstasy of a transcendental kind. We will ignore, for a long moment, those politically significant dramas in which the characters involved have bodies of the same genital type. Our consideration of heterosexual eroticism, nevertheless, will owe a great debt to a lesbian feminist critique of any eroticism combining pleasure and power, as well as to a very different lesbian feminist attack on the idea that such a combination must be always oppressive. Furthermore, it will conclude by asserting the deep meaninglessness of the body – an assertion that points to the provisional character of the categories "heterosexual," "lesbian," and "homosexual" and so to the tendencies to decomposition of any heterosexual norm or ideal.

Before we embark on a course of imagining heterosexual eroticism's conformities to and departures from phallocentric designs, we should warn ourself against certain mistakes we almost certainly will want to make. We strongly will be tempted to concoct characters who are as purely resistant to received notions of sexual pleasure as heterosexual characters can be. We will want to invent lovers who in every pore of their bodies subvert the phallocentric rule, so that a single description can capture the whole of their erotic temperaments. We will require that they be self-reflective and intentional in their rebellious desires. We will demand that their passions be mirrored in one another; that there be no misunderstandings between them, no incongruence in their conceptions of what they are doing together. Finally, we will want to convince ourselves that the relations between these lovers will be uninspired by power motifs.

It seems to me that we must fortify ourselves against the charm of all of these inclinations. It is exactly our task to search for subversions of the received eroticism in small incidents, slight physical movements; pleasures that are spontaneously and unselfconsciously taken against the phallocentric grain; a lack of synchronization between the self-images of the lovers; and plays of control and vulnerability dissociated from the rule of Masculine/feminine. We must try to imagine not only fully revolutionary passions but deviant nuances and shadings of desire, because there is no reason to assume that an erotic sensibility at odds with the sensibility celebrated in public does not leave at least a partial mark on ordinary instances of heterosexual passion as well as a deep mark on extraordinary ones. And we must try to imagine erotic plays of control and vulnerability that are unaccompanied by the rule of Masculine/feminine, because there is no reason to trust that the play is solely the function of that rule – as if passion between women and men outside the phallocentric pale would be necessarily, in every sense in addition to *that*, nurturant or just or "good."

8

Power, Desire, and the Meaning of the Body

1.

If we retain the notion of a phallocentric culture that is hegemonic but not totalitarian, and give up the notion that the body must have natural significances fixed to it, four dramas of heterosexual eroticism come most immediately into view. In each are featured two kind of bodies. The one kind is probably but not inevitably larger, stronger, more roughly hewn than the other, with its center of arousal a length of flesh that swells and softens on the outside of itself, visible in its apathies and excitements to general view. The other kind is probably but not inevitably the slighter, more lithe, and agile. It has several secondary centers of arousal both inside itself and on its surface, with its major center a fiery point hidden from the eye of the other and in that sense secretive and self-contained in its boredoms and delights.

With the first drama in which these bodies are engaged we all are overly familiar. This is the story conforming to hegemonic prescriptions, and it has been recited to us through dominant cultural forms again and again. It is preserved inside the concepts of virgin, mistress, slut, and whore; animated in movies of romance and marriage, and sex and violence; made palpable in the plastic arts; brushed onto canvas and then reinterpreted on the printed page ("There before us," writes the journalist of de Kooning, "was his notorious 'Woman I': mythic icon and modern idol; compost of flesh, flowers and razor blades, Virgin and whore; love and loathing; sex and death."[1] Well, we have been spies in the house of love painted by the dominant culture long enough to know that house as if it were really our own.

Perhaps it would be more refreshing to view this phallocentric dream in the form of its anti-hegemonic double: to be voyeurs in radical feminism's nightmare of heterosexual erotic encounters.

In the nightmare as in the dream, the pure facts of the flesh have a rigid and unbending significance to them that hardly can be overstated. The two bodies – one rough, one slight, one visible, one secretive – are the physical ground for an extraordinary set of oppositions to do with the impetus and occasions for sexual arousal, the experience of the self as a demanding presence or waiting absence, and the enjoyment of or prohibition from the active exercise of power. To the first kind of body is attached an eroticism infused with aggression and force. This body is aroused when confronted with a body it sees as more vulnerable than itself. Its excitements occur through the enticement of that body into a posture of submission. But it is not simply the body that must be enticed, or, if enticement fails, forced. It is the will of the self that must be made to say "Your will is more powerful than mine, I surrender myself to you, I make myself into your object, I am *for* you." The fusion of the body and the will on the part of both dominating and submitting selves is crucial to any eroticization of power. But what is distinctive about the fusion here, is that the dominating will identifies the mainspring of its dominance with a special part of its body, with – we can say it now – *his* body, with his center of arousal, that length of visible flesh. From his insistence that power emanates out from the fleshly penis, the other elements of heterosexual intimacy follow. The masculine self sees the second kind of body, whose fiery center is hidden from view, as "lacking" a penis, and in addition as slighter in will because slighter in physique than himself. On it – the "feminine" – he seeks to achieve his pleasure through exerting his power. He penetrates the body, he subjects it to his force; at the moment of his climax, he sees himself as having the body, taking it, conquering it, possessing it, and using it. The feminine self only can be masochistic and self-abasing in her desire for a self whose own desire is a cauldron of sex and violence, pleasure and domination, release and exploitation. To enjoy erotic entanglements with the masculine self is to enjoy bowing down before the supremacy of the phallic subject and find excitement in being had, taken, conquered, possessed, and used as an object by him.

For phallocentric culture and radical feminism alike, this is the only possible drama of heterosexual eroticism. In actual fact, it directly if secretly points to another. In this second drama, the self whose center of arousal is the visible length of flesh has exactly the same erotic temperament as it did before. But things are very different with the other self. It is, to be sure, the same *body* as before – the difference does not occur at the physical level. Rather, this feminine self does not experience herself or the masculine self in the same way that the masculine self does. She does not look on his bodily movements as the movements of conquest, possession, invasion, nor does she consider her own moves of passion to signify submission and self-annulment. She does not see herself as the object of pleasure for him, nor does she take her own pleasures in abasing herself before him. To the contrary! She sees her physical agility as a trait quite as admirable as his physical strength. She delights in the powerful demands of her own bodily points of arousal, for which his body may provide pleasure but is never the owner or final purpose of that pleasure. She would laugh at the crudeness of his perception, were she to discover that he could see action only where there was visible physical movement, and that he would see passivity where there in truth was a physical charge of shattering inwardness, magnitude, and depth. She would shout with derision were she able to hear him boast that only *he* acted on *her*, as if the host of interesting ways in which she also acted on him had simply vanished from his memory. As for that one action that he would glorify as the emblem of his physical possession of her – she would see it as only one out of any number of provocative erotic acts, and she would call it, instead, her receiving of him, her taking him in, her accepting him – not as one accepts a conqueror, but as one accepts a supplicant.

The intimacy between these two lovers, in sum, is based on the most profound kind of interpretive discordance. It is made of the mutual attraction of two bodies and souls who are entirely different for themselves from what they are for each other. Only the feminine self has an objective interest in unearthing the incongruity between them. It is more than possible that she never will know that the incongruity exists. She may only suspect that it does, or may be made suddenly aware of what she had been ignorant before. Then again, she may be quite astute about the way she is seen by the masculine self but nonetheless choose to use him for her own pleasure, while secretly scorning him for his vanities and self-delusions. In any event, the physical union of lovers whose hearts and minds are so hopelessly at odds would be perhaps merely comic, were it not for the fact that the one's interpretation of desire has the allegiance of a whole culture behind it, while the other's is unsupported by anything grander than itself. The cultural reserves that the masculine self finds at his disposal are so great that the moment he steps out from close intimate quarters into an airier public space, he sees his vision of desire confirmed wherever he looks, while the feminine self sees her vision constantly negated. Does the worst moment for her come when she finds that the radical critics of masculinity have embraced *its* account of her eroticism rather than her own?

The third drama is marked out from the second by the presence of a feminine self who is far less ebullient and proud, and who fares much worse in the intimate milieu. She is, to be frank, defeated, but not because her desire has come to complement that of her masculine lover, nor because she is even more blind than before to interpretive discordances between them. She is all too aware of these discordances, and it is precisely because of her hyper-awareness that her relationship with the masculine self takes the punishing form that it does.

Here is a feminine self alert to the sensual delights to be had equally in wielding power and in yielding to it, keen to claim both kinds of delights for herself, and happy enough to extend them to her lover. She may be, at the same time, enticed by the finer shadings of power for lending a greater intrigue to passion than do its crude exaggerations. Such nuances, in addition, are not dependent on asymmetries of physical strength and do not jeopardize her notion of herself as a free self (not a master or a slave) beyond the bedroom wall. But although her desires spontaneously run the gamut from commanding to succumbing in love, and although she may be aroused by the refinements, not the extremities, that the gamut has to offer, she is stopped short in her pursuits before a masculine self who on the old grounds of bodily difference claims for himself the sole prerogatives of the active, the dominant, the masterful, and insists that she take up the position of the passive and the yielding. He also imposes on their mutual situation images of control and vulnerability that are fairly coarse-grained.

In sum, the masculine self allows the feminine only one-half of the pleasures she seeks for herself, and he allows her these pleasures in a form only passably interesting to her. If she tries to wrest the others from him by exercising her will to power, or if she tries to redesign all the pleasures to suit her taste for the delicate gradation, he withdraws his desire from her. If she withdraws her desire from *him*, she receives no pleasures at all. In this drama there is only one other course open to her, and it is the course she ultimately takes. She reduces her expectations and trains her behavior to conform to the relatively blunt notions of acting and waiting, taking and succumbing, that he has conceived for them both. She resigns herself to enjoying the real but partial pleasures of waiting and succumbing. After concealing from him her own will to power, she listens in silence as he brands her the inherently passive sex. As a final penalty, she witnesses his contempt for her as one whose essential delights lie in sexual subordination. In her supreme sensitivity (if only she were less perceptive, or more cynical and thick-skinned), she sees and feels this contempt fully. Isn't this the truest erotic defeat: not to be rejected in love, nor to be its pain-seeking victim, but rather to be forced to press the expansiveness of one's desires into stultifying limits, to consent to love within those limits for the sake of the partial pleasures they permit, to be defined as one who naturally indulges only in those pleasures, to be ridiculed for the indulgence, and, finally, to take one's pleasures precisely with the perpetrator of one's predicament?

Let us close the door on this unpleasant scene of heterosexual eroticism. It will be a relief to leave behind its claustrophobic atmosphere, closed in on a desire that is tightly, tightly confined.

So at last we arrive at the fourth scene, and what immediately will impress us about it is its freedom and its egalitarian ambiance. Well, it is really a curious kind of egalitarianism and freedom. Relations between the two lovers are not at all the intimate analogue of relations between citizens in a democratic state, who ideally at least treat one another in a perfectly reciprocal way. Erotic freedom and equality come rather as the absence of phallocentric impositions on the two lovers' experience, with a consequent multiplication of sensual possibilities between them. It comes, in other words, as a sharp disconnection between the pure facts of the flesh on the one hand and, on the other, the impetus and occasions for arousal, the opportunities of the will, and the self-conception of the desirous self. The body, of course, is still of great importance: the scene would not be a scene of eroticism otherwise. But neither the self whose center of excitation is the visible length of flesh (shall we continue to call this, for simplicity's sake, the "masculine" self?) nor the self whose primary center is the secret fiery point (shall we call this the "feminine" self for the same reason?) ascribe any fixed and given meaning to the physical differences between them. They read no established script for the playing out of desire on their bodily surfaces and depths, so that the flesh becomes for them a field of adventure, unfenced by rules stipulating specific eroticisms for specific bodily types.

What are the kinds of adventures on which the two lovers are able to set out? Let us begin with the masculine self, who so strikingly departs from his previous guise. And let us look at him during the actual moments of genital intercourse – the moment of heterosexual "truth" according to phallocentric culture and radical feminism alike. Certainly during these moments the masculine self is likely to exult in his physical power over the feminine, to exhibit that power in his thrusting movements, his possibly but not inevitably larger, stronger body descending like a wild bird over her own. But just as easily and quickly this same masculine self forsakes the use of his physical strength, offers himself up to the feminine self, abandons his body to her. By the merest relaxation of his grip, the turn of his head, the quiver of his mouth, the change in the look in his eye from imperiousness to pleading, he places himself under the mercy of her will, to be controlled in the ebb and flow of his passion by her movements, to be actively aroused, excited, placated, and stilled as she decides and commands. And yet there is one more attitude that, depending on the vagaries of mood at the particular moment, the masculine self is likely to assume. He may be swept up with the feminine in a mutual ecstasy of identity and fusion. Suddenly their physical merging will signify not the explosion of opposition and difference between the most intensely inward and the most intensely outward domain of the body, but the utter dissolution of opposition and difference.

The masculine self's contentment and excitement in moving from a posture of power and strength to one of abandonment and vulnerability to one of reciprocity and fusion does not simply signal an expansion of his erotic repertoire. It also transforms each of its specific moments, so that his enjoyment of power and strength does not have the same meaning that it did before. How can he experience his movements over and on the female body as acts in an episode of conquest and exploitation, orchestrated by him and for his own sake, when the moment after he exults in his force he succumbs to the force of the feminine self, and the moment after that he joins with her as if they were a single self with a single erotic perspective?

As for the feminine self during genital intercourse: precisely the same trio of attitudes is offered to her. She may become the commanding, the succumbing, or the fused self, although the different facts of her flesh will mean that she will embody these attitudes in her own distinctive way. But genital intercourse is hardly for her the only or key moment of "truth." That she derives pleasure from her lover's thrusting movements inside her, or from her taut and driving movements on him, or from the reciprocal rhythms of their physical union is only part of the story of her sexuality. The idea that it is the whole story is perhaps the supreme phallocentric delusion. With respect to her more intense and absorbing moments of physical passion, she can assume the attitude of one who forcefully takes her pleasure upon her lover, or who is served by him, or who gives herself up to his will and control. And how can her self-abandonment be called her subjugation, when she moves so freely from that stance to another during her most acute experiences of pleasure no less than during his?

I would have liked to conclude our inspection of this erotic scene with an account of the many physical movements inside it that can manifest power and control. The thrusting of the penis has been so extraordinarily over-equated with the expression of power in eroticism by phallocentric culture and radical feminism alike, and I would be pleased if I were able here to set the record, quite explicitly, straight. But a cryptic approach is required instead, in part because the same physical movements so often can, in sexual situations, have the most varied significances and meanings, so that a mere description of the movement as a movement would not suffice to show whether it was an expression of power or not. In turn, sexuality is secretive and also idiosyncratic enough that the outward signs of an assumption or forsaking of the attitude of power often cannot be read correctly from the outside. One would have to be one of the lovers to notice a barely perceptible shift in the body of the other and to know just what that shift in the body meant. Then again, certain physical signs of assuming or forsaking power are so graphic that it would take a poet or pornographer to describe them. Let me, a mere theorist, make only this small suggestion: that the lover knows immediately that his lover is assuming a stance of power the moment he catches an expression of slightly cruel concentration on her face, the moment he is beset by the searching movement of her hands, the moment he feels the hard pressure of her touch somewhere on or inside his body.

This is, I think, the appropriate point for us to withdraw to a less over-wrought, more exterior place to consider the signficance of what we have seen in the intimate domain.

2.

Of course, there is no reason to limit the imagination to four dramas of erotic desire, or six, or ten, once one admits to the chance of an imperfect fit between hegemonic culture and lived life. One might posit an infinity of possible eroticisms, or at least as many as human ingenuity and eccentricity can support, even though most of them might show up only very rarely. But it was never my intention to present you with a truly catholic catalogue. My choice of offerings instead was guided by dominant dictations for eroticism on the one side and by oppositional musings on sexuality on the other.

The oppositional musings that have left their most vivid mark in feminist circles have been radical feminism's own. I hope I have conveyed a strong enough sense of the good reasons why this should be so. I do think that, for all its sharp perception in unmasking the cultural valorization of the phallus and revealing the ugly practices associated with it, radical feminism has been more intimidating than convincing in its pronouncements on the nature of actual heterosexual encounters. As we shall see later on, those pronouncements, transfigured, have reappeared as political prescriptions for lesbian eroticism and as wholesale condemnations of active homosexual passion. It strikes me that radical feminism's astute analysis of the phallocentric logic of the larger culture, in combination with its mean understanding of felt life, presents a crucial challenge to feminist theory. Can theory make room for the varieties of desire in actually felt life that depart from the hegemonic rule, not just as odd and insignificant exceptions to it but as telling instances of sexual pleasure, at the same time that it preserves the recognition of hegemonic power and remains a partisan of radical cultural–sexual critique?

The conviction that theory *could* do this, and that feminist theory *must* do this, led me to search for the exact weak spot in the radical account of heterosexual desire. It became increasingly clear that one key to the problem lay, ironically, in radical feminism's understanding of the brute body as a fundamentally determining force. Now, in looking in on radical feminism's nightmare of heterosexual eroticism, one initially might think that radical feminism thinks that the lovers there simply, if catastrophically, have the wrong idea of why their caresses take the dichotomous forms that they do. One might think that radical feminism thinks that it really is *not* the pure body that determines the flavor of their intimate engagements, in which only one takes, while the other is taken – that it is not the dynamic of having and lacking the fleshly penis that lends that peculiar piquancy to their every embrace. After all, radical feminism often appends an afterword to its story of heterosexual eroticism, to the effect that the penis has no intrinsic drive to domination of its own but rather is culturally translated and transformed into the source, sign, and instrument of power. Once again, Stoltenberg follows the feminist lead when he declares that "What 'feels natural' about sadism to males or what 'feels natural' about masochism to females is that these behaviors are sensorily consonant with the cultural specifications of phallic identity and nonphallic identity, respectively."[2] Yet it would be quite naive of us to take such pronouncements on the original innocence of the physical genitalia at face value. For in the radical feminist nightmare, the penis enjoys such a perfect identity with the phallus (every penis acts the part of the phallus, every possessor of a penis behaves as the phallic subject), phallic power over the female is so total and complete, and the erect penis is so directly evocative of violence and aggression, that the very movements by which one body enters, and one body takes in, the other, become irredeemably brutal and brutalizing. That force is "the essential dynamic of sex," not merely for the masculine self but for the male body, that the female is a pssive and pain-accepting body whenever an erect penis is present – these disquieting impressions of an anatomical compulsion behind masculine force remain behind when one awakens from radical feminism's troubled sleep.

The second key to the problem turned out to lie, just as ironically, in radical feminism's depiction of women's sexuality in the heterosexual context as a foil for or outright function of men's. Radical feminism thus deduces from the premise that men's sexuality is aggressive and invasive the conclusion that women's sexuality in the company of men must be submissive and self-annulling. But surely, even if male sexuality *were* inevitably aggressive and invasive, that does not make it the author or director of female desire in the heterosexual plot. Nor does anything in the murky atmosphere of sexual intimacy, where physical movements so often are unaccompanied by words, provide for an automatic synchronization between the consciousness of two lovers. Nothing, as a consequence, guarantees that if the first lover sees his movements as signifying conquest and possession, the second must see them in the same way, or that what makes for dominance in the self-experience of the one makes for submission in the self-experience of the other. A lovers' agreement on the meaning of sexual actions could be taken for granted only in situations where the one's actions were so brutal that no one but the brute who was also a liar could demur over their conceptualization; or in situations where an openness of heart between the lovers reflected a far more mutual relation than the relation that would obtain if one of them believed that only he had the natural right and ability to command. In all other cases, why should we suppose that when a man experiences himself as commanding, his lover does not experience him instead as entreating, or as meeting her power for power, or as merging with her beyond all notions of power, or as stupidly self-deluded in his arrogant view of himself? Why suppose that when a man experiences his lover as submitting, the woman does not have her own quite independent view? It is not that she *could* not see herself and him in the way that he did, but that she just as plausibly might have her own reading of their interactions – a reading no less inherently privileged (however heretical it might be in the eyes of the larger culture) than the man's or the culture's in defining the substance of their particular erotic relation.

It also seemed to me (to continue my justification of the small sampling of eroticisms I presented to you) that nothing in an intimate encounter of which it *could* definitively be said that the man acted as forceful subject and the woman as lure and prey, ruled out the possibility that the woman's passionate proclivities were more expansive than she freely was able to show. After all, the entire thrust of phallocentric culture, condensed and reiterated in the person of her lover, would work to prohibit her from indulging in all varieties of pleasure, regardless of the routes her inner desire might take. Only if one self is thoroughly autistic or already assured by the larger culture that *its* is the authoritative view can it "control" without bothering to make sure there is a requisite response on the other's part. In every other case, "control" implies that another succumb in some way. It seemed as likely as not that the man's refusal to succumb to the sexual control of the woman, in conjunction with the woman's acute awareness of that refusal, was at the root of what happened and did not happen in this heterosexual scene, rather than the absence of a sexual will to power on the woman's part. To the extent that this in fact proved to be the case, radical feminism's account of that scene would be off the mark. Its two favorite principles would be off the mark as well: first, that the sexual will to power is intrinsically male;

and second, that, being male, it is under all circumstances vicious and contemptible.

But if a phallocentric culture might have an imperfect hold on women's desire, how could we suppose it must have a perfect hold on men's? Dictates that valorize the phallus and posit female sexuality as its compliant object can be expected to be more seductive for the sex those dictates do everything to affirm than for the sex they do everything to negate. But once we assume cultural impositions do not reflect anatomical truth, there is nothing to prevent a man from making his escape from them. To the extent that he manages to do so, it would be supremely unkind of us to refer back to the given portrait of the phallic subject in order to understand his experience of sexual pleasure. The occasions of his arousal, the opportunities for his will, the meaning of his physical movements, his self-image as a desirous self – all these, being open questions for him, must become open questions about him for us. It also would be unfair of us to take it as a sure sign of phallocentric loyalties on his part, were he to feel arousal at the sight of his lover's vulnerability and self-abandonment, strike a stance towards her of sexual command, find a portion of his pleasure in his own forceful movements on her body, and see himself during these times as a powerful desirous self. The mark of the loyalist rather is the refusal to forsake, from one moment or hour or night to the next, the pleasures of force for those of vulnerability in his encounters with the "feminine" self, on the grounds that force is only for *him* and yielding to it only for *her*. The masculine rebel, then, is distinguished not by a renunciation of the eroticism of strength and control, but rather by his utter familiarity, ease, and excitement in exchanging this eroticism for its opposite through giving himself up to the command of the "feminine" self; by his delight, additionally, in his moments of identity with her; and finally by the internal transformation of his experience of power in consequence of his experiences of self-abandonment and fusion.[3]

The passion between this self and the "feminine" self whose sensibilities do not mesh with those sensibilities culturally authorized for her, runs a course unconstricted by phallocentric dictations. The free sensuality between them may occur, importantly, not in some utopian future but in the present. Its logical possibility under given, unemancipated social conditions has a curious significance for feminist theory and practice. It means that actual heterosexual desire may be less oppressive under those conditions than it originally was declared to be. It means that the chances for an egalitarian sexual regime may be less bleak, there being no reason to rule out the possibility that intimations of such a different future are already, in the present, in place. But it also means that erotic life may be lived against the grain in the intimate sphere without any larger cultural–political repercussions – without, that is, disturbing in a major way the public face of sexual relations in general and the public portrayal of eroticism in particular. To the extent that it is caught within the privacy and secrecy of a milieu in which no one but the implicated lovers are present, an unfettered heterosexual desire offers in itself no public challenge to a shared language, the idioms of speech, and cultural artifacts; to the costume, cosmetics, and bodily cultivations that distinguish masculine sexual predator and feminine sexual lure; or, finally, to the myriad social practices in which the idea of masculine subject and feminine object is expressed, preserved, and extended. Such passion, in sum, is compatible with a culture that is phallocentric, hegemonic, and effective, although, to the degree that it is an actually lived passion and not just a logically possible one, it is a stamp of the culture's failure to achieve total closure in one of the most fundamental of social domains.

Let me turn to radical feminism's reading of eroticism outside the heterosexual milieu.

Convinced that the will to power is no more and no less than the expression of the phallic personality, and either convinced or strongly suspicious that that personality is a necessary function of the male body – radical feminism at first very naturally assumed that power would be severed from desire once the fleshly penis were banished from the erotic scene. It also, by the way, could and more and more frequently did conclude on the basis of these convictions that power would be doubly fused with desire in situations of homosexual eroticism, where two lovers were phallic selves instead of one. That these possessors and worshipers of the phallus engaged in erotic plays of masculine and feminine, and thereby derived pleasure from a theatrical subjugation of the feminine (and what else would any sexual interlude of command and submission be but this?), only made things worse.[4] The dynamic of lesbian eroticism would work necessarily in another direction. The simple mirroring of the lovers' bodies would ensure that no anatomical difference could become the ground of an opposition of dominant and submissive wills, of prerogatives and prohibitions of power, of contemptuous and contemptible selves – an opposition that always had meant the oppression of female eros. That simple mirroring also would allow each lover to be able to elicit a sensation in the other that perfectly echoed and anticipated her own and to be able to expect from that other the same eliciting of sensation for herself. The physical empathy secured by this parallelism of the flesh would save the two lovers from all the discordances and antagonisms that can spin themselves out of gross incongruities between bodily types. But most important, the mirroring of the distinctively female body, whose center of arousal was that fiery point hidden from the eye of the other lover but no longer from the other's inner sight, would ensure that these lovers would find their pleasures in reciprocity, mutuality, and nurturant love, rather than in the exercise of power.

No sooner, however, did the paint dry on the portrait of a reciprocal lesbian eroticism than a new, drastically different representation arose to counter it. Arriving tempestuously on the feminist scene like an uninvited and unwanted guest, lesbian sado-masochism declared that reciprocal desire was merely one possibility for female eroticism outside the boundaries of phallic rule and not the most exciting possibility at that. Far from being the natural effluence of the mirroring, identity, and empathy of the bodies of female lovers, reciprocal desire was said to hinge on a willful playing off of that mirroring, an active intensification of that identity, a purposeful raising of the pitch of that empathy. It was said to hinge, that is, on the making of the body into a metaphor for the sexual will. Given its contingent, not essential, relation to the body, female desire just as easily could travel down a different path: towards the willful stimulation of opposition between lovers, the active provocation of tensions, the purposeful sharpening and refinement of contrary urges.

The dramatis personae of the new representation of lesbian eroticism still were two bodies that mirrored each other. Consequently, no genital-anatomical difference could become the ground for the dictation of dominant and submissive wills; and each body could elicit from the other a sensation perfectly echoing and anticipating its own. The pure facts of the flesh here, however, invested the dynamic of arousal, the opportunities of the will, and the self-conceptions of the desirous selves, no more with a mutual and egalitarian ethos than with an exploitative and inegalitarian one. To the contrary, the two lovers with the same kind of body enjoyed opposing kinds of sexualities: one of command, the other of a vulnerability before it. Moreover, the specific expressions of these sexualities were, on both lovers' parts, intentional and pronounced.

To exact the most intense sensations from their mutual encounters, the lovers purposefully plotted out and acted out the dialectic of power and desire. They sought after and exploited the possibilities of differentiation; they deliberately heightened and emphasized their opposed positions; they jointly pursued all the aspects, physical and emotional, of acting and being acted upon.[5]

Obviously enough, lesbian sado-masochism posed its challenge not to a hegemonic but to a counter-hegemonic regime of truth. It pitted itself not against the rule of women's sexual submission to men, but against all prohibitions on how pleasure can be sought and received outside the reach of that rule. It condemned the chaining of female desire to a new truth and rule: the truth that erotic passion is in its essence, and the rule that it must be in an emancipated world, nurturant, egalitarian, and kind. As a corollary move, it debunked the idea of any compassionate and peace-loving female nature. It also refuted the idea of any logical relation between erotic taste in an intimate setting and socio-political sympathies in the world at large. And what could radical feminism do in response to such an unruly, defiant sexual desire, but charge it with having been cultivated in a patriarchal milieu; with having been crippled by the symbolic if not the real presence of the phallus; with reproducing the masculine attitude towards sexual pleasure; with mimicking the logic of male/female relations; with remaining unreflectively imprisoned by the dominant culture's eroticization of power and powerlessness?[26]

3.

Surely radical feminism's great insight into eroticism in our own times is its exposure of a massive cultural force pressing to constitute female eros as feminine desire – a desire prostrated before the phallic subject. But are there, simultaneously, key insights into eroticism to be gained on the other side, from the multiple dramas of felt heterosexual life and from the representation of lesbian sado-masochism?

The plainest lesson the heterosexual dramas have to teach is that it is quite possible for there to be, in the erotic encounter, a break between the phallus and either the will to power or the successful execution of that will. The derisive hoot of laughter we heard from the second feminine self on discovering that her lover always has seen himself as her sexual master testifies clearly enough to the imperfect success of his control. Meanwhile, the third feminine self, who hides her own will to power from her lover to secure his desire for her, is living if secret proof that the will to power is autonomous of any bodily type. Open proof can be found in the "feminine" and "masculine" lovers who delight in exerting power and yielding to it outside the bounds of any rule for what kinds of bodies can enjoy what kinds of things. The importance of such breaks between power and the phallus is this: they suggest that eros' being cut entirely free from the dictates of Masculine/feminine might issue in an expansion, not contraction, of the possibilities for an interplay of power and pleasure. It would mark not the end of power's co-mingling with eroticism, but the lifting of prohibitions in the intimate setting against the female body's enjoyment of sadistic impulses and the male body's enjoyment of masochistic ones.

That the emancipation of eros from the entrenched order of power would enhance, not the frequency or intensity but the variability and fluidity of what traditionally have counted as personal vices or as psychological perversions and what more recently have counted as political sins, is only at first glance an odd position for feminism to take. The premise underlying that position is that there are dimensions of the will to power and wish for yielding to it in intimate erotic experience that are not a function of Masculine/feminine at all. These might go deeper than it; they might be more resilient and intransigent than it; and, to the extent that they do not weigh on the side of any one social population against another, they would not be, in themselves, politically contemptible. One such dimension may have to do with the fact that the first conscious sensual relation of any self to another is the relation of a child to an adult, so that, quite apart from the adult's particular motivations and actions *vis à vis* the child, the eroticism of the latter and thus (having once been a child) the former is stamped forever by the dynamic of vulnerability and power. Another dimension must have to do with the distinction every self comes to make between itself and the object-world outside it.[7] Such a distinction brings for the self the twin possibilities of detachment from and engagement with the world. It brings these triple possibilities for engagement: the impulse to control the object, the impulse to give in to the object and be controlled by it; and the impulse to merge equally with the object into one.[8] A weakening grip of Masculine/feminine over the body would mean the crumbling of one detailed set of dictations and constraints for the playing out of such impulses in the intimate erotic situation.

From a different vantage point, the representation of lesbian sadomasochism reiterates the logical possibility of a dissociation of the will to power from phallic pretensions. Whatever the meaning of any of its particular and graphic details, the abstract significance of the lesbian sado-masochistic scene is its revelation of the possibilities for sexuality outside all rules and truths elaborated on the genital-anatomical distinction. Such possibilities may include incidences of real cruelty and abasement in passion, but they expose, by the same token, the contingency and severity with which erotic impulses of sadism and masochism have been divided up and parcelled out to different bodies under the old regime. These impulses might have flowered more anarchically and creatively if that regime had not been in place. Lesbian sado-masochism also holds forth the emancipatory ideal of free play for all erotic impulses,[9] refuting not only the hegemonic rule of heterosexual desire and truth of that desire as one of male dominance and female submission, but also the counter-hegemonic rule of lesbian desire and truth of that desire as one of reciprocity, equality, and loving-kindness.

The heterosexual dramas and lesbian representations we have been discussing thus far immediately indicate other dramas and representations: a purely reciprocal and nurturant eroticism between bodies of two different genital-anatomical types; a sado-masochistic eroticism between those different types of bodies that is not rooted in genital-anatomical associations; a spontaneous exchange of erotic stances of command and submission between genitally similar bodies, and so on. A juxtaposition of all these together provokes the additional thought that what we have been calling distinct *dramas* or *scenes* may be instead, in actual life, different moments of a single erotic encounter. There certainly is no reason not to expect interruptions and displacements of some major theme of an erotic episode by some different minor chord. Indeed, if there is an essential instability to passion – an inherent susceptibility to changes in mood, sentiments and self-conceptions (and isn't that part of the meaning of the term?) – we dare not speak about a given episode of desire in any phrase that cannot be instantly modified or reversed. We dare not say, for example, that there can be no moment of reciprocity in an episode of phallocentric passion, or that unfettered heterosexual desire could not be plagued by a resurgence of phallocentric demands, or that lesbian reciprocal desire never could give way to the impulse to command or succumb. Perhaps every episode of sexual desire is as often as not a contradictory *melange* of different erotic modes with one perhaps dominant but never absolute.

I want to conclude this discussion with a summary of the ways that given concepts of power, the body, passivity, equality, and above all masculinity and femininity have clouded our understanding of erotic life.

Let us begin with "passivity." As it has been traditionally marked out, this concept conflates two very different, indeed antithetical, sexual postures: the first a posture of boredom and indifference, the second a posture of receptivity and languor. It thereby obscures the truth about the body in its receptive and languid state: that it is extraordinarily alert and sensitive in the anticipation of having pleasure bestowed upon it and active in being acted upon. Its arousal is no less heightened and its sensations no less intense for their issuing in no grandiose physical movements. In truth, every posture of bodily arousal, including the posture of self-abandonment, is supremely active. Passivity is not a mode of eroticism at all but a mode of apathy and antipathy to eroticism. As such, by the way, it has been the characteristic female strategy of resistance to eroticism governed by the phallocentric norm. The hegemonic claim of an essentially passive female sexuality, and the radical claim that female sexuality is necessarily passive in the heterosexual setting, of course only aggravate the original conflation. They also camouflage the infinite number of ways in which the female body can act forcefully or grandly, as well as receptively and intensely, in erotic life.

We already have gotten some inkling of how the crude equation of power with domination, and domination with an overwhelming physical force that can be the privilege of the stronger of two bodies alone, conceals the complexity of power in eroticism. Almost every expression of power and vulnerability, first of all, is dependent on the meanings that lovers ascribe to physical movements, and almost no physical movement can be called invasive or submissive in and of itself. Secondly, wielding and yielding to power are far from simple and self-evident kinds of acts. They have multiple forms and gradations, each with a significance that varies depending on whether or not there is movement from one position to another on both lovers' parts. These forms, gradations, and significances require us to make fairly refined conceptual discriminations. Control, vulnerability, commanding, succumbing, yielding, strength, and self-abandonment – these concepts, you will remember, which surfaced in the drama of anarchic heterosexual desire, may be appropriate to any drama in which bodies indulge in a fluidity of pleasures. Conquest, subjugation, violation, exploitation, and self-annulment help describe the nightmare of phallocentric eroticism. For the drama of sado-masochism that is not based on anatomical difference, theatrical images for the sexually motivated imposition and bending of the will come into play, of which "master" and "slave" are the most stark and emphatic. Has a vocabulary of love and power yet been devised that is delicate enough to capture all erotic possibilities – their distinctions, but also their points of overlap?

We already have discovered, too, that equality in the sexual context is not simply synonymous with mutual and reciprocal relations. The principle of equality in desire does not preclude the dialectic of power and vulnerability from intermingling with sexual pleasure. It precludes only a fixity of sexual stances, prohibiting either or both of two lovers from refusing to give up one set of pleasures for the other. As to whether erotic emancipation requires an equality of desire between lovers in this expanded sense, once all systematic, socio-cultural impositions on power and pleasure disappear – well, this is, fortunately perhaps, not the kind of question cultural–political theory is designed to answer.

The concept of the body presents us with new complications. For the dominant culture, of course, this concept is entirely straight-forward. Its "body" is divided into two sexual types, genitally distinct and asymmetrical with respect to delicacy of features and physical strength. Affixed to each type is a detailed script, empirically unobservable but visible to the mind's eye, that assigns a clear, authoritative meaning to every fact of the flesh. The script's being read and the meanings' deciphered directly issue in all the conventional cultivations of the body (the development or stunting of its various parts, the training of its physique to assume a particular form, the production or inhibition of specific capacities), as well as its acceptible costume and cosmetic decoration. These elaborations of the body, according to the established concept, are instructed by the body for its own presentation in the world, rather than being instructions to it of what it must be made to be like.

A concept of the body that includes the idea of the pure flesh and the idea of a script naturally attached to it makes the interpretation of actual bodies and their movements an easy task. One simply reads from the script. The penis means aggressive power and strength, the opening of a body to the penis means that body's submission to that strength, the embrace of a large body and a small one means the possession and protection of the second by the first, and so on. My own method of procedure has ruled out any use of such a simple device. Against the dominant culture I have represented the body as having in truth no script of its own, no meaning intrinsic to its fleshly parts. Against a kind of feminism not much more nuanced for calling the script a cultural, not essential, phenomenon that has been absolutely effective for "the whole of patriarchal history," I also have represented the body as having no cultural significances fastened to it so mercilessly tight that there is no possibility of evading or subverting them. My argument has hinged on the presumption that fleshly difference inherently signifies nothing in particular. I have hinted that almost any of the body's points can be used to exert force on another body, and almost any point can be acted upon. I have said that any body can become the commanding, the succumbing, the fused self: that the decisive factor is not the physical factor but the culturally pressured and limited, but not thereby determined, will of that self, and, very crucially, the will of the self with which it is passionately involved.

Yet it would be deceptive of me to conclude in this way, by juxtaposing to the highly restrictive concept of the body in the dominant culture, and the not much less restrictive concept (but with all the valuations reversed) in radical feminism, an entirely open concept of my own. I do have a lingering doubt about whether there is an indelible significance, not to what is really an incomparable genital difference, but rather to the perfectly, even prototypically comparable differences in overall bodily stature and strength. Such a doubt makes me think an expansive notion of the body must have certain of its avenues closed off. Am I right to suspect that the sheer bulk of a body, its larger presence and greater prowess relative to another body, leaves its stamp on any situation in which the body *per se* plays a central part – and so on every erotic situation? I have said that commanding and succumbing in love have fundamentally to do with a dialectic of the will, and that nothing prevents a self that is physically stronger from becoming the succumbing self. It still is the case that the stronger self must forswear the use of its physical strength in order to succumb. It silently must proclaim that it will be forced, or commanded, or controlled not on the basis of the slighter self's brute physical power, but on the basis of its will, self-conception, and the paths its desire happens to take. Does this very refusal to make differences in physical size and power the crux of the erotic drama testify to their irrevocable – if bracketable – significance? Does the fact that the refusal is the prerogative of the physically stronger self testify to the same irrevocable truth?

It would be a mistake, of course, to suppose that the distinction between a large and a slight physique is synonymous with the difference between a male and a female body, and analogous to the distinction between masculine and feminine. Physical stature is as implacably a differential factor body to body within each sex as it is a differential factor between them. To a great extent it is the consequence of cultural and economic influences. The weak and sedentary figures in the post-industrial city are at least as sharply set off from the thick and burly figures in the pre-industrial countryside, and figures that perform heavy physical labor in each type of society are at least as sharply set off from those that do not, as physiques that are male are set off from those that are female. In addition, the extraordinary differences in physical size accompanying differences in racial and ethnic stock, the fortuitous fortunes of individual birth, variations in individual and cultural taste for athletic pursuits, and finally the potencies and ravages of age, all combine to produce an array of bodies whose stature or prowess is not at all simply a function of their sex. In fact, the world of bodies is so little a mere world of male physical power and female delicacy, that if physique were legislated as the sole criterion of gender, the border between masculine and feminine would be laid in a new and iconoclastic place.

The imperfect fit between the facts of sheer physical presence and the sexual facts of the flesh signals a secret corruption in the meaning of "masculine" and "feminine." Here is one sense at least in which the distinction proposed by the two concepts turns out not, after all, to have its real location precisely at the gender line. Does the concept conceal other corruptions to do with eroticism as well? "Masculine/-feminine" purports, of course, to tell the vigorous truth of the erotic dynamic, and in a much fuller, more comprehensive way than "passivity," "power," and "the body" were able to do. It claims to set forth the difference between the sexual facts of the male and female flesh; the difference between the strong and the delicate physique; and the polar sets of meanings attached to the two types of bodies that authorize the sexual tension between aggressing and submitting, forcing and yielding, acting and being acted upon. It declares that all of these differences congeal as two discrete and opposite selves, so that, although one exists for its own sake while the other exists to serve and satisfy it, each is what it is in and of itself. Feminism long since has revealed the apparently separate and externally related notions of "masculine" and "feminine" to be internal dimensions of a single, self-mystifying conceptual whole. If separate masculine and feminine selves are the typical selves of the actual world, it is only because that self-mystifying whole already has left its stamp on lived and felt life.

But if the *multiplicity* of erotic dramas have made any sense to us at all, we surely must be prepared to go further than this. That multiplicity has taught us that "masculinity" and "femininity" are highly problematic terms in the heterosexual context and so in any lesbian or homosexual one superficially seeming to mimic heterosexual relations. We must preserve the terms to describe aspects of erotic life conforming to the hegemonic rule and discard the term to describe aspects departing from it. The endemic instability of passion means we can never be sure that only the conformities, or only the departures, animate any given erotic interlude. And what can we extract from the dynamic of heterosexual eroticism to say about the nature and desire of the feminine self, when that self has proven to have such diverse natures and desires from one erotic drama to the next? What can we say with any constancy about the masculine self, given the fact that the meaning of "masculine" has become increasingly obscure the further the masculine self moves away from a rigid stance of sexual command – the male body present in its fleshly maleness all the while?[10]

These deteriorations and evaporations of "masculine" and "feminine" press us to end on an ironic note. On the one side, they are signs that the body produces no instructions out of itself for the orchestration of desire. It provides no ground for an ontological duality of erotic experience, and no grid to which a cultural regimentation of experience can be fixed so perfectly tight that the erect penis becomes identical with an eroticism of aggression and domination. Conversely, the deteriorations and evaporations expose the body as the only real sediment of essential truth in the masculine/feminine distinction. All else besides the pure facts of the sexual flesh and the highly qualified facts of physical stature and prowess owes its debt to a system of invention and elaboration. The system is massive and demanding, to be sure, yet exactly because it is a cultural–political system, it cannot prevent its own circumvention. The ever-present chance for desire's freedom from phallocentric pressures and constraints is held out by the body itself – not in its being, in some privileged way, the source of the liberatory impulse, but rather in its deep meaninglessness, its implicit existence as a free field for adventure, its openness to the interpretive imagination. We know this for the opposite reason that radical feminism knows phallocentrism to be a cultural system of power. We know it not through all the stunning evidence of the system's impositions on desire, but through all the ways that desire can escape from those impositions and can set off in other, undictated directions.

Is a postscript on the politicization of eroticism in order? Certainly the drive to politicize questions of sexual desire will appear to traditional political theory to be beside the point of both politics and sexuality, the first putatively having to do with the public arrangements of ruling and being ruled, the second with private pleasures. To introduce as a matter for social debate the ways desire ought to be felt, the paths it should take, and the kinds of objects in which it should find its satisfactions, may very well seem a dangerous prelude to the imposition of collective constraints on what had been a "free state." Of course, as scandalous as it might be for political theory, the association of "rule" and "sexual pleasure" always has been a standard truth for psychoanalysis. The association of *this* association with the primacy of the phallic subject has been a standard truth for it as well. However, orthodox psychoanalysis located these truths squarely inside a psychosexual developmental process closely if obscurely allied to anatomical fact. By this single stroke, it denied any political meaning to phallic authority. It also became one of the great legitimators of phallocentrism, the primary agent of its scientific articulation, and – through the clinical work of psychotherapy – an instrument of its practical enforcement.

The way traditional psychoanalysis interpreted forms of desire that were at odds with the phallocentric rule followed from its interpretation of the rule itself. It could not contemplate a desire unconstituted by the rule, over which the rule could enjoy only the retrospective power of distortion by redescribing it in phallocentric terms – the kind of power that psychoanalysis itself, as theory and as clinical practice, was in an admirable position to exert. It also could not understand desire in revolt against the rule as anything other than some tragic abnormality (and life, it well knew, was full of *those*) generated out of the harsh demands of psychosexual development. It could not, that is, see such desire as a practical denouncement of socio-sexual regimentations: as an instance of dissidence, defiance or rebellion neither fully shaped by nor fated to fail as a result of a relentless psychosexual dynamic. This blindness to, on the one hand, the gratuitous imposition of the primacy of the phallic subject on social life, and, on the other, the political integrity of a desire unscarred by or in hostile conflict with the rule, has been especially severe where female sexuality is concerned.

Exposing, if in this problematic way, the rule over sexual desire, psychoanalysis provided feminism's own connections between "imposition," "authority," and "sexual pleasure" with clear theoretical precedents. Feminism had only to contest the fixity and effective power of the rule by testifying to its contingent and provisional character, and challenge the legitimacy of the rule by unravelling its ideological mystifications and justifications, to turn the whole discourse of sexuality in a political direction. Such a turn, which feminism had to make before it could emancipate sexuality from what it saw as oppressive pressures and constraints, obviously belongs in the catalogue of adventures making up the modern quest for equality and freedom.

At the same time, by revealing the secret and malignant determinant of desire, feminism opened the question of how desire ought to be determined anew. This question provoked, as it almost inevitably would, a host of prescriptions for the orchestration of sexual experience, all poised to supplant the rule in place. Thus the authoritarian designs on desire by the dominant culture have been joined by equally censorious, if far less potent, designs on radical feminism's part, this time in the name of the need for vigilance against any new outbreak of erotic exploitation. Both entrenched regime and emancipatory movement show their tyrannical impulses in the same cultivated limitation of vision: a staunch refusal to hope for, search out, and see instances of life that in some way contradict a prescription or rule. If the dominant culture bestows its recognition on phallocentric eroticism alone, radical feminism allows itself to see only that eroticism on the one side and reciprocal lesbian desire on the other. It has been no more interested than the culture at large in looking for or finding a multiplicity of eroticisms all lived out, in different ways, against the grain.

Do disobedient eroticisms have repercussions for social life beyond the bedroom wall? Earlier I noted that disobedient eroticisms in the intimate sphere need have no public reverberations. This is not to say that they will not have political significance, but it is to say that the significance will tend to be of a secretive sort. Very differently, this also is not to say that a whole mass of rebels may not deviate from the rule of Masculine/feminine in other spheres of life in addition to the intimate erotic sphere, in such a way that their public and private deviations constitute a relatively distinct and coherent mode of life.[11] That mode may be marginal to established social arrangements, but it is still a source of potential pressure on life as it is ordinarily lived out.[12] It may stand as proof that extraordinary ways of thinking, desiring, and acting are not impossible ways; it may flaunt in the face of the dominant culture possibilities that culture has prohibited to itself; it may actively do battle with the hegemonic order.

The interlacing of a defiant eroticism and an alternative culture, militant to a greater or lesser degree, means that experience at odds with Masculine/feminine will not be confined to the close and narrow ambiance of intimate quarters. A much broader and more open terrain of thought and action now comes into play over which it can be said that hegemonic impositions of Masculine/feminine are constricting but not choking. Alternative and oppositional cultures occupy this terrain collectively. But might not unassociated individuals also occupy it as fragments? Might they not think and act not only in intimate but in public settings that in various ways are out of kilter with the cultural–political rule? And might not their unassociated deviations, in conjunction with the more dramatic counter-cultural ones, pose to the whole order of things some kind of counterweight?

Fragmentary and counter-cultural moments at odds with the entire regime of Masculine/feminine deserve our attention, but we are not ready to consider them yet. First we need to sort out another set of problems about the regime itself. These have to do, not with the reach and extent of its power, but with that power's point of origin and operating method. What is the motive force behind the rule of Masculine/feminine? How does that rule subsist and perpetuate itself? Let us return, for our starting point, to radical feminism's side once again.

9

A Regime without a Master

1.

We have seen how radical feminism succumbed to one simple idea by presuming, in the ordinary case, a direct correspondence between the dictations of phallocentric culture and the actually lived life of the desiring body. Now we will see how it succumbed to another simple idea. It did this by explaining the sex/gender system in terms of men's self-conscious authorship, and women's conventional thoughts and actions in terms of men's manipulations; and by making a sharp division between power, which it connected to vice, and powerlessness, which it connected to virtue or innocence.

The hyper-conspiratorial example of this kind of explanation and division, which a host of feminist writers have cited appreciatively for its germinal influence upon them,[1] is Mary Daly's *Gyn/Ecology: the Metaethics of Radical Feminism*. Stripped of its entertaining wit, Daly's argument is this. There is a world-wide system of power, and its planners, controllers, and active agents are male. All historical periods, cultural forms, and political movements, all customs and rituals, all social practices and public events, are manifestations of the same "planetary" plot to subjugate and deplete the energy of women. Male "myth-masters" and "enforcers" condition women to submit to male rule by implanting "false molds" in their minds, reinforced by "ego-depressing follow-up fixes," while the same myth-masters condition men to become the victimizers of women, giving them follow-up fixes that are "ego-inflating." Contemporary patriarchy takes on the monstrous form of a "phallotechnocracy," attracted to all that is "dead, robotized, mechanical," spewing out nuclear bombs, chemical weapons, carcinogenic food additives and mind-pollutants to poison the earth. "Lobotomized" and "mentally castrated" to be the passive pawns of such a necrophiliac order, women essentially are, nevertheless, life-loving, creative, energy-producing, aligned with the natural rather than with the man-made world.

Daly's thoughts on an engendered antagonism between nature and scientific culture need not concern us here. Rather, we should note her causal monism: a single power relation animates all of history and civilization, and every particular event, practice, and institution is explicable by reference to this relation. We should note her one-dimensional view of thought and action: good or evil, manipulated or free, thoughts and actions are one thing *or* the other. They are never internally contradictory, never mixed in motive or meaning. The only crucial exception to the rule is the thought and action of women who are making their way from patriarchal mystification to truth – but here, while a particular thought or action may be "partly one thing and partly the other," the way from mystification to truth is not. It is a single way, with a fixed beginning and a fixed end. We also should note Daly's mechanism: with the exception of "hags" and "crones" who have exorcized their patriarchal delusions and have recovered the "wild," "uncultivated" depths underneath, women receive the contents of their minds from the outside. Their ideas are placed in them by other human beings, who are as self-conscious, calculating, and aware of the full significance of what they are doing as the women whose minds they condition are unreflective and manipulated. Finally, we should note Daly's essentialism: men are by nature predatory, violent, and death-loving; women by nature love peace and life.[2]

If not so boldly formulated or baldly put, and not so tightly wound into a single knot, these explanatory predilections turn up in the works of other major feminist writers, as well as in the pamphlets and broadsides that circulate in women's communities, and in women's speeches and conversations never immortalized in print. That men are not merely the privileged beneficiaries of the sex/gender system but also its self-conscious authors and powerful agents; that the entire social world emanates from their desire, purpose, and will; that in all of history, women have been the blinded victims of male machinations; that in their true, unmystified, and uncontrolled state, women are essentially good – these are the core premises of radical feminist social critique. Susan Griffin's *Woman and Nature*, is a highly elaborate exposé of men's subjugation and domestication of women as the secret of history and culture. Catharine MacKinnon puts it more tersely: "[M]ale power produces the world before it distorts it."[3] The single-minded, malicious, and thoroughly vigorous efforts of men to dominate women extend out in every possible direction. Male power manipulates female desire: "the enforcement of heterosexuality for women," states Adrienne Richy, is "a means of assuring male right of physical, economical, and emotional access."[4] It disciplines the female body: "physical bondage was the real purpose of high feminine fashion, claims Andrea Dworking." The lady's costume was a sadistic invention designed to abuse her body."[5] It creates and imposes the sexual organization of labor: the barrier keeping women in and men out of the service sector, declares Marilyn Frye, is "erected and maintained by men, for the benefit of men."[6] Finally, it issues the conceptual rules for classifying and valuing all things: "Male/female, mind/body, subject/object, man/nature, inner/outer, white/black, rational/irrational civilized/primitive – all serve to explain the way in which patriarchy has ordered reality," notes Sheila Collins. " . . . the left hand side of each equation has assumed a kind of right of ownership over the right."[7] The correlate of men's total power can be only the abject powerlessness of women. "The patriarchy used dichotomies such as 'feminine' and 'masculine,' 'black' and 'white,' 'personal' and 'political' *to weaken us*," asserts Hallie Iglehart.[8] MacKinnon announces: "The substantive principle governing the authentic politics of women's personal lives is pervasive powerlessness to men."[9] This powerlessness is, as MacKinnon sums it up, "both internalized and externally imposed,"[10] so that woman in her very identity is the passive creature of men's active designs. "Women have been the nature, the matter, the acted upon, to be subdued by the acting subject seeking to embody himself in the social world."[11]

All originative thought and action being, in patriarchal society, the thought and action of men, any evil done must have men's authorship and agency behind it, even when women are not its direct target and indeed may seem to be its co-perpetrators. The facts of men's ceaseless responsibility and women's unrelenting innocence are, after all, part of what it means to say that men are the active subjects and women the conditioned objects of social life. More drastically, men have a special propensity for doing evil: there has been nothing else that they *have* done. It typically is argued that the masculine self, for bio-psychological and/or deep cultural reasons, experiences himself in separation from and opposition to everything outside himself and can secure his inviolability only by subjecting everything else to his will. All of men's projects have the drive to domination at their core. Men first became addicted to power in the sex/gender domain and afterwards extended the scope for its play by inventing other axes of domination and subordination. "[T]he alienation of woman from man – because it was the first and still is the longest lasting form of human alienation," says Sheila Collins, "can be seen as a primordial paradigm from which all other unjust relationships derive."[12] Rich concludes in "Compulsory heterosexuality" that "the power men everywhere wield over women . . . has become a model for every other form of exploitation and illegitimate control."[13] Griffin argues in *Woman and Nature* that instrumental reason, capitalist exploitation, and scientific management all express men's fear of and defensive aggression against everything outside their calculative control.[14] Nature, the body, and women are the archetypal, intimately allied instances of "the wild" that threatens the male self-construction as a self in control of itself and thus necessarily in control of all outside itself.[15] Dworkin lists "those forms of social injustice which derive from the patriarchal model of male dominance" as "imperialism, colonialism, racism, war, poverty, violence in every form."[16] In her best Dworkinesque prose, she asserts that "[t]he will to domination had battened on female flesh; its muscles had grown strong and firm in subjugating women; its lust for power had become frenzied in the sadistic pleasure of absolute supremacy . . . Once female slavery is established as the diseased groundwork of a society, racist and other hierarchical pathologies inevitably develop from it."[17]

I have said that radical feminism presents history and culture as man-made and evil, with women the manipulated victims of men's designs, responsible, therefore, for neither their own thoughts and actions nor the larger shape and face of social life. At the same time, radical feminism has identified places outside the bounds of the man-made world in which women could be said to think and act autonomously. Feminism has speculated about a matriarchal "prehistory" in the mists of time prior to the beginning of patriarchal civilization. It has celebrated the emergence of women's communities in the contemporary period. Finally, it has uncovered a subterranean field of women's disaffection from and disloyalty to the established order, including all women's episodes of madness, protest, defiance, and outright rebellion, along with the bonds of love women have forged with one another under the shadow of the phallocentric law.

Shining through these outlawed episodes of female autonomy is a bright, compelling goodness: when women are what they truly are, they are nurturant, caring, co-operative, and egalitarian, embodying the peace that comes with a cyclical rather than teleological attitude towards life. For all of this, they are innocent of the will to power. This life-loving female principle is declared to have animated matriarchal "pre-history" and to typify women's culture on the edge of modern times. It is said to infuse the activities of women that always have been vital to men: the mother's nurturance of the child, the wife's alert attention to interpersonal relations, the female lover's impulse towards interconnectedness and inclusivity ("the sense of having no boundaries in the postorgasmic state is often described by women as a peaceful, expansive mindset, by men as fearsome, vulnerable, or even terrifying . . . the little death."[18]) Finally, this principle is said to rule women's subterranean life within the patriarchal order – a life in which women act in instinctual sympathy with all victims of domination, provide asylum and solace for those who have borne the brunt of male abuse, and enjoy mutually respectful and loving relations among themselves that stand in stark contrast to all they suffer through men.[19]

Women who are thoroughly self-determining are thus also thoroughly good, virtuous above all – to allude to an earlier subject – in their eroticism. They are sexually impassioned only by other women as the embodiment of good and, *as* women, they are visited by none of the sexual vices that would afflict them if they, like men, had a will to power of their own.[20] Haunani Trask sums up this whole train of thought when she celebrates the "return to the mother" and the "feminist eros" as generative of a radically new kind of power. This power is, in Trask's words, "integrative" – "a posture which continuously seeks to balance the human and the natural, the natural and the cultural, the intellectual and the spiritual . . . This integrative, synthesizing impulse arises in opposition to the splintering, divisive *power over* attitude of the patriarchal Self." It is "collective" – "a practicing sisterhood, refusing patriarchal collectivities based on the dominating Self . . . a sisterhood . . . with special attention to nurturance and care." Finally, it is "beneficent" – "an encompassing characteristic unifying all other aspects of feminist power . . . the power of continuing, protecting, and enriching life and the life instincts. In the largest sense, this quality opposes the patriarchal Thanatos of aggression, cruelty and destruction."[21]

Radical feminism's anatomy of power is perhaps nowhere on more condensed, conspicuous, and politically incendiary display than in its account of racism and white supremacy. That racial power relations make up – if we may borrow a Marxist turn of phrase – merely a secondary contradiction follows from the principle that male supremacy is the original sin out of which all other sins historically arise, and is, at any given moment, the primary cause of evil. Patriarchy is not only the seedbed of and model for white supremacy, but, when both oppressions are present, always has the stronger effect: "The condition of the black woman in slavery was determined first by her sex," Dworkin declares, "then by her race."[22] That white men are the sole authors and agents of white supremacy follows from men's being the sole authors and agents of everything, and from everything's being, for that reason, full of cruelty and exploitation. On the authorship of racism, Marilyn Frye declares: "Those who fashion this construct of whiteness, who elaborate on these conceptions, are primarily a certain group of males. It is *their* construct."[23] And on the agency of racism: "For hundreds of years . . . white men of European stock have been out, world-wide, conquering, colonizing and enslaving people they classify as dark . . ."[24] As for imperialism's neurotic motive force: it is "white men's anxiety for the survival of their race . . ."[25]

In her essay, "Disloyal to civilization: feminism, racism, gynephobia," Adrienne Rich underscores white men's instrumentality and white women's innocence, not to say virtue, in the American slave system. While admitting that white women often held black women in the deepest contempt and could behave inhumanly to slaves under their command, Rich declares that it "compounds false consciousness"[26] for white women to shoulder the guilt of slavery, when they "did not create this relationship" but rather were "impressed into its service" as "the active and passive instruments" of white men.[27] White women did not think or act freely when they helped perpetuate racial brutality. They were, however, self-determining when they fought against it; their fighting against it is precisely proof that they did not act under men's control. Rich strongly implies that if the men of the dominant race were the true protagonists of white supremacy, the women were, in that race, its sole antagonists. She conjures up that subterranean field in patriarchy of women's autonomous if ill-fated efforts on behalf of the good, when she emphasizes that "strong anti-racist female tradition" that persisted "despite all efforts by the white patriarchy to polarize its creature-objects, creating dichotomies of privilege and caste, skin-color and age and condition of servitude."[28] Moreover, she hints at there being a fount of anti-racist sentiment in all women – a natural predisposition to egalitarianism – by citing Frederick Douglass on the kindness shown him by his white female owner, a kindness to which, when she married, her husband quickly put a stop. It was the woman's entrance into matrimony, Rich asserts, that eventually instilled in her "false power and false loyalty to a system against which she had at first instinctively revolted. . ."[29]

On this innate virtuousness of women, distorted under conditions men alone have made; on women's blindness to men's machinations (white women did not understand that their privilege was only "skin-deep"[30]); and on the origins of white supremacy in the male will to power, Rich almost but does not quite rest her case. She goes on to argue that if white women were to pierce through racist ideology, they would discover their true sisterhood with black women – a sisterhood "patriarchal fragmentation did not intend . . . for us to see in each other."[31] She thereby intimates that racial power relations have as their true function the mystification of the more fundamental, sexual fault-line in social life. Men designed white supremacy as a delusory antagonism to divide white and black women who were in truth on the same side, and they thus prevented the real blow against power from being collectively struck. I say "men," but I should say, as Rich does, "white men," black men having dropped entirely and conveniently out of view. They are too obviously the target of white supremacy to be placed in the category of male oppressor, yet they are just as obviously no part of that "sisterhood" white supremacy putatively was designed to conceal, feminism to uncover and sanctify.

Surely, if there is any choice of method to be made, one would not have thought radical feminism would have rushed to embrace the most exaggerated sort of instrumentalist approach. One would have thought it would do anything it could to fix on some other mode of explanation than one which treats every male fantasy of omnipotence and omniscience as if it were not fiction but fact. Maker of the social world, perfect knower, effective power: this is man presented as demi-god, poised above the world in which he is simply a man. As for women peered at through the same lens – they are, except in their biologically determined proclivities and their rare moments of rebellion against patriarchal control, mere ciphers of men, always the tool or effect, never the originator of the deed.

But how unpleasant it is to describe men in a way that rivals anything men have had the pomposity to say on their own behalf! How humiliating to describe women in a way that rivals all the contemptuous things men have said against them! How laborious to re-read all of women's cruelties – the injuries inflicted on black slaves by white mistresses, the condescension shown to servants by women of a privileged class, the petty snobbery and crass inhumanity levelled at members of a colonized people by imperial wives – to show that they were really men's cruelties! The sheer exhaustion in treating every play of power except those openly to do with sex and gender as a disguise beneath which some other play of power is at work, and the boredom in finding that other play always to be the same one, should be enough to drive anyone with a horror of monotony and repetition in search of a new explanatory method.

There is another reason to be driven: to say good riddance to the idea that any subordinate is incapable of thinking and doing ugly things of its own accord, which almost always accompanies the idea that every ugly thing a subordinate actually thinks or does can be traced back to the evil genius of its dominator. The capacity to choose autonomously to do evil – in the sense, that is, that one has the capacity to choose to do anything "autonomously" at all – is surely one of the more interesting things about being human, adult, and *compos mentis*. Innocence is the child's prerogative, and even then it is an innocence guaranteed by the smallness of the child's world and the narrow boundaries of its knowledge, rather than from any natural purity of its desire and will. Unmitigated goodness, even worse, is a quality signifying something so spiritless and static that the vital and vigorous are all too happy to impute it to populations they especially despise. Radical feminism's romanticization of women as essentially innocent or good may be more benign than the dominant culture's degradation of women, and it may be more well-meaning than that culture's idealization of women in a backhanded way that suggests they are really the weaker and less dramatic sex. Still, it is absolutely infantilizing and embalming. It implies that women are not complex enough in desire, sophisticated enough in imagination, and dynamic enough in will to act in vicious as well as virtuous ways, out of passions, predilections and motive forces that are not men's but their own. It denies, in short, that women have the fundamental capacity for every possible emotion and desire and so for being able to think, will and try to do despicable things.

It strikes me that a discourse that declares itself a "discourse for women" ought to be, above all, perverse. It should be happy enough to search out women's worst interventions in social life, and it should refuse to censor in advance the sense that can be made of them.[32] A discourse for women also should extend the range of permissible interpretations of women's apparently good thoughts and deeds. It should greet them with a half-admiring, half-jaundiced eye, as if to say: "You cast yourselves in an honest and generous light, and you may be exactly what you present yourselves to be, but I will probe you for inner dissemblances." It should do so not because they are women's, but because they are seemingly good. There is nothing, as Nietzsche has shown us, so suspect as *that*. But women's thoughts and actions are suspect, too, simply because they are thoughts and actions. That is, they are rarely of a single piece so that a single word like "good" could sum them up, and they are rarely disconnected from their own, at least partial, negation – from some prior temptation not to pursue that particular idea or course of action, some hesitation during the event, some after-pang of regret, some curiosity for what was not thought of or done after all. Then again, all thoughts and actions are worthy of methodological cynicism in that they never are stamped with proof of their being what they appear on the surface to be.[33]

2.

The attraction of an instrumentalist analysis of power – and there is, after all, an attraction – is that it is highly gratifying, in certain ways, to subordinate groups. It allows them to say: "They have done this to *us*; *we* are innocent, *they* are guilty; *they* are evil, *we* must be good!" And in any relation of domination and subordination, there will be a great deal of truth to these charges. Dominant populations do enjoy a heightened agency, an awesome effectivity, a directive authority; they do possess, through their overbearing material, cultural, and psychological position, a greater responsibility than subordinates for the course and content of collective life. But it is a long leap from the claim that a dominant group exerts a tyrannical agency in society to the claim that it exerts sole agency. It is an even longer leap from the claim that one group wields mastery over another in a system of social power, to the claim that that group is master of that system:

that it has concocted the idea for it, designed it, executed it, and that it craftily has inculcated the group it oppresses and exploits with appropriately submissive beliefs, tastes, and preoccupations.

When the dominant group controls the production of public culture, as it almost invariably does, it so patently puts forth the ideas that are reproduced on the public scene, and those ideas so characteristically celebrate its superior status, that they seem to be, on the face of things, its own. But life is not always what it appears on the face of things to be, and we must ask whether those enjoying the prerogatives of social power are by the same token the self-conscious authors and masters of socio-cultural life. Do those who control the production of public culture always design in an originative and knowing way, the whole universe of classifications, ideas, desires, and purposes in which a subordinate group is imprisoned – to the extent that it is imprisoned there?

Surely the sordid history of domination and subordination, in which the powerful have proved to be at least as much in the dark about the real source and significance of their thought and action as anyone else, points in the opposite direction. But the logical argument is just as telling. For think what self-conscious authorship in domination would mean. It would mean, of course, that the dominant group would produce and reproduce hegemonic ideas with energy and fervor. That group would strike up self-aggrandizing conversations, present sermons on its natural right to rule, print tracts on the weak character of its subordinates that require them to be governed for their own sake. Alternatively, it would testify to the achievements of individual equality and freedom as if no systematic power in social life actually obtained. If it did not spew out this constant stream of ideas on its own behalf, certainly no one else would. But as it would have devised such ideas in a calculating way for the purposes of delusion and manipulation, it would be fully aware of the deceit. And as it quite knowingly would have carved the whole established classificatory order out of the perhaps infinitely wide universe of possible orders, it would understand that order as something invented and artificial. The recognition of a regime of truth as deceptive in that it functions to obscure the realities of dominative power, and as fortuitous in that it has no objective ontological or cosmological ground, by definition occurs outside the pale of that regime. There it can precipitate all sorts of iconoclastic adventures or it can stop with itself, but in either case it is a fundamentally heretical recognition. Thinking outside the truths it has devised for the purpose of mystifying others, uninhibited in its private musings by its public pronouncements, any master of a regime of truth thus would be its first heretic at least in the intellectual sense.

The declaration that men are the self-conscious authors and masters of patriarchal culture signals that women's imaginations are imprisoned while men's imaginations are unfettered and free-ranging. It must have been the distastefulness in giving male consciousness so generous and undeserved a compliment as that of hyper-intelligence and wit that pressed Mary Daly to make a fleeting but telling distinction between two sorts of men: the mass of them, conditioned to think and act on behalf of the masculinist cause; and the few self-determining male "conditioners," "enforcers," and "mythmasters." This distinction hardly arose out of a close study of how power sustains itself through the medium of ideas rather than the medium of force. It was merely the most obvious way to hold on to two opposite and oppositely advantaged accounts of male power at once. One was an account of that power as so self-originative, intentional, and effective that it could be charged with being the first cause of every abominable idea and event in the history of civilization; the other, an account of that power as no less conditioned, manipulated, and blind than female powerlessness, so that men, while having greater might on their side, would not be more admirable in understanding and vision.[34]

Now political thinkers have toyed occasionally in the past with the idea of splitting the subjugating consciousness into two separate figures – the brainwasher who devises and directs the drama of social life, and his protégé-pawn, in whom he has implanted the ideals of domination – as a way to avoid crediting a dominant group with a superior intelligence, as well as to make up for the lack of a good explanation for how that group came to think the way it did. But it was a solution that always turned out not to work, and it did not work for Daly at the usual point: when some allusion had to be made to the genesis of the brainwasher's own ideas and purposes. As soon as Daly remarked that a few of the "conditioned" men would become the "fatherly" mythmakers and enforcers of the next generation, the bit of scaffolding holding up the analysis of patriarchal consciousness collapsed.[35] Logically, the true pawn never can become the true brainwasher, who is set apart from those in whom he implants "ego-deflating" or "ego-inflating" ideas by the fact that he, unlike they, must know (and in the grandest sense of the term "to know") just what he is doing and why. His intelligence must be extra-ideological.

The tension between the ideas of an autonomous and a conditioned male consciousness runs like a twisted thread through all of radical feminist analysis. As a rule, however, it appears not as a distinction between two contrary sorts of men, the brainwasher and the pawn, but as two contradictory claims about the same men. In one breath, all men are described as authoring, designing, controlling; in the next, as having been socialized, conditioned, brainwashed. The persistence of the tension, and the difficulties that appear like a cloud of flies whenever it is said that men have made and imposed patriarchal culture on women, should be taken as a sign that the relation between dominative power, agency, and consciousness must be thought out in a different way.

So let us start over again, and let us take as our first premise only the point of there being a regime of truth that imposes itself on the sexed body. If we want to consider sex and gender as a system of power, this much, I think, must be granted in advance. Like the classificatory order Edward Said charted in *Orientalism*, this one makes its fundamental distinction between "Self" and "Other," demarcating the former by establishing the latter as its negative illumination, its intimate opposite, its "underground self."[36] The distinction thus has its origins in itself, but it presents itself as if it corresponded to the truth outside itself of two natural, separate entities. In the case of sex and gender, the difference between Self and Other is articulated not as Occident/Orient but as Masculine/feminine. Its classic exposé is not Said's *Orientalism* but Simone de Beauvoir's *The Second Sex*. It is, "strictly speaking," not a "field of learned study"[37] populated by writers who leave signed texts behind them – "poets, novelists, philosophers, political theorists, economists, and imperial administrators"[38] – but an interpretive regimen for popular, hence anonymous, self-experience. It will leave its deepest and most clear-cut imprint on the body and psyche rather than the page.

Masculine/feminine is disciplinary first in the fairly benign sense that, like every classificatory order, it is particular and so is less than infinitely permissive. Through supplanting sheer chaos, fluidity, and boundlessness with relatively fixed identities and thus relatively stable possibilities for desire, will, and action, it curtails the utter creativity of thought and action, at the same time as it enables them to occur. The order is disciplinary in a second, malignant sense that it speaks in the particular language of overweening social power. It delineates as the two star characters in its cast, a masculine subject to whom it assigns the prerogatives of the seer, the thinker, the doer, the law-giver; and a feminine object constituted by the subject's gaze, his conceptions, his acts, his rule. The regime of Masculine/feminine is coherent as a consequence of these internal designations and assignments, but it is not subjugating simply on their account. Any madman or sadistic dreamer, after all, can conjure up a fantasy made of conceptual indicators for domination and subordination. The terms of the classificatory whole must be reiterated in social arrangements to be "subjugating" in a meaningful way. They must be hegemonic over the living of actual life. A real population designated as masculine must enjoy the prerogatives of active Subject, and a population designated as feminine must be forced to act the part of the object for him. The feminine population not only must behave as Other and witness constantly images of its otherness on the cultural screen – it must understand itself as Other to a masculine Self in the specified ways that the regime traces out. That is, its secondary stature *vis à vis* a masculine Self, and its ascription of supreme subjectivity to that Self, must be part of its own directly felt identity. It must cling to the rule of Masculine/feminine with all the loyalty that self-love (in its case, the love of the self-obliterating self) can induce.

The existence of a regime of Masculine/feminine is in one sense a central premise for radical feminism as well as for us. Radical feminism, after all, is nothing if not de Beauvoir's intellectual heir in viewing "the feminine" not as a natural and singular identity, but as a logical requirement for and appendage of "the masculine". It would be more adamant than we (but no more adamant than de Beauvoir) that the rules of the regime govern, in a total way, established social life. On the other hand, radical feminism in the main would reject this second premise, which also follows from de Beauvoir: that there is no deeper truth to which Masculine/feminine in a distorted way corresponds, no real essence of the male and female, no distinction between two different sorts of principles, spirits, or selves – nothing beyond brute and meaningless bodily difference at all. But it is a third premise I want to discuss here (one on which, I think, de Beauvoir tacitly, but only tacitly, counted): that Masculine/feminine as a regime of truth has no originative genius or master behind it. The self-identity and self-understanding of the population assigned the position of the Masculine master are generated out of the regime rather than the other way around, so that men can think, speak, and write the terms of Masculine/feminine, and decorate, refine, and extend them, without being their true author or first heretic at all.[39]

It should be pointed out that "a regime without a master" is not a new way of declaring that all men as well as all women have been, by patriarchal culture, brainwashed or socialized. That declaration still would suggest the hidden presence rather than the absence of a master-brainwasher – no longer in the form of a concrete individual or group, but rather as a culture doing the work of indoctrinating its members under its own, impersonal steam. The notion of culture as master-brainwasher retains the crude notion that culture and mind are externally related, so that any mind can be assumed to have gotten its ideas via inculcation and implantation; and the peculiar image of inculcation as a conveyor belt, with virgin hearts and minds at one end, minted hearts and minds at the other, and a hovering master-conditioner at the controls – in this case the dominant culture as a whole. Any master-conditioner being, by definition, free of the habits of thought and tendencies of desire it imposes on others, the culture here must be understood, very curiously, as being free of itself, as if it were a logically separate and distinct figure from its own classifications, specifications, and rules.

To the contrary, the notion of a regime without a master means that rules of classification and practical permissions and prohibitions are not authorized or imposed by any self-consciousness at all – not by an entire group, not by a few individual mythmakers and masters, and not by the culture impossibly stepping into the brainwasher's place. This notion has, as its preliminary truth, the point that any individual always begins to think, desire, and act in terms specified for it by an established order of things, elaborated for it by past generations of individuals who began their thinking, desiring, and acting in the same way. Thus there is a great deal to thought and action that is not the willful product of any thinker's designs and intentions – designs and intentions which indeed are more likely to issue out of the established order of thought than the other way around. The inevitable traditionalism of thought and action means that there is always a very large element of objective (which is not to say "material") determination about it. This element characteristically does not become the object of reflective attention, so that any particular figure is likely – but not fated – to spend its life inside a world whose terms it never thinks to think about.

The unwitting and unintended in every mode of thought and so in every mode of action, the settling in of beliefs, tastes, values, aims, and tendencies of practice for no reason that anyone ever devised, as the result of no indoctrination process that anyone ever decided to begin, is of great significance for us. It means we must recognize an element of sheer givenness on the part of a regime of truth and blind habit on the part of those who think, desire, and act within its terms. This is so even with respect to regimes specifying terms of mastery and servitude as fundamental identities of social life. This is exactly the recognition that the notion of a regime without a master requires from us, and more. It demands we see givenness and habituation as a (although not "the") primary means of its own entrenchment. Now, the perpetuation of any order of things through the absence of considered reflection about it, its refinement through the extension and embellishment of lines of thought and permissions of practice already firmly and unnoticeably in place, does not mean that any of its individual figures cannot be more rather than less self-conscious and calculating in helping things to continue on in the same vein. Nor does it mean that an order of things cannot be more, rather than less, lax or slipshod: that it cannot be relatively open rather than relatively closed to experimentation, ingenuity, and shifting identities. But when a regime of truth imposes terms in strict relations of entailment with one another, when its internal specifications have a tight coherence and relentless logic to them – when, that is, stringency is added to givenness and habituality, it can be said to wield a tyrannical sort of mastery over those who think, desire, and act under its rule. The crucial point is that its own mastery must be distinguished very sharply from any social mastery to which it gives conceptual life.

The power that a regime of truth *exerts* over its members obliges us to make the initial assumption that it is a power "from no one and nothing." It disciplines those it may assign, on the basis of characteristics it has delineated as signifying a particular "type," to a dominant social position no less than those it assigns to a subordinate: the content of both regimentations will be different but the fact of regimentation will be exactly the same. On the other hand, the power that the regime *specifies* for certain of its members of, say, a dominant Self over subordinate Other obliges us to assume that the exercise of that power is the prerogative of a specific group or groups, so that its workings can be traced back to specific sources and sites, and that its effects on a target population can be counted as injuries and punishments. At the same time, we must remember that while a dominant social group may exert institutional authority of every kind, monopolize the production of public culture, make and enforce the law, engage with impunity in violent and exploitative adventures, there is nothing in the concept of "overweening social power" that entails that power lies entirely on the dominator's side. Moreover, the dominant group cannot be supposed to wield mastery over the regime of truth, which we are obliged to treat initially as the "meta" power of the thought, word, and deed. Nor, consequently, can the dominant group be supposed to wield full and true mastery over the consciousness of the subordinate. To the extent that that consciousness is mastered, it will be so in the most fundamental sense as a comrade of its dominant counterpart under the same discursive regime, breathing the same ideological atmosphere, which is not to say (in fact, it is to say quite the contrary) that the regime and the atmosphere dictate identical self-images, proclivities, and passions to both parties.

If the attribution of a regime of truth to the original genius of a dominant group is the classic error of the instrumentalist analysis of power, the presumption behind the error is the belief that human thought and action can occur outside any particular classificatory and practical order at all. Thus, the first question it strikes instrumentalism to ask is how a certain group (a subordinate group) came to think in a certain way (a way confirming its subordination), as if thinking in a certain way instead of "freely" is the greatest puzzle of all to work out. Thus, too, the first answer it strikes instrumentalism to give is that a dominant self-consciousness has implanted in its subordinates specific desires, beliefs, and intentions, as if, had the subordinate group not been indoctrinated by the dominant, it would be free in consciousness, unhinged from any givenness and objective determination. As soon as one disentangles discursive from social power, one is able to pose questions about how consciousness is determined in a different way. What, one can ask, are the dominant culture's basic classifications and assignments of identity, its range of conceivable practices, its encouraged sensibilities, its prohibited trains of thought? That is, what is the nature of the order of things both dominant and subordinate populations inhabit? What are the stances towards that order it is possible to take? Which of these stances are most likely to lead the way out, and which populations are most likely to be led, not to some free zone of thought and action, but from the hegemonic set of specifications through their subversion into some other, different sort? How is the dominant culture kept alive, reproduced, and expanded? To what extent is instrumentalism correct when it claims that it is the subordinate population that must be, in normal times, most thoroughly captivated by hegemonic ideas, or that it is the dominant group that always plays the pre-eminent part in keeping the given order intact?

One is pressed also to follow a new methodological rule of thumb. The initial movement one looks to trace is not from outside the bounds of an order of truth *in* (the sort of movement by which virgin minds are inculcated with hegemonic ideas), but from inside the bounds of that order, where every mind begins, out. What lies beyond those bounds, in turn, must be expected to be never a "free land" but rather another order, if not discovered as already existing in some other geographical place, then emergent out of the dissolutions and transfigurations of the old. An emergent order originally will likely have much that is unruly and highly charged about it, an exuberance that comes in the absence of rigid rules for how things must be thought about and so what can be thought to be done. But to the extent that it acquires any real coherence, complexity, and strength, what began as an anarchic *melange* of shifting conceptions and practices will harden into a counter-cultural hegemony in its own right. This is only to say that every vigorous counter-culture is bound to end up exerting its own discipline over life. It is not to say that discipline must be one of social mastery and servitude.

The reverse truth of the inevitability of every individual's situation inside a specific cultural order is the possibility of any individual's making its way out, to some different and perhaps antithetical tendency of thought and action. This possibility is rooted in the human capacity for not merely going on in the same direction as before but for critical reflection and creative transformation. Its signficance for us is that a member of a dominant social group never is precluded logically from coming to think and trying to act outside the pale of an order that has elaborated and justified the terms of its dominance to it. A break from the dictations of Masculine/feminine, to take up our specific subject again, is not women's prerogative alone, as though only bodies of a certain sort could have outlawed desires or disloyal ideas, or as if subordination were the only position from which criticism and rebellion could come. At the same time, the initial presumption that men and women are situated inside the regime of Masculine/feminine allows us to register in theory what any glance at practical life already should have shown. This is the fact that is is women rather than men who are the less likely (which is not to say they are unlikely) to be captivated by the notions of

Masculine Self and feminine Other; who are the more likely (which is not to say they are extremely likely) to view the dominant Self with a jaundiced and cynical eye that does not see in the same way that the conventional eye does, and that on occasion breaks entirely with conventional vision. And in fact received truths generally will prove less potent for those at the bottom of any hierarchy than those at the top, although this rule has a proviso to which I will return in a moment.

That the subordinate group will not, after all, be the more thoroughly swayed by ideas legitimating its subordination hardly should strike anyone as surprising. Certainly, subordinates are injured externally and internally by power relations. What else would their subordination be about? But there is much in the daily getting of those injuries to make them suspicious of the self-glorifying terms in which the larger culture represents and understands itself. Their inferior social position does not allow them that indolence of thought that is the luxury of the complacent, self-satisfied, and smug. Then too, they are over-exposed to the shocks and agonies that can lead to fatalism and despair but alternatively can trigger a sea-change in received intepretations. Minimally, then, and against the instrumentalist view, the dominant group is no more apt than the subordinate to think beyond established bounds. Maximally, it is not only not the regime of truth's most autonomous and free-ranging master but also is its most abject – that is, unreflective, uncritical, and unimaginative – servant.

There is, as I said earlier, a reservation to the rule of the dominant group's distinctive obsequiousness before hegemonic principles. This group tends to have two special chances for a restless, expansive thought, desire, and will. First, as it typically is relieved of biologically necessary toil, and as it is unhampered by all the legal, customary, and material constraints to which subordinate populations are specially subjected, it will have a greater freedom than anyone else to wander outside its native geographical domain. Individual members of a dominant population are, then, well placed to undo their ties to their concrete situation and to set out on a journey from the familiar to the strange potentially corrosive of old tendencies and habits. They can pitch themselves into ways of life so different from their own that they return – if they return at all – seeing everything both strange and familiar in a new light. The promise of such self-dislocation is no less real because expeditions from the familiar to new and strange modes of life so often actually, in modern times, have worked out differently, with the new and the strange being forced into a relation of servitude to the culture of those journeying abroad, assuming a position designed by it of that which is "exotic," "primitive," "depraved," a "pleasure palace." But however acutely the modern era has seen the expansion of a culture's reach out into new territory on the individual adventurer's heels, it is just as possible for that culture to lose its hold over that adventurer. Only if every territory in the world were absorbed into a single culture, so that adventurers could come upon no "living rule" in opposition to their own, would those with the prerogative of geographical mobility not also have the prerogative to come to think and so to think to act in radically new ways. At this point, the phenomenon of the "adventure" would pass out of the practical lexicon of social life.

The second prerogative that the dominant group in a literate culture characteristically enjoys is that of taking an intellectual journey from the familiar to the strange. This is the prerogative of reading, thinking, and questioning in a prolonged and serious way, not the better to execute some particular task or to acquire social graces and skills, but for understanding's own sake. It is an exercise in reflection as the primary thing rather than as something done in the process of doing something else, a decomposition of common sense and regular notions, a broadening and deepening and undermining of the ordinary proclivities of thought. As useless or dangerous as reflective learning can appear to a dominant group to be, it typically is its special preserve. It comes to be so through the dominant group's having the leisure and material wealth to support a sustained course of study; through the restriction of general access to libraries and schools; through the establishment of private academies of learning; through the imposition of censorship on popular audiences; through the prohibition of literacy for the subordinate group; through the heaping of scorn on the idea of the educated subordinate; through the social isolation of subordinates who become educated against the rule, or alternatively through their absorption into the ranks of the dominant population; through the transformation of public education into technical education.[40]

Paradoxically, its monopolization of reflective learning specially invites the dominant group to a rebelliousness and self-destructiveness of thought. For often even more than physical travel, written words have the power to erode the inherited and habitual understanding. They can draw their reader further and further from familiar conceptual and imaginative territory: from the ordinary notion, the acceptable idea, the permitted point of view. At the same time, they have a stability about them through being fixed on the page that allows them to be mulled over, cited, consulted, appended, and expanded upon. To be sure, just as a strange mode of life can be forced to submit to the desire, conception, and will of the traveller's native regime, so the written word can be forced to submit to the desire, conception, and will of the reader's own hegemonic culture by being read in strict obedience to established rules of what constitutes meaning and meaninglessness; truth, distortion, and "mere" fantasy; good sense and madness. Even more obviously, the written word can have been composed under the tutelage of received rules in the first place, so that for it to be understood in accordance with them requires no act of interpretive discipline by the reader against the tendencies of the text.

The extreme parochialism, conservatism, and unreflectiveness that can characterize members of a subordinate group usually signal that the geographical and intellectual routes out of an inherited order have been closed off to them. Ironically, that closure hardly has been corrected by modern mass communications and mass transportation. Their joint consequence has been a transformation of the Different into the Same: an ideological representation of the Different to suit the Familiar's prejudices, and a physical reconstruction of the Different to suit the Familiar's desires.[41] Mass education has been more mixed in its effects. While iconoclastic notions have appeared in the public curriculum at least as liberally as in the private, the thrust of public education has been away from reflective studies towards technical instruction – that is, towards coursework in the detailed maintenance of the established social order. There is reserved for subordinates, of course, always that third route of a *practical* education: the getting of a critical consciousness through the hard living of life. This route offers its travelers neither the thrill of adventure nor the leisurely pace of intellectual study. What can be said in its favor is that it is highly democratic, and that it leaves an indelible imprint on those who go its way. The parochialism, conservatism, and unreflectiveness that can characterize members of a dominant group testify to the fact that everything in life conspires against their discovering this third route, and that their taking either of the other two is far from a sure thing. To have the prerogative to plunge into the new and the strange is not to use it; to use it is not to use it well. The overwhelming tendency of dominant individuals has been not to take advantage of their prerogatives but to deepen their own abasement before hegemonic dictations (and the sheer pull of interest comes in obviously here), so that those few who make their way out are quite aptly called by the rest, "eccentrics," "subversives," "traitors," and "queers."

10

Loyalists, Eccentrics, Critics, Traitors, and Rebels

What are the stances that can be struck towards Masculine/feminine as a cultural–political regime? At first glance, it might seem that we must make our primary distinction between the stance of "woman" and the stance of "man." And certainly with respect to the interior of Masculine/feminine, the line between "women" and "men" is drawn in exactly the right place. Everything changes, however, as soon as we step outside that interior to consider the ways it is possible to receive the regime's presentation of itself as speaking a vast, foundational truth. At this point, there is every reason not to base one's classifications on established classifications – not to draw automatically one's lines of division along the lines that the given order has etched out. How odd to remain faithful to the terms of Masculine/feminine just at this point! How odd to obey a rule when one is looking to show the rule's political tyranny rather than categorical truth – and more, when one is looking to show that tyranny's less than total triumph over life! We must discriminate instead between sensibilities of heart and mind that are "sympathetic" and "antipathetic" to the hegemonic regime. These are sensibilities to which the body's cultivation is so closely allied that the word "posture" perhaps is more apt, referring indifferently as it does to positions of thought, feeling, and physique.

If we begin in the heartland of Masculine/feminine and make our way out, the first posture we will find is that of "native loyalty." This is the stance in greatest identity with the terms of the established order, or, to put it differently, in grossest subservience to them. The naive loyalist sees the world of Masculine/feminine as natural, simply given, the summation of all possible worlds. It has not thought about ordinary things at any distance from ordinary proclamations about them, and it is loyal to the dictates of Masculine/feminine regarding manner and gesture, skills and proclivities, physical decoration and all varieties of taste. Its naiveté rests in its unreflective acceptance of those dictates and its belief that they flow out of the body. However punishing its own situation inside the larger situation may be, its understanding of neither has been irremediably shattered. Habituated to the comforts and torments of its familiar landscape, and uninclined by curiosity or restlessness to think past that landscape and back on it from some outside point, the naive loyalist remains lodged in its customary place.

This first, sympathetic posture has its pure and impure forms. Even pure forms, of course, are so only in abstraction from actual life, where they are unsullied by the hesitations and ambivalences of living human beings. Remembering, then, that we are moving in the realm of concrete condensations of abstract ideas and not in the empirical world, I want to consider the military Marine and the fashion Model as supreme naive loyalists of Masculine/feminine. the Marine and the Model are a theoretically exquisite pair: opposites inside the hegemonic order, comrades in their bond to it, both of them embracing – more, embodying in their very flesh – its claims to truth to the same exaggerated degree. The one strong and hard, the other slight or voluptuously soft, their bodies are the site of a unified system of meaning, a physicality ripe with intimations of aggression and allurement, vitality and vanity, brute command and an invitation to invasion. The Marine and the Model have been crafted out of rougher material into refined specimens of the Masculine/feminine idea through analogous disciplinary processes, the one located in the barracks and the bootcamp, the other in the modelling school and the photographer's stable. While the first purpose of neither the political/military nor the commercial/communicative apparatus of power is to manufacture masculinity and femininity, they each readily would acknowledge that precipitating out, respectively, "unmanly" qualities and qualities "undesirable in a woman" was something that they regularly did. The Marine's and the Model's loyality, to be sure, is not wholly the effect of these particular precipitations. The Marine originally had been lured into the treacherous abyss of obedience, authority, and regimented violence by the promise that every trace of the feminine would be eradicated from him – that he would be turned "from a boy into a man." The Model had set herself on a course that clearly would strip her of every vestige of an active will by training her in the multiple postures of the exposed and self-exposing object of the gaze. Whether they chose their ordeals through the wish to become perfect specimens of masculinity and femininity or not, the two could see those ordeals as suitable choices for them because their self-understandings as masculine and feminine were already in place. Their naiveté also both precedes and follows their hyper-cultivation as classificatory exemplars. A critical examination of the whole system of classifications, after all, was hardly preliminary to their special training. Even less is it its natural afer-effect, criticism's being in direct opposition to the substance and function of the exemplary figure.

Through their simple presence in the public world, the Marine and the Model help sustain the given order of sex and gender. The Model is no less active in that sustenance than the Marine, even though she plays the part not of forceful warrior and adventurer, but of the immobilized object of enticement. Together the pair serves as Masculine/feminine's most luminous instruction, its crassest epitome, its measuring-rod against which others can be judged to fall short. This is not to say that the two have the regime's reproduction as their conscious intention and plan. Some of the most vivid brutalities and vanities, cruelties and submissions are displayed by exemplars such as these. But any evil that they do or compliantly suffer is likely to stem from some prototypical vice of masculinity or femininity, not from the prior vice of creating and imposing Masculine/feminine as a system of vice and so also a system of virtue. Can we at last put it this way? What they do will be symptomatic of masculinity or femininity as a disease – it will not be the original sin of germinating the disease and inoculating the human race with it.

Let us shift our sights from the naive loyalist in its pure to its impure form. This second figure is attached to the Masculine/-feminine in a way that is altogether less stark, less pronounced, less the result of rigorous institutional orchestration. A yawning gap commonly separates its talk about life from its living of it, not because this naive loyalist condemns Masculine/feminine in words while embracing it in action, but because it proclaims its truth in speech, while its practical adherence to that truth may be inconstant, erratic, cavalier. We all have met such contradictory figures in concrete life. There is the man who concurs that men are made to be masters but turns out not to wield mastery over women at all – not through a failure of nerve or an ineffective will, but because the exercise of mastery over women is actually repugnant to him. There is the woman who assents in all honesty that men are made to be masters but in day-to-day life never submits to any man, being strong-spirited, formidable, ready and able to counter men's every overbearing move. Both of these figures are loyalists paramountly in the ideological sense. They sustain the hegemonic rule through their reliance on idiom and homily when summing up the general sense of sex/gender relations. They erode the rule by living their lives in discordance with it. Their naiveté rests in their being oblivious to their contradictory condition, in their clinging, out of psychological resistance, intellectual laziness, or an impatience with introspection, to ideas about life that are at odds with their ideas in it.

Thus when it is not thinking and speaking about life as a whole – when it is thinking and speaking in doing rather than on the significance of what has been done – this naive loyalist often strays outside the hegemonic rule. Only when commenting directly on the truth of the rule does it strenuously take the hegemonic side. Even then, its avowals are not programmatic but conversational – the odd sentence spoken and dropped. It never gives the matter of Masculine/feminine serious attention, so that thoughtlessness rather than willful deceit is its tell-tale flaw.

Thoughtlessness is exactly not the flaw we find when we come to the next posture in our series. This is also the posture of a sympathizer, but one who has "thought round" the classificatory regime, has considered its claims to truth, has reflected on its requirements and prohibitions, and subsequent to all of this has embraced it in some significant way. The very reflectivity and intentionality of the embrace, however, bespeak a certain tense reserve about it. This loyalist's identity with the given order is not immediate, spontaneous, or total. Its breadth of vision is wider than the order's own; it knows there are different ways of thinking and acting; it is denied the bliss that comes, not from contentment, but from believing that there are no other possible arrangements of things besides the arrangements one happens to find oneself in. An interior distance separates the self-conscious loyalist from all that it hopes to be loyal to. It can cross the distance only by plunging back from reflective into habitual thought.

In addition to feeling a general loyalty laced with estrangement, self-conscious loyalists may be plagued by quite different specific contradictions. One loyalist chatters away in harmony with the dictates of Masculine/feminine while evading those dictates in its practical life – not, this time, out of naiveté but out of cleverness and the desire to deceive. Fully aware of the retaliations conventionally used against those who stray outside conventional bounds and fully intending to stray there itself, it fixes on practical disobedience obscured by verbal deference as the safest course for it to take. Thus in concrete life we find the woman who declares that men are made to be masters, not sincerely but to conceal from men her strong and independent will, which they would set out to crush were they forced to see it face to face. We find the man who does not incline towards acting the master in his relations with women, but who boasts of his mastery to safeguard his relations with men (knowing well what arouses their ridicule and disdain) by sounding "like a man" in their company. We meet the woman or man whose erotic passions are felt for members of their own sex, and who make a show of hegemonic allegiance to avoid those severe punishments devised for use against sexual desire at odds with heterosexual prescriptions. All of these figures are loyal to the established order only through being liars in front of it. Still, the appearance of partisanship no less than the real thing helps to keep ordinary life on its ordinary course.

A self-conscious loyalist who must be counted for opposite reasons as a liar denounces the truth of Masculine/feminine in words while being faithful to it in deeds. This figure is almost always a man, who in public questions the legitimacy of male power (but with *civility*, *moderation*, and *tact*) and in private conducts himself more circumspectly, perhaps, than other men but with their same purposes and interests at heart. By this strategy he hopes to win gratitude and admiration from his subordinates and to convey all around the air of a man who is progressive and broad-minded, while he continues to indulge in the pleasures that sexual domination afford.

But not all those who in some way affirm the established order are cynics, fugitives, or hypocrites who say one thing and do another. They may be as consistently true to Masculine/feminine as it is possible for any self-conscious loyalist to be. Surely the most strategically placed of *these* are professional cultural or political workers. For the most part, of course, theologians, scholars, film-makers, novelists, grass-roots organizers, orators, and officials reiterate established notions of sex and gender in a naive and unreflective way. But at least a few are likely to have devoted themselves to a serious consideration of "the opposite sexes" – intellectuals and activists always are putting their minds to a serious consideration of something or other, after all. And more than a few of those few are likely to become, as a consequence, not disenchanted but newly astute in their loyalties to ordinary ideals and conventions. Their sermons, essays, films, novels, political platforms, and speeches then become distinguished from others on the public scene by having been deliberately tailored to show the rightness or usefulness or necessity or normalcy of the given order of things. The point of the show may be to give the established terms of sex and gender one tighter turn of the screw, to fortify them against criticism and experimentation, or to elaborate and decorate them for the sheer pleasure that embellishment gives the embellisher.

But even with respect to such self-consistent and loyal members of the intelligentsia, there are interesting incongruities and incoherences. These vary according to sex. The woman, first of all, who fights on the side of Masculine/feminine by marching, debating, lecturing, or leading cannot help but stand against the rule in the course of standing for it. To enter into the public arena, to strike a militant pose, to make appeals through political argument, to organize masses of people – all to uphold woman's rightful submission, dependence, domesticity, and submergence in the life of the body! This is a deep contradiction, and the position of the active woman loyalist always will ring, as a result of it, false. The false aspect of the man who is an intellectual and a loyalist is this. While he defends Masculine/feminine more eloquently than any other sort of man, he is less likely than any other sort to correspond in his cultivated body, mannerisms, and style of speech with the masculine idea. Certainly as a bodily type (and we are talking only of types) he is cruelly bested by the marine, the football player, the blue-collar worker. It is through the fact of his inadequate embodiment of his own ideal that the male intellectual who is a loyalist so often is fascinated by that whole pantheon of mythic figures including the soldier, the athlete, the hunter, the adventurer, and the outlaw. He is fascinated, that is, as long as they are *men*: to be bested in masculinity by women is something he only can see as grotesque. The ferocity of his ideological tie to the given order and the relative delicacy of his physical self, by the way, should put us on guard against assuming too easily that the outer body signals and corresponds to any particular set of interior commitments. We cannot be sure, then, that a burly and muscular male physique will signify an ideological attachment to the masculine idea.

It should be obvious by now that members of the intelligentsia who thoughtfully and intentionally support that regime are not by that token its authors and masterminds. They only have taken the opportunity, available to anyone at all, to reflect on the given order's claims to truth before engaging in activities to prevent those claims from being, by others, reflected upon. The self-consciousness in their loyalty, in other words, comes after their initial attachment to Masculine/feminine, not before. Likewise, the themes that acquire publicly visible form in their work originate inside the established set of discourses, not out, even if that set takes on a newish cast as the result of their making their mark on it.

But enough of these loyalists! They are so predictable, so ordinary in their vices and virtues, so stolid, unimaginative, and resigned. There are so many of them in actual life (and isn't there something of the loyalist in each of us?). Let us move on to that more striking quartet: the eccentric, the critic, the traitor and the rebel.

Every dominant culture has its mavericks, its eccentrics: figures who do not fit its specifications but are not moored at any other identifiable site. The eccentric is one who early on drifted far away from ordinary conventions. Yet it never drifts towards any group of rebels at odds with the given scheme of things, and it does not study that scheme long enough for it to count as a solitary critic. The eccentric simply goes along in its own peculiar way, not bothering to hide its peculiarities from open view. To all appearances, at least, it is unfazed by a larger order that so badly suits it and that it so badly suits.

Before Masculine/feminine became, first, medicalized by psychoanalysis, then politicized by feminism and the gay movement, its eccentrics often were those out of kilter with the rule of heterosexual desire – except when the rule was not, in fact, heterosexual at all. This particular eccentricity *as* "eccentricity" largely has been obliterated, on the one side by the rise of a battery of distinctions between sexual "normality" and "perversion" and the host of medical and academic institutions thriving on their basis; on the other side by the emergence of counter-hegemonic sexual politics and cultures with their own distinctions between "straight" and "gay," "homosexual" and "lesbian," "male-identified- " and "woman-identified women." The eccentric, after all, is not one through belonging to either a deviant or counter-cultural group. But there always have been other kinds of "queer fish" where sex and gender are concerned: figures who, in their sensibilities and predilections, or in their mannerisms and dress, or in their interests and skills, seem to be aligned with the sex that is not their biological own; or are thoroughly ambiguous, a hybrid of the genders; or are altogether beyond any familiar sex/gender description. Once again, many such figures have been swallowed up, conceptually speaking, by medical science and sexual politics and turned into members of groups with shared qualities: psychological abnormalities or political virtues, as the case may be. But although scientific and political classifications may have shrunk "the maverick's" scope of play, they can never entirely eliminate it. It will always be possible for a new oddity to arise, or for old qualities to combine in a newly odd way. I can offer no general summary of the eccentricities of our time – eccentricity is, after all, precisely that which shows itself as true singularity and uniqueness, as qualities thrown together in a particular arrangement only once. You must look around for the concrete instance for yourself. Only do not, in real life, expect to find someone who is a maverick through and through. You are much more likely to come across the impure case: someone, for example, who has pedestrian ideas about men and women in their mutual connections but who lives as much as possible outside those connections, beyond the furthest point of what is commonplace for either sex; or someone who cuts the most ordinary physical figure but in its every other relation to the sex/gender system is completely unorthodox. The strange and the commonplace can meet in a single figure in a hundred different, undictated ways.

The critic of Masculine/feminine is more likely than the eccentric to conform in manner to hegemonic specifications. At the same time and unlike the eccentric, the critic is intellectually attentive to those specifications out of a strong desire to undermine them, and has the sharpest understanding of how they malignantly work. If the eccentric, with no larger point to make, *does* not obey the rule, the critic, to the extent that it can help it, *will* not. Its antagonism stems not from any oddness on its part (however magnificent true oddness can be) but from a clear-sighted, hard-headed intelligence about and distaste for all the established order entails. The essence of the critic is just this intelligence and distaste turned into talk – into an immense, ceaseless volubility. The critic talks to reveal and to denounce everything: the rule of Masculine/feminine as an authoritarian imposition, and its own particular conformities (bodily, emotional, dispositional) as evidence of how deep the rule actually goes.

The critic's revelations and denunciations must be counted as actions on its part. This is so because of the real strenuousness with which it keeps them up. But it is also because speech so classically makes an incision in social life, and the human world so centrally has to do with what is said in it. To be sure, the critic does not confine its actions to verbal commentaries. Its iconoclastic outlook invades its way of conducting friendships, love affairs, and family relations (which is why the critic makes such difficult company for everyone else); it affects to a certain extent the way it prepares itself physically for public view; and it determines the kinds of practices in which it chooses to take part. Still, the critic's capacity for radical analysis overstretches its capacity for self-transformation. It is tied tightly, if corrosively, to the given scheme of things. It extends itself as a negative rather than a new positive, striking blows against the established regime, and against what it already has been pressed by that regime to be.

Broadly speaking, there are two sorts of critics of this particular regime. The first is the critic "in life." This is the posture of, specifically, a woman, who spontaneously and glancing no further than her own particular and immediate situation, refuses to assent to her subordinate assignment. She openly violates the established rule with insolence, with anger, with pride. The critic in life is most forcefully herself not in front of massive economic and political institutions with their great powers of forbidding, censoring, firing, and imprisoning – but in contexts more miniature, more domestic, more private. In the street, in the house, in the bedroom, she announces her intention to live exactly as she pleases and not at the command of a male master. She arranges her life to suit her own purposes, she guards herself against those who would want submission from her, and she seeks pleasure on her own terms. Her immense volubility as a critic occurs in ordinary conversation, in the form of advice, warnings, beratings, tirades, admonishments, derisive laughter, and ironic asides. She presses her own demands with the fierce independence of the self-certain self, presenting herself as a force to be acknowledged, reckoned with, placated, and occasionally begged to. She meets her match when she is met by another figure who is prepared to acknowledge, reckon with, placate, and when necessary beg to her: not as a servant begs to a master, but as one equal sometimes must beg to another for something that it badly wants or needs, the deep equality of their relation forbidding it the privilege of command.

The second, very different sort of critic comes to its position not in the spontaneous course of living its life but rather through distancing itself from its immediate situation. From a temporarily detached point, it surveys the larger order, investigating how precisely that order works, and it sides with all of those the order has most harshly used. In sum, it becomes politicized in its understandings and interests. The politicized critic (who is likely to be a woman but who also can be a man) does a great deal of its talking in casual conversation. Its special forte, however, is the formal argument, the plotted-out speech, the public action taken against the established order, the cultural form created in contrast to it. This figure goes far against the regime but not infinitely far. Its most vociferous attacks are launched largely at the level of talk and antagonistic action. The regime still is powerful enough to keep it somewhere still under its sway: the critic's political convictions are not matched by its thorough metamorphosis of the self.

The man who comes to a critical understanding of sex and gender through reflection and politicization inevitably holds a modest place in the critics' camp. He learns from and follows the lead of women – the negative impulse along this particular axis of power is after all so paramountly theirs. But there is another, independent route to criticism a man can take, more akin to the route of the critic "in life." This is the route of the traitor. The traitor is a figure who, in the simple course of being and living, betrays the interests at the heart of the sex/gender regime. This figure is necessarily a man, as no woman intelligibly can be said to betray interests that have worked against her from the start. The distinction between a man who is a critic and the man who is a traitor lies in the difference between a point of view and a temperament, a set of ideas and a character, a train of thought and an intellectual–emotional disposition. The traitor lives out instinctively, so to speak, a renunciation of any right to mastery over women. His turns of phrase, bearing, sympathies, and desires are innocent of the phallocentric urge. This is not to intimate that he is someone whose urges do not draw him towards women at all, who out of mere apathy and boredom does not bother to tyrannize over them. The passions fueling the desire for and the desire to dominate women, to be sure, both may be absent from the traitor in the individual case. Still, this absence is not the traitor's distinguishing mark, nor is it proof that a man betrays masculinist interests in his general outlook. That the traitor renounces mastery over women, to make a different point, does not mean that he has no sharp edge, is incapable of a severity of mood or stubbornness of will, or takes no pleasure in exerting strength and force. It is rather that he sees no special prerogative for him in sharpness, severity, stubbornness – no exclusive right to strength and force invested in him by his biological sex.

The traitor finds other men quite disagreeable for what the conceit in their sex has worked in them. He often keeps the company of women. He need not exhibit or be enamored of the feminine vices, but vanity, triviality, a narrowness of vision and concern will strike him as being more tolerable than arrogance, emotional crudity, and the constant impulse to control. Thus he is happy to put up with the vices – or morbid symptoms? – of femininity where he comes across them, in order to enjoy among women a comfortable flow of conversation, an easy play of personality, a jousting – not warring – of wits. The traitor in fact shares a whole range of sensibilities with women, or at least with women who have not acquired, through a change in their structural position, the classic sensibilities of men. His delights – for example, in the sensuous detail, the delicacy of character, the intimate connection – are frequently identical with theirs. So are his irritations. All in all, the traitor very naturally takes women's point of view, and, in their antagonisms with men, their side.

At last, we come to the rebel: that figure in whom antipathies to the hegemonic regime are most graphic, whose refusal to fall in with prevailing assignments is most extreme. The rebel challenges – sometimes in its spoken self-reflections, always in its self-presentation and lived life – the truths about the body that the cultural order has to tell. Does the male body signify power, intelligence, and aggression, and the female weakness, innocence, and allurement? the rebel scoffs at such pretensions. It actively crosses the boundary between masculine and feminine to claim for itself the posture, manner, and dress said to belong to the body of the opposite sex. Or it dissolves the distinction between masculine and feminine in its physique, proclivities, and tastes, so that it lives and breathes outside all familiar classifications. In its crossings and dissolutions, the rebel has the undisciplined air of someone at play: for isn't it the tedious plodding along according to a rule that is the real essence of work? Like all people at play, the rebel is constantly poised between the polar possibilities of becoming either utterly frivolous or deadly serious in its pursuits. On the one side, its forays against Masculine/feminine can degenerate into sheer theatricality and a narcissistic focus on the making of physical appearances. The rebel's fascination with that artificial aspect of Masculine/feminine *par excellence* – the costumes, decorations, and cosmetics that help mark out the "woman" and the "man" – may lead to its complete seduction by artifice for artifice's sake. The rebel seduced gives itself up entirely to the voluptuous pleasures to be had in posing and ornamentation. Then again, on the other side, rebellion can escalate into a game played for political stakes, an engagement undertaken to subvert the larger sex/gender regime. This escalation occurs when the rebel joins to its attack on the line between masculine and feminine an attack on the masculine prerogative. Then it pits itself not merely against the dictation of two different scripts for two different physical types, but against the fact that one script and not the other gives dramatic license for subjectivity, independence, and power.

In seriousness or frivolity, the rebel challenges the given order as its special project, its life's play. It understands that order very thoroughly, very profoundly, with a keenness of insight far surpassing that of the most perfect loyalist, who never thinks about the order which it is loyal to. It is this keen insight that most clearly distinguishes the rebel from the eccentric (which it may resemble in other respects) and most closely unites it with the critic. Yet, the rebel goes much further than the critic in its desire and its cultivation of the palpable self. Beyond the critic's furthest horizons, the rebel moves, energetic and dynamic, drawing a line between masculine and feminine on its very self in some outlawed way, or altogether giving up those ghosts that are said to come attached to the body.

What, in the end, is the political significance of these various concrete types?

Clearly the naive loyalist is key to the perpetuation of socio-sexual life in its old form. In the practice of its vices – or virtues, if one take the hegemonic point of view – the naif keeps afloat all that is conventional and routine. Its general vice, you will remember, is that blank indifference to reflecting back on its situation. For the hegemonic regime, this is the great virtue of immediate and unconditional allegiance. The naif's gender-specific vices vary across a wide and rich range. On the one side, it might exhibit egotism, the love of force, and a worship of authority (the hegemonic virtues of masculine self-assertion, physical courage and obedience); on the other, it might display vanity, a superficiality of interest, and the passive submission to direction (the hegemonic virtues of feminine beauty, charm, and the desire to please and to serve). The naive loyalist, however, is politically key to Masculine/feminine through maintaining it not politically but in its spontaneous living of life. If we wish to find the true political champion of the old order, we must look to the self-conscious loyalist, who intentionally argues or lobbies or riots or legislates to keep the regime intact.

The figures in most acute opposition to that regime are the politicized critic and the rebel. They are the locus of cultural–political resistance to power, but this does not mean that they are more virtuous, knowing, or free than the rest. They have their characteristic vices, for a start. The critic leans hard against the entrenched order in its thought-out principles and planned-out actions but leans hard towards it in many of its proclivities and tastes. Its ambivalence can verge very nearly on hypocrisy and cowardice. And we have seen how the rebel, through delighting in its own iconoclasm, can succumb to sheer dramatics and narcissistic self-absorption. Very differently, the rebel in league with the critic can grow to love the exercise of power over others and become tyrannical in counter-hegemonic settings. On the positive side, the critic can be said to be admirably knowing through having a developed political understanding – but then, the self-conscious loyalist enjoys such an understanding too. And while the rebel is freer of the imprint and pull of established dictations than any figure except the eccentric, it is not free in some absolute way. If it performs its rebellion solo, it will suffer the constraints of isolation. If it rebels in a mass of others, it will be hemmed in by a host of stringent new expectations and demands.

What uniquely mark the critic and the rebel are not moral purity, superior wisdom, and abstract freedom, but a negative relation to the socio-sexual order that is clearly willful together with an understanding of its situation on not just the personal but the grand, collective scale. The rebel is a living image of the dissolution of the old regime, a visible denial of hegemonic truth, a declaration in the body that at least *here* the rule is dying or decayed. It points in its being to possible schemes of things beyond the given: schemes that are not natural or rational or true but radically different – and a radical difference from Masculine/feminine is surely good enough. The critic points beyond the boundary of the given not as much through the body as through the word. It denounces and debunks Masculine/feminine, it issues a call to arms against it, it analyzes the forces of power lined up on the hegemonic side, and it designs strategies for oppositional action.

Their different qualities of opposition are precisely what make these two figures politically vital for each other. The rebel provides the critic with a provocation for its imagination. In the rebel's absence, the critic very likely would think and dream near the edge of entrenched ideas and practices but not over the edge. The critic, on its side, is essential to the politicization of socio-sexual resistance, both because words have a public clarity to them that simple self-presentation does not, and because sexual rebellion alone too readily takes the form of mere individual perversity or subcultural exoticism. The unity of critic and rebel in opposition to the order of things is not only a unity of a negative and a startling new positive, but also an odd variant of the unity of theory and practice. The critic analyzes and agitates against hegemonic pressures and constraints, while the rebel surpasses them but also refers back to them by living as a strange self inside the old world.

The lines of political division between loyalists, eccentrics, traitors, critics, and rebels, crisscross the two populations of male and female. The question of political alliance in the realm of Masculine/feminine thus becomes very complex. As the subordinate population of that realm, women will be the main subjects and must be the main objects of every effort of political mobilization aimed against it. But women will not situate themselves necessarily on the opposition's side. Although they are far more likely than men to become critics and rebels of Masculine/feminine, they are not more likely to become critics and rebels than to become loyalists. And of course they are not the only possible critics and rebels around. Thus it is that women who are actively at odds with the dictations of Masculine/feminine may be closer in their sensibilities to the few men who are traitors or rebels than to the many women who are loyalists. Any sexual politics of resistance ultimately will be brought face to face with that fact.

Conclusion

On Practice

1.

Lovers whose desires do not run a straight masculine or feminine course break the rule for eroticism behind the bedroom wall. Eccentrics, traitors, and natural critics are fated by sensibility and temperament to think and act in unconventional ways. To these spontaneous resistances against the socio-sexual order, we now must add the collective and political resistances of self-conscious critics and rebels.

Radical feminism calls the target of such sexual–political resistance "The Patriarchy," but that term is off the mark for us. No other term so strongly conveys a sense of male power – indeed, of all power – as something wielded from a single center, in an absolutely monolithic and intentional way, working in the same interests for the same goal in every period and place. Moreover, "The Patriarchy" rests on "woman" and "man" as categorical givens, whose separate identities are more fundamental than the fact of patriarchal rule.[1] The notion that there is and has been no other rule but this one, when combined with the notion that women's and men's identities are foundational while the rule is ultimately not, means that patriarchy's end would signify nothing other than the emancipation of women as a natural, universal, essential group. In contrast with this, we have concluded that power is inherently fractured, that emancipation is always provisional, and that identity, being something constructed, is forever on the edge of dissolution.

What also makes "The Patriarchy" suspect for us is that it represents men's rule over women in the form of "the rule of the father." Sometimes this rule is taken literally to mean the domination of wives and children by men through their position as heads of households – an odd meaning to make everything else hinge upon, given that this kind of domination is specific to times increasingly distant and regions increasingly far from late industrial social life. Sometimes, instead, the term is meant metaphorically to stand for an abstract law of the father which operates quite independently of whether actual fathers rule families or not. This law, as we noted in another discussion, is said to insert itself between the natural unity of mother and child, forcing out of an inert and instinctual relation language, culture, and civilization on the level of the history of the species; and the self's sense of itself as a separate self, its desire for the Other, and the moral regulation of that desire on the level of the individual biography. Sometimes, lastly, patriarchal power is said to signify the rule of the father in the functional sense, the locus of that rule's having been displaced in modern times from the kinship group to the centralized state. But whatever the particular sense of "the rule of the father," male rule is taken to be synonymous with it.

Now, power need not take a single form in order to benefit a single group, and it is not at all self-evident that it takes a single form in our case. To be sure, the power men enjoy along the axis of sex and gender has asserted itself as father-right over wives, children, servants, and wealth; it has reserved for itself, on the basis of that right, the prerogatives of public rule; and it has exerted its control by means of paternal authority and morally sanctioned punitive force. But that power also has elaborated itself on the different basis of the male physique and particularly the male genital organ, representing that physique and that organ as the site of physico-sexual prowess and the source of male superiority in every other thing – strength, courage, intelligence, ingenuity, and independence. In this form it has asserted itself not as patriarchal right over a household but as phallic right over the objects of its purposes and desires. It has ruled both through violence – that is, through the physical force with which it does and takes what it wants without any moral authority behind it – and through consent that it may do and take what it wants, which it has gained as a result of the cultural impression of the superiority of the phallic subject upon the consciousness of a whole society.

The double possibility of masculine power should not surprise us, once we remember that there are two great thematics of sex and gender, not one: the thematic of species reproduction, and the thematic of sexuality. The imperatives of kinship ties and erotic passion function in a close yet tense relation with one another, and so do the imperatives of patriarchal and phallic right. As two different sides of masculine power, patriarchal and phallic right supplement each other, yet the first operates on the side of hierarchical order and discipline, and the second on the side of individualistic anarchy and self-gratification. The patriarchal principle indeed obstructs the full vigor of the phallic principle, in that the moral-paternal law forbids any subject, including the phallic subject, from pursuing its pleasures as it pleases.

That masculine power has a fissured, partly contradictory make-up is an analytic point, but there is an historical point to be made as well. For it is clear that the contemporary West is witnessing at least a partial eclipse of masculine power as patriarchal power in familial and public life. This eclipse has come largely as the result of the logic of capitalist development and the solidification of the modern ethos – tendencies originating outside but having fundamental consequences inside the sex/gender domain.

There has been, first of all, a decay of the father's economic power in and over the family with the move of production out of the domestic sphere and the absorption of wives, sons, and daughters into the social labor force.[2] There has been, secondly, an erosion of the legitimacy of a fixed hierarchical order in which women had a restricted and subservient if also a protected and sanctified place, as moral–political principles of autonomy and atomism supplanted principles of obedience and obligation. There has been a whittling away of the spatial base of patriarchal relations through the increasing fragmentation of the family under the pressure of both economic and cultural factors, to the point at which the father often disappears entirely from the familial scene. Finally, there has been a replacement of paternalistic rule in society at large by impersonal, bureaucratic authority. While such authority may be exercised at the higher levels by millions of men through the strong residual effects of patriarchal right, it is as far from being "father law" as one can imagine. Modern bureaucratic power is wielded anonymously, not personally; it is divided and subdivided, with the power of every specific office objectively delineated and tightly confined; and its positions are filled on the basis of competitive achievement rather than inherent characteristic or inherited position. Moreover, it arose in the political sphere precisely to ensure the equal treatment of all individuals against particular privilege, including, ultimately, patriarchal privilege; and in the private sphere to enhance the efficiency of an industrial capitalism that itself was corrosive of patriarchal right.

One almost might suspect that it was as a way to recover from the damaging blows to the reign of the father that masculine power began to shift its legitimating ground from a familial position to a brute bodily attribute. One might suspect that this shift was the way that a power threatened by depletion conserved and saved itself. Yet the very historical transformations that led to the atrophy of the patriarchal principle (and, by the same stroke, to the rise of feminism, which then pressed its weight further in the same direction) paved the way for the pre-eminence of phallic over patriarchal right. The scientific disenchantment of desire, objects, and action produced a profane world in which nothing is sacred and "everything is permitted." The liberal championing of individual freedom worked to emancipate from traditional prohibitions what were seen as man's natural inclinations, including what were seen as his natural sexual inclinations. Eventually, the utilitarian belief in the satisfaction of individual desire as the highest good combined with late capitalism's stimulation of infinite desire to issue in the public glorification of sexual gratification in certain highly manipulable, that is, commodifiable, forms. One thus could argue that the triumph of phallic right was as much the consequence of as the antidote to patriarchal right's decline.

The public incitement of desire, along with a liberalization of public discourse that allowed and then encouraged an explicit articulation of the sexual theme, have provided perhaps the most important cultural accoutrements of the contemporary phallic self. Modern communications systems, in turn, have provided perhaps its most important technical conditions. Through television, radio, the cinema, and the repetitive production of newspapers, records, billboard advertisements, and magazines, the symbolic depiction of phallic right has been able to occur continuously, on a massive scale, and in a wide variety of cultural forms, saturating both the public arena and the private sphere. Such an onslaught is critical where phallic power is concerned. A bodily organ is an especially fantastical ground of social prerogative, and, as it rests there, phallic power requires for its maintenance a whole mythologizing apparatus, effective over the great breadth of social life. And yet, while the penis is a far more fantastical ground of prerogative than the paternal position, it is also a less mystified one. Phallic right openly shows what patriarchal right had shrouded under so much spiritual drapery:

that the regime of Masculine/feminine, which enabled fathers to claim the position of master as being rightfully theirs in the first place, founds itself at base on brute bodily difference. It is as if, after centuries of pointing upwards and talking sanctimoniously about the divinely prescribed moral superiority of the father, the phallic self coarsely points downwards and declares: "Here – this has been the only real basis of masculine power all along!"

With the ascendence of phallic over father right, we would expect power to be dispersed from males who rule as authorities over hierarchically ordered households to males *per se*, with the usual complications of class and racial power leading to new twists on sex-based power, the precise nature of which we may not yet be in the historical position to analyze.[3] At the same time, that dispersed power will be much reduced in significance, as no submissive dependants, descendants, household economy, or property is guaranteed to come with it. In addition, we can expect phallic power to be effective more sporadically than patriarchal power but also more unpredictably in so far as it is exerted through outbursts of pure violence. We can expect it to be effective far more indirectly and diffusely than patriarchal power in so far as it is exerted through its winning of popular consent. The securing of this consent requires phallic power constantly to take a long detour through its own cultural representation, and there is no assured position of institutional rule for it at the detour's other end.[4] Nevertheless, consent in and of itself spells a great cultural victory for phallic power in that it signifies not merely an intellectual agreement to phallic right on the part of the consenting population, but the continued constitution of that population as actual masculine and feminine selves. The opposite kinds of erotic desire that each of these selves has for the other vividly testifies, when every other testimony has failed, to the difference between women and men, to the mastery of men, and to the sexed body as the source of that difference and mastery.

In sum, however tightly patriarchal and phallic right are connected together, and however much they might thrive off each other in specific circumstances, they still are two rights, not one. The first is a refined and mediated manifestation (in that it claims to be based on a familial position, which in turn rests on the possession of a particular kind of body), the second a crude and immediate manifestation (in that it claims to be based on the possession of a particular kind of body alone) of an underlying cultural–political regime. Whether in a twice- or only once-obscured way, this regime rules by exerting interpretive power over the brute body. It fashions masculine subjects and feminine subject-objects that are highly specified and elaborated out of sensuous details that, like all sensuous details, have no meaning in themselves.

Moreover, patriarchal right is a quintessentially (which is not to say solely) traditional form of power, and phallic right a quintessentially (which is not to say solely) modern form. To put the point more starkly, what seems to emerge from the decay of patriarchal rule is not freedom along the axis of sex and gender or even the preconditions for that freedom. The grand cultural meaning of the move from traditional to modern society is, to be sure, the victory of a permissive natural individualism and gratification of desire over a repressive natural hierarchy and moral prohibition. But that victory at once signifies and mystifies a reorganization of power over the sexed body. The dominative regime of Masculine/feminine is transfigured, not obliterated, as the sexed body comes to assume the position of biological source of the impulses to and imperatives of mastery and submission.

The fact of this reorganization may never be so obvious again as it is while it is still in process, before the new world comes to seem like the natural and true world. It is in this ambiguous and contradictory period that feminism fights its pitched battles on what are largely two different fronts. Against patriarchal power, it fights for the right to abortion and birth control, and for the end to the sex discrimination and the sexual division of labor. Against phallic power, it fights to stop sexual harassment, pornography, prostitution, rape, and the sexual use of children by adults. At this same contradictory moment but on behalf of antagonistic masculinist interests, patriarchal power and phallic power fight these battles out between themselves.[5]

2.

The years between the decline of one principle of power and the solidification of another are uniquely turbulent and expansive. In those years, political practices are bound to surface that intimate transformations far more fundamental than anything dominative power ever would bring about.

At our own place and moment, what might be the practices that intimate a real obliteration rather than a mere transfiguration of the Masculine/feminine regime?

The struggle to equalize women's and men's economic and political positions in bourgeois society cannot be counted unequivocally as a practice of this sort, whether that struggle is waged with liberal or ultimately socialist ends in mind. After all, we have seen that the phallic principle becomes pre-eminent in tandem with just such an equalization. The opposite practice of creating a women's culture at the margins of social life to uphold women's "true difference" is no less equivocal in its implications. The hegemonic power will continue to flourish right beside it, and women's culture, as hegemonic power's living negative, will be in large part hegemonically defined. Moreover, that living negative will be pressed to impose an iron will on its small world to make sure that nothing shows up there but what it has declared to be women's essential truth. It will have to shrink the infinite possibility of desire, proclivity, and taste to a single set of possibilities: it will command its members to enjoy only *these* desires, *these* proclivities, *these* tastes.

Yet both the struggle for economic and political equality between women and men, and the creation of a separate women's culture to assert women's difference, contribute to the decomposition and radical recomposition of the entire sex/gender domain. The victories of equality help to erode fixed feminine and masculine identities and so the popular certainty of just what, with respect to their productive capabilities and political intelligence, "women" and "men" really are. Women's separate communities force open – or at least keep alive the possibility of forcing open – the imagination of the larger social whole. They exhibit in front of that whole a different valuation of bodily selves, a different rule over those selves' erotic relations, a different aesthetic, a different moral law, a different political commitment, and a different living of everyday life.

Thus egalitarian practices on the one hand and separatist practices on the other participate implicitly and ambiguously in the radical cultural–political project. What does a sexual politics do that takes up that project in an explicit and complete way?

Such a politics wages a struggle over the common-sense presumptions of a whole society, over its elements of imagination, and over its philosophical principles as they have influenced popular life. These ordinary beliefs, imaginative elements, and philosophical principles will appear in speech – that evanescent but all-important substance of cultural life. They will appear in the self-presentation of bodies – in costume, decoration, gesture, cultivated physique, and habits of movement. They will appear in words and images that are fixed in newspapers, novels, textbooks, music lyrics, and paintings; produced and disseminated by schools, churches, professional associations, government offices, and the mass media; portrayed on billboards, news-stands, and in shop windows on the street. Finally, they will appear embodied in everyday practice. A radical politics challenges these hegemonic truths in settings as open as possible and battles for room to exhibit its own different conceptions in public and private places. It acts always in a two-pronged way: criticizing old forms and creating new ones, provoking popular debate on conventional thought and action and pursuing new thoughts and actions beyond the pale, inciting a desire for and giving birth to strange possibilities, extending in thought and practice the range of identities that the sexed body is permitted to take.[6]

At the same time that a radical politics tries to erode the power of the dominant culture through negative critique and positive creation, it refuses to take the strength of that power at face value. It is alert to all the details of domination but also the escapes from those details. It does what it can to appreciate those escapes and to enlarge its notion of the counter-hegemonic on their basis. It tends towards expanding itself through an invitation to the outside, not purifying itself through expulsion from within; towards incorporating, not splintering; towards becoming not more and more intolerant of strange and new forms, but more and more adventurous and relaxed. For a political movement to be alert and adventurous in this way is sure to have its immediate rewards, for hidden in the crevices and cracks of the social order are likely to be all sorts of traitors, eccentrics, spontaneous critics, and even ambivalent loyalists; and invisible in the intimate sphere, female desires that take different routes than the route of the mere object of desire, and male desires that do not conform to phallocentric prescription.

Still, a politics would not be radical if it went no further than recognizing and celebrating what is maverick and marginal to a hegemonic order. It must be out to demolish that order altogether. The fundamental transformation of an entire cultural–political regime, of course, is bound to seem fantastical at any time and especially at this time, when such regimes have mammoth forces of replenishment and remobilization at their disposal. But the great advantage of cultural–political transformation is that it can be prepared, as Gramsci and Foucault both put it, "molecularly." In relatively unhinged epochs such as our own, and with respect to systems of power stretching as far into mundane and intimate spheres as does the system of Masculine/feminine, molecular changes may occur constantly in the spontaneous living of everyday life. They may occur more definitively as women begin to move into positions of power in major institutions of cultural production, where they have the chance to undermine the representations of Masculine/feminine on a grand scale. But we must remember that women in general are more likely to be loyalists than critics of the established order, so that women in culturally pivotal positions are more likely to reproduce the terms of that order than not. Moreover, everything about cultural production at the center militates against criticism and rebellion, even for critics and rebels (and traitors and eccentrics) who manage to make their way in. Here, after all, cultural production is most centralized, bureaucratized, and encrusted; most committed to profit-making; most unattuned to the political implications of cultural forms; most bound to the dominant regime.

While individual acts of subversion just might happen inside hegemonic institutions, they are more likely to happen en masse from without, in the more hospitable and experimental (if also potentially repressive) settings of marginal cultures. Especially under contemporary conditions and especially on the terrain of sex and gender, marginal cultures appear to be essential to any hope of a real transformation of cultural–political life. Here, departures from all sorts of socio-sexual norms and conventions can flourish. Here, too, cultural forms and institutions can spring up relatively freely to challenge their hegemonic counterparts.

The question remains of whether alternative cultures as they organically arise and develop can be, in and by themselves, a real force against the given scheme of things. On even the molecular level, can alternative cultures be effective enough in challenging the dominant rule? Will they be strong enough gradually to constitute a second universe that can woo away from the first the eccentrics, critics "in life," traitors, and naive loyalists as well? The answer is very obviously "Not likely." A great cultural–political battle waged over the long run requires a continuity of purpose, a harmonizing of efforts, a sense on the part of those at each local point of resistance that they are participating in something much larger than their own particular adventures. It requires, too, not mere non-conformity with the rule but active opposition to it, infused with a critical understanding of why opposition must take place – a unity, in other words, of theory and practice.

We already have seen that political theory in general and critical political theory above all loses the source of its inspiration and vitality once it breaks its connection with practice. It cannot, after all, pull new ideas and the passion for criticism endlessly out of itself. We also have seen that the theoretical contemplation of political problems becomes potent only if it returns to contribute to "good sense" in practical life. On the other side, a counter-culture that has no tie to political theory is likely not to come to more than a naive understanding of its own situation. It may hold to the most parochial conceits of the age on every social and political question but its own, through not understanding how the larger society is made of a variety of axes of power, not just the sex/gender axis, that combine in a sometimes complementary, sometimes contradictory way. Finally, even on its own terrain it may end up reversing hegemonic values but maintaining hegemonic classifications, however much it had meant to negate them, through lacking a systematic way to break their hold.

In the contemporary Western context, an additional and perhaps prototypical danger for cultural unconventionality uninformed by a political theoretical point of view is that it so easily can decay into a mere "alternative lifestyle," characterized by the consumption of commodities and the enjoyment of leisure pastimes marketed and advertised as "daring" or "avant garde." Well, perhaps not even political-theoretical knowledge can prevent local points of cultural resistance from being absorbed so ignominiously back into the bourgeois mainstream. These points may have been doomed to failure in any case. But it still is true to say that the fragile quality of alternative cultures – their tendency to appear and disappear, or to resist and then comply, or to surface in the open and then secrete themselves in some crevice of society without further disturbance to public life – can be alleviated to the extent that they have a theoretically informed notion of their own purpose and potential significance, and are conscious of being part of a broad-based challenge to the given scheme of things.

In any cultural–political struggle, however, the role of theory is even more central than this. For theory's natural medium is language, and if any particular language is always a system of specific constraints which limit what can be thought and so done, it also opens the way out of those constraints. Each of its categories of identity suggests the possibility of something that escapes beyond its bounds; each of its distinctions between opposite sorts of things suggests a third sort of thing somewhere between the two. A critical theory that combines the evocative and the analytical is uniquely poised to bring to light these suppressed and subversive possibilities. It can pull out of language the words to mark figures and episodes that escape or transgress sharply drawn conceptual lines. Against a regime of power that works through the imposition of meaning and the rigid confinement of the actual and imaginable, these released figures and episodes will have their own expansionary, anarchic force. Critical theory plays a direct role in practice through activating that force. In our own case, it plays a direct role in helping to contest the authority of Masculine/feminine as a regime of truth and to explode the identities of mastery and servitude that the system dictates.

If the unity of theory and practice is especially crucial to cultural–political struggles, how to ensure that the union takes place is still an unsolved problem. How is it possible to pit against a hegemonic order something more forceful and astute than a transitory cultural fragment? Gramsci offers one solution to this problem when he says that a revolutionary party can and must build up, little by little, a universe of conceptions, desires, rules of conduct, practical tendencies, communicative organs, and lines of authority, to stand against and eventually replace the hegemonic universe. At the same time, that party can provide for the constant interaction of a theoretically sophisticated leadership and the masses subordinated under the old regime. In this way the leadership can derive the problems for theoretical analysis and political struggle from the everyday lives of the masses, and the masses can be stimulated to move from common sense to good sense, and from being the passive objects to being the active subjects of history. But if a unified party with a coherent plan, clear direction, centralized organization, and intellectual leadership has more stamina, weight, and insight than purely local, purely cultural resistances against the entrenched order, it has its serious drawbacks too. Foucault has given us a good indication of what they are, but any glance at twentieth century history would have done so as well. A unified and centralized party is instantaneously a new field for the operations of power. As a resistance movement, it imposes a single analysis of power, a single line of division between oppressor and oppressed, and a single strategy of action over local points of resistance that are far more fluid, multiple, and mobile.[7] As a victorious new state, it becomes a regime of power in its own right, provoking new local points of resistance against it. From start to finish, the reservation of the prerogative of leadership to those with a theoretically superior grasp of the world inevitably will smack of a will to power on the part of an intellectual elite. In an age of the decay of father right, can we expect radical popular movements to be less hostile than anyone else to the very distinction between leaders and led?[8]

Clearly radical politics has arrived at an impasse on the question of how to organize itself, and by "radical politics" I mean here not only feminist tendencies but all radical tendencies in contemporary times and late industrial places. Radical politics nearly comes to another impasse as soon as it considers what the final point of opposition is to be. Radical feminism has talked in terms of breaking with an oppressive past and present to create a future in which no one will wield power over anyone else, and each self will be "whole" in relation to itself and harmonious in relation to the world at large. But the chasm between absolute domination and absolute emancipation surely is too wide to make one's way across. Isn't there, as well, something deathly in the wish for the end of all contradiction? On its side, critical theory largely has given up on the notion it had been seduced by not long ago, of a necessary historical movement from domination and exploitation to equality, solidarity and freedom. In the main, the various tendencies of critical theory have become resigned to the fact that new modes of life always will be sites of new forms of power, unpredictable and so unforestallable from the old vantage point.[9]

Can so thorough a pessimism of the theoretical intellect still be united with an optimism of the practical will? This brings us back to the question we had put off answering much earlier, of whether theory can attend to the shades of grey in social life without contributing to a depoliticization of practical interests. Now we can pose the question to suit our more particular concerns. What effect must critical theoretical thinking have on the passion to oppose a given order of things? Surely it must have a supremely mobilizing effect through its analysis of the hidden workings of power, its exploration of the possible forces and avenues of resistance, its development of appropriate strategies of subversion and transformation, and its insistence on the possibility of a dramatically different kind of life. But just as surely it immobilizes. It does so first of all by obscuring any clear-cut line between enemies and friends in its insistence on the complexity of the present situation. It does so, second, by calling into question the point of any special effort to wrench a new situation out of the old one, through its warning that the very best that can be hoped for as a consequence is the surpassing of actual inequities but not all possible ones.

Very likely we will have to wait for practical life to find some third oppositional attitude between romanticism and fatalism, just as we will have to wait for it to invent some third oppositional strategy between centralized party and local resistance points. But let me venture a few theoretical suggestions in advance. If history does not turn out to be a matter of an inevitable or even a possible progression from domination to freedom, it does seem to move in a jolting way between ordinary and abnormal times. If we can take those terms a bit further than Gramsci had meant them to go, isn't it possible to say that history fluctuates between periods when things continue on, at least on the surface, very much as they had been before, according to the same rules, encouragements and constraints; and moments when for a variety of possible reasons order becomes disorder, and entirely new desires, identities, ideas and actions become explicitly possible and quite conceivably actual? Might it not be such abnormal times that we still can hope and work for inside a mode of life that is oppressive in the way that the atmosphere in a room can be both ugly and close? And might not the molecular changes a cultural–political movement seeks to make under the surface of normal times be directed towards generating abnormal times like these?

And perhaps critical theory, with its mobilizing focus on the secrets of power and chances for resistance, and its immobilizing focus on the complex present and imperfect future, is suited best for the period of molecular preparation, when it is imperative to have a deep knowledge of the antagonist, a "long view" (as the communists used to call it) of historical change, and a protection against utopian fantasies. Perhaps it is in this extended period too that a collective party can preserve a sense of the continuity of struggle among fragmentary efforts, provide the local level with a larger picture of things, and lend institutional support to the unity of theory and practice. But in that moment of explosion when the larger order falls apart, or when a great surge of creativity and experimentation bursts out beyond counter-cultural margins onto the general scene, critical theory and the organized party are bound to lose something of their magnetism and stature. Their discipline, stolidity, realism, and caution will mark them as being too closely aligned with the old scheme of things. Adventurousness, spontaneity, iconoclasm, even a certain simplicity of thought, will be more in keeping with the heat and rush of the moment.

The part a collective party might be called on to play after extraordinary times have passed will depend on the particular, unpredictable course of actual events. But we can say this about what is to be hoped for from critical theory. As soon as the elements of disorder begin to coalesce in a new way, critical theory should reappear in the guise of a gadfly, to agitate on behalf of the exuberance of life against a too-avid fixing and freezing of things.

Notes

Introduction: Things in Two's are Sometimes, but not Always, Dichotomies

1 I will be using this phrase to signify a system of power that operates by declaring the natural, foundational truth of two separate and complementary figures, the masculine self and the feminine self; but that actually creates these truths one as the reverse of the other and imposes them on the sexed body. I use the upper case letter for the "M" alone to remind us that the masculine and the feminine are in fact contradictory, internal aspects of a single whole; and to underscore the positive constitution of the masculine as opposed to the feminine self. This positivity consists most importantly of the masculine prerogative of mastery over the feminine. (For a fascinating illustration of the constitution of the feminine out of the reverse elements of the masculine – fascinating because the illustration appears to have been so naively done – see Jean-Jacques Rousseau, *Emile*, trans. Barbara Foxley, London: J.M. Dent and Sons, Ltd, 1974, with special attention to the education of Sophy.)

2 For a discussion of what ill can be said against it, see Robert Darnton's "Pop Foucaultism" (a review of Pierre Darmon, *Damning the Innocent; A History of the Persecution of the Impotent in Pre-revolutionary France*), *The New York Review of Books*, 33: 15 (October 9, 1986), pp. 15–16.

3 One shift is all-important: from radical feminism in its first phase, in which it urges active political war on the patriarchal order, to radical feminism in its second and still present phase, in which it denounces political militance and conflict as prototypically male and looks instead to create a peace-loving women's culture outside the bounds of the patriarchal culture. This is a case in which a transformation of analysis is a transformation of almost everything. I discuss the consequences of the shift in more detail in my article "Wordless emotions: some critical reflections on radical feminism," *Politics and Society*, 13: 1 (1984), pp. 27–57 and especially p. 32.

4 Again, see "Wordless emotions" for my original formulation of these ideas as they inform feminist cultural practice, especially p. 28. The principles of therapy, pedagogy, and athletics generally are anti-hierarchical, anti-competitive, and relational; the political strategies generally are non-violent; the appropriate cuisine, vegetarian; the appropriate dress, androgynous; the appropriate eroticism, lesbian and egalitarian.

5 Kate Millett, *Sexual Politics*, New York: Ballantine, 1978, was really the key classic text to situate itself at this intersection; radical feminism followed on from there.

6 For example, Alison Jaggar, Michele Barrett, and Christine Delphy all explicitly hold to the constructionist view of gender identity. However, their materialism does not lie in their holding to this view. Rather, it lies in their focus on the material consequences of the construction: the distribution of food at the table, the super-exploitation of women's labor by capitalism, men's control of women's sexuality to guarantee the paternity of children, and so on. See Alison Jaggar, "Human biology in feminist theory: sexual equality reconsidered," in Carol Gould (ed.), *Beyond Domination: New Perspectives on Women and Philosophy*, Totowa, New Jersey: Rowman & Allanheld, 1983, pp. 21–42; Michele Barrett, *Women's Oppression Today: Problems in Marxist Feminist Analysis*, London: Verso Editions, 1980; Christine Delphy, *Close to Home: a Materialist Analysis of Women's Oppression*, Amherst, Massachusetts: University of Massachusetts Press, 1984.

7 Primarily in chapter 5, I use the term "critical theory" more narrowly to refer to theory that unabashedly makes some kind of appearance/reality distinction, as opposed but not entirely unrelated to theory that is deconstructive. The context, I think, makes the special usage clear.

8 It is Herbert Marcuse who is still, to my mind, the most brilliant theoretician of cultural domination in the late capitalist United States, even though he presents far too monolithic a portrait of popular affirmation of the established order. See his *One-Dimensional Man*, Boston: Beacon Press, 1964. For a superb account of the cultural turn in Western Marxism, see Perry Anderson, *Considerations on Western Marxism*, London: Verso, New Left Books, 1976.

9 The best-known post-colonial critic in feminist circles is Gayatri Chakravorty Spivak, who however works out of a different combination of theoretical traditions than Said does. See Spivak, *In Other Worlds*, London: Methuen, 1987.

10 That it is *a* good, however, seems to be contestable only by the kind of complex argument that Rousseau makes when he exposes the corruptions that accompany complexity of every sort. Jean-Jacques Rousseau, *The First and Second Discourses*, trans. Roger D. Masters, New York: St Martin's Press, 1964.

11 Simone de Beauvoir, *The Second Sex*, New York: Vintage Books, 1974.

12 Gayle Rubin, "The Traffic in Women: Notes on the 'Political Economy' of Sex," in Rayna Reiter (ed.), *Towards an Anthropology of Women*, New York: Monthly Review Press, 1975, pp. 157–210.

13 Millett, *Sexual Politics*.
14 For two excellent essays that do just that, see Biddy Martin, "Feminism, criticism and Foucault," *New German Critique*, 27 (Fall, 1982), pp. 3–30; and Judith Butler, "Sex and gender in Simone de Beauvoir's *Second Sex*," in Hélène Vivienne Wenzel (ed.), *Simone de Beauvoir: Witness to a Century*, Yale French Studies 72, New Haven, Conn.: Yale University Press, 1986, pp. 35–49.

1: Consciousness and Culture

1 Edward Said, "Traveling theory," in Said, *The World, the Text and the Critic*, Cambridge, Mass.: Harvard University Press, 1983, pp. 226–47.
2 Antonio Gramsci, *Selections from the Prison Notebooks*, ed. and trans. Quintin Hoare and Geoffrey Newell Smith, New York: International Publishers, 1971, p. 407. See also p. 469.
3 ibid., p. 441.
4 ibid., p. 9.
5 ibid., p. 323.
6 ibid., p. 323.
7 ibid., p. 445.
8 ibid., p. 447.
9 ibid., p. 445.
10 ibid., p. 447.
11 Stuart Hampshire, *Thought and Action*, New York: The Viking Press, 1959.
12 ibid., p. 26.
13 ibid., p. 223.
14 ibid., p. 21.
15 ibid., p. 11.
16 ibid., p. 68.
17 ibid., p. 91.
18 ibid., p. 208.
19 ibid., p. 39.
20 ibid., p. 234.
21 ibid., p. 234.
22 ibid., p. 31.
23 ibid., p. 242.
24 ibid., p. 241.
25 ibid., p. 242.
26 Raymond Williams, *Marxism and Literature*, Oxford: Oxford University Press, 1977, p. 115.
27 ibid., p. 111.
28 ibid., p. 111.
29 ibid., p. 87.
30 ibid., p. 87.
31 Gramsci, *Prison Notebooks*, p. 184.
32 ibid., p. 242.
33 ibid., p. 247.

34 ibid., pp. 341–2.
35 Williams, *Marxism and Literature*, p. 116.
36 ibid., p. 136.
37 ibid., p. 115.
38 ibid., p. 117.
39 ibid., p. 132.
40 ibid., p. 131.
41 ibid., p. 134.
42 Edward Said, *Orientalism*, New York: Vintage Books, 1979.
43 Gramsci, p. 344.
44 ibid., p. 377.
45 Said, *The World, the Text and the Critic*, p. 227.
46 ibid., p. 236.

2: Dominative Power

1 Gramsci, *Prison Notebooks*, p. 247.
2 Williams, *Marxism and Literature*, p. 108.
3 Said, *Orientalism*, p. 11.
4 ibid., p. 11.
5 Michel Foucault, *Power/Knowledge: Selected Interviews and Other Writings 1972–1977*, New York: Pantheon Books, 1980, esp. pp. 58–60.
6 Gramsci, *Prison Notebooks*, p. 12.
7 ibid., p. 196.
8 ibid., p. 350.
9 ibid., p. 447. While "East" and "West", for example, seem to describe some universal geography, they in fact have "crystallised" from "the point of view of the European cultured classes who, as a result of their world-wide hegemony, have caused them to be accepted everywhere. Japan is the Far East not only for Europe but also perhaps for the American from California and even for the Japanese himself . . ." p. 447.
10 Said, *Orientalism*, p. 14.
11 Williams, *Marxism and Literature*, p. 110.
12 ibid., p. 108.
13 ibid., p. 110.
14 ibid., p. 110.
15 ibid., p. 110.
16 Michel Foucault, *The History of Sexuality*, vol. I: *An Introduction*, New York: Vintage Books, 1980, p. 93.
17 ibid., p. 93.
18 ibid., p. 85. That the ideas are not identical can be seen by a glance at Foucault's description of the tortured body in Part I of *Discipline and Punish: The Birth of the Prison*, New York: Random House, 1979. The power of torture comes from a central, royal point but is not merely a prohibitive power (although it is very importantly that too). It produces a positive truth on the tortured body as well as exercising negative coercive punishment over it.
19 Foucault, *The History of Sexuality* vol. I, p. 85.

20 ibid., p. 85.
21 Williams, *Marxism and Literature*, p. 110.
22 ibid., p. 110.
23 ibid., p. 111.
24 Especially in texts like *The Order of Things*, New York: Vintage Books, 1973, and *Power/Knowledge*.
25 Said, *Orientalism*, p. 23.
26 And he could have as easily taken it from Weber or Althusser's Marx.
27 Foucault, *The History of Sexuality*, vol. I, p. 94.
28 ibid., p. 92.
29 ibid., p. 93.
30 Foucault, *The History of Sexuality*, vol. I, p. 99.
31 ibid., p. 93.
32 Foucault, *Power/Knowledge*, p. 96.
33 ibid., p. 39.
34 Williams, *Marxism and Literature*, p. 112.
35 ibid., p. 116.
36 ibid., p. 116.
37 Said, *Orientalism*, p. 1.
38 ibid., p. 3.
39 ibid., p. 2.
40 ibid., p. 8.
41 ibid., p. 6.
42 ibid., p. 12.
43 Foucault, *Power/Knowledge*, pp. 131–2.
44 Foucault, *Discipline and Punish*, p. 194.
45 The spirit of anonymous power Foucault captures with the phrase, which he uses to describe a narrower and more specific situation: "any individual, taken almost at random, can operate the machine," ibid., p. 202.
46 ibid., p. 136.
47 ibid., p. 25.
48 ibid., p. 26.
49 ibid., p. 184.
50 ibid., pp. 178–9.
51 ibid., p. 304.
52 Foucault, *The History of Sexuality*, vol. I, p. 68.
53 ibid., p. 106
54 For a sense of the exhilaration and expansiveness of that release, see Marshall Berman, *All That Is Solid Melts Into Air: The Experience of Modernity*, New York: Simon & Schuster, 1982.
55 The Third World working population theoretically is only a temporary exception, to the extent that industrial capitalism penetrates the economy and culture of the globe.
56 This of course was the point of Marcuse's argument on repressive desublimation in his *One-Dimensional Man*.
57 Can the New Right be understood as a movement against the contemporary ascendence of the deployment of sexuality, and for the

traditional deployment of alliance – that is, as a residual movement struggling to restore a decaying organization of power in the field of sexual relations?

3: Criticism and Resistance

1 Hampshire, *Thought and Action*, p. 40.
2 Williams, *Marxism and Literature*, p. 125.
3 Said, *The World, the Text and the Critic*, pp. 246–7.
4 Williams, *Marxism and Literature*, p. 130.
5 Gramsci, *Prison Notebooks*, p. 452.
6 ibid., p. 450.
7 ibid., p. 326.
8 ibid., p. 327.
9 ibid., p. 337.
10 ibid., pp. 336–7.
11 ibid., p. 333.
12 ibid., p. 333.
13 ibid., p. 337. Gramsci aims this barb at mechanistic Marxism, but it would be equally well aimed at many critical theoretical tendencies in our own time.
14 Perhaps the most brilliant depiction of the enlargement of breadth and depth of a situation that comes through the reflectivity of its participants can be found in a section of Paul Scott, *The Day of the Scorpion*, entitled, aptly enough, "The Situation," New York: Avon Books, 1968, part 1, book 2.
15 Herbert Marcuse in *One-Dimensional Man* and George Steiner in "Text and context," in Steiner, *On Difficulty and Other Essays*, Oxford: Oxford University Press, 1978; intimate such a point, each in his own distinctive way. Marcuse lambasts the cultural and intellectual banality of a society that reduces all ideas and texts to the same level, offering all as equivalent commodities in the marketplace. Thus individuals can browse through *How To Be Your Own Best Friend; Scruples; The German Ideology*; and *Discipline and Punish* in the book section of their local supermarket, with Bach-made-musak playing pleasantly in the background. In this utterly tolerant cultural setting, there will be no edge to one's choice of one book or idea over another, no negative encouragement to take one's own thought seriously, and no mental quiet in which to think profoundly. Steiner similarly argues that the "free" hubbub of the capitalist marketplace and consumption culture is a constraint on thought rather than a provocation to it. "The pace of being, the surrounding noise-levels, the competitive stimulus of alternative media of information and entertainment (a plurality notably lacking in the Soviet Union) militate against the compacted privacy, the investments of silence, required by serious reading (*On Difficulty*, p. 10). Looking at the same question from the opposite political vantage point, Steiner suggests that serious oppositional thinking finds its most favorable milieu where, on the one side, the dominant order is a canonical one that combines a deep respect

for textual knowledge, a sanctification of a particular textual tradition, and an outlawing of counter-canonical literature; and where, on the other side, there is a penetration of literate values in the society at large that extends back before the lifetime of that dominant order. The entrenched canon and the long-lived literate cultural tradition together stimulate a highly cultivated, rigorous, underground counter-discourse. Steiner declares: "The primary reflex in Marxist feeling and political-social application is that of citation, of re-reading." But if "this essential bookishness . . . is the medium of power and official discourse, it is, no less, that of opposition. The antecedents here are plainly pre-Bolshevik; they lie in the very fabric of suppression which defines Russian history as a whole" (ibid., p. 6). There has been a "paradoxical gain" to the state suppression of a counter-literature. "No society reads more vehemently . . . Czarism and Stalinism are incommensurable structures of obscurantism and chastisement, yet structures proportionately vulnerable to, shaken by, the adverse text. . . What Western regime flinches at a poem?" (ibid., p. 7).

16 See, for example, Richard Rorty in his "Hermeneutics, general studies, and teaching, *Synergos: Selected Papers from the Synergos Seminars*, George Mason University, vol. 2 (Fall 1982), pp. 1–15.

17 Gramsci, *Prison Notebooks*, p. 381.

18 See, for a sense of this kind of thinking, ibid., pp. 275–6. Marxism gets around the problem of fascism by calling it not an emergent movement but a defensive and reactionary one – another of those morbid symptoms of the crisis of the old order that Gramsci talks about.

19 See Foucault's interview comments in *Power/Knowledge*, for example.

20 ibid., p. 60.

21 Peter Winch makes the best argument on this point. See his *The Idea of a Social Science and its Relation to Philosophy*, London: Routledge & Kegan Paul, 1970.

22 Gramsci, *Prison Notebooks*, p. 194. Gramsci here is referring specifically to the creation of a collective Party will, but the description applies as well to his more general notion of the development of an intellectual–moral unity of a whole historical epoch.

23 ibid., p. 119.

24 The stragetic primacy of such a long preparatory cultural development is even more evident in our period than in Gramsci's. For a detailed analysis of the ambiguity and problems in Gramsci's notion of the "war of position" and the extent of Gramsci's prescience here for our own age, see Perry Anderson, "The antinomies of Antonio Gramsci," *New Left Review*, 100 (November 1976–January 1977), pp. 5–78.

25 Gramsci, *Prison Notebooks*, p. 243.

26 In a paper read at the Symposium on Caribbean Cultural Identity, Havana (July 18, 1979), René Dépèstre offers a provocative account of how socio-economic relations were transfigured during the period of American colonial slavery into racial ones, with the consequence that racial categories were codified "as the products of *nature*, when in reality they belonged essentially to the society and to its political and economic

history (p. 2) Such a codification lived far beyond the life-span of the slave economy that elaborated it. Ultimately, I would argue (perhaps against Dépèstre), it took on its own autonomous life, so that it no longer could be seen as simply the disguised form in which class relations presented themselves.

27 Foucault, *The History of Sexuality*, vol. I, p. 95.
28 ibid., p. 96.
29 ibid., p. 96.
30 Williams, *Marxism and Literature*, p. 112.
31 ibid., p. 114.
32 ibid., p. 122.
33 ibid., p. 114.
34 ibid., p. 111.

4: Theory's Practical Relation to the World

1 i.e., by starting with bourgeois political economy and the appearance of exchange relations.
2 Gramsci, *Prison Notebooks*, p. 347.
3 ibid., p. 323.
4 ibid., p. 419. Every reader of Gramsci will know how slipshod he actually is in his use of "spontaneous philosophy" and "common sense" – sometimes speaking of the latter as if it were the primary determinant of the former, sometimes as if it were one element of it, sometimes as if it were its exact equivalent.
5 ibid., p. 323.
6 ibid., p. 324.
7 ibid., p. 419.
8 ibid., p. 330, Gramsci's footnote.
9 ibid., p. 422.
10 ibid., p. 323.
11 ibid., p. 419.
12 ibid., p. 424.
13 ibid., p. 326, editor's footnote 5, quoting Gramsci.
14 ibid., p. 348.
15 ibid., p. 338.
16 ibid., p. 323.
17 The British conservatives surely are right to make this point. They would, of course, include politics at the top of the list of skills and crafts, and everything to do with women at the top of the list of the organic and cyclical, but we need not go all the way with them to go a short distance. See Michael Oakeshott, *Rationalism in Politics*, London: Methuen, 1984. For a gem of a non-conservative defense of tradition, see Verta Mae Smart Grosvenor, "The kitchen crisis," in Toni Cade (ed.), *The Black Woman*, New York: Mentor, 1970, pp. 119–123.
18. *Prison Notebooks*, p. 324.
19 ibid., p. 348.
20 Such a repetition of hegemonic classifications and principles is especially

likely to occur when a counter-cultural movement dismisses history as being so absolutely seared by domination that its detailed study is entirely unnecessary; and when it condemns contemplative theory as being, in its abstractness and logical rigor, fatally condescending towards concrete, practical life. Then it will not be overly likely to be aware of its links to any other oppositional movements prior to itself or of the most secret ways in which it is connected to the dominant order. It will not be likely to move restlessly, out of the perverse joy of negative thinking, to criticize its own most cherished counter-conceptions and counter-practices. Lastly, it will not be able through historical research or theoretical abstraction to escape the parochial limits of the here and now.

5: Theory's Contemplative Relation to the World

1 Another variation on the same theme is that "good" theory is "experiential" – meaning not just that it begins with experience but that it continues to treat experience as the source of truth. See, for example, Nannerl Keohane's Foreword to N. Keohane, M. Rosaldo and B. Gelpi (eds), *Feminist Theory: a Critique of Ideology*, Chicago, Ill.: University of Chicago Press, 1982. Keohane writes: ". . . feminist theory is fundamentally experiential. Its subject is women's lives . . . " (p. vii). Also see Catharine MacKinnon, "Feminism, Marxism, method and the state" in the same volume, in which the author makes a host of obscure and problematic connections between women's experience and feminist theory (pp. 1–30).

2 Certain of these points on theory's weaknesses and strengths I have made before, in my essay "Suspicious pleasures: on teaching feminist theory," in Margo Cully and Catherine Portuges (eds), *Gendered Subjects: the Dynamics of Feminist Teaching*, Boston: Routledge & Kegan Paul, 1985, pp. 171–82.

3 So many feminist academics work off cultural representations that the specific mention of any of them would be arbitrary. Among the radical feminists who do so are, most prominently, Andrea Dworkin, *Pornography: Men Possessing Women*, London: The Women's Press, 1981; and Susan Griffin, whose *Woman and Nature*, New York: Harper & Row, 1978, is one of the most startlingly original and stylistically breathtaking *tours de force* in contemporary Western writing.

4 In an especially revealing and disturbing instance, Brenda Verner uses her vast collection of nineteenth- and twentieth-century greetings cards, playing cards, cereal-box illustrations, and so on, in a slide show presentation, to show how white culture has represented in images and captions the black woman and man for white consumption. These images also were dictations to blacks of how they were to present themselves before whites in practical life. Brenda Verner (Verner Communications, 7319 South Luella, Chicago, Ill.).

5 The significance of this black blues and jazz tradition for sexual politics cannot be overstated. The lyrics and self-presentations not only of many female but of certain male singers portray a world in which, far from being subordinated object-victims of male desire, women are sexual

subjects, independent and demanding, and in which men recognize women as those same sexual subjects and are quite willing to address, plead with, and beg to, them. The distance of that world, populated by female as well as male subjects of desire, from the world portrayed in dominant cultural song lyrics and their singers' self-presentations is infinitely great.

6 Karl Marx, *Capital* vol. I, New York: International Publishers, 1967.

7 Together Marx and Freud bequeath to us the most sophisticated methods of analyzing purposes and beliefs that are at once manifestations and mystifications of "something underneath." In the first case, the ideology of the marketplace is held to both express and conceal the secret logic of the capital–wage–labor relation. In the second case, conscious purposes and beliefs are held to both express and conceal unconscious motives and desires.

8 Hannah Arendt, *The Origins of Totalitarianism*, New York: Harcourt Brace Jovanovich, 1973.

9 ibid., pp. 79–88.

10 ibid., p. 87.

11 ibid., p. 80.

12 ibid., p. 80.

13 ibid., p. 80.

14 ibid., p. 80.

15 ibid., p. 83. That is, Proust's Swan.

16 ibid., p. 87.

17 ibid., p. 86.

18 ibid., p. 87. Although Arendt does not place responsibility for the genocide of the Jews only on "those strata of society which had known Jews most intimately and had been most delighted and charmed by Jewish friends" (p. 87) – on those "'admirers' of Jews" who "finally became their murderers" (p. 86).

19 Once again, in Paul Scott's *Raj Quartet* we find a superb rendering of thousands of movements of force from one local, capillary, point to another. Often they are so local and capillary as to be no more than a flicker of reaction by an Englishman's wife to an Indian lawyer introduced at her table, and his silent registration of that reaction, in what had been in the days of the Raj a white British officers' club, but which after Independence had a mixed membership. The wife "still protectively immersed in the shallow enchantment of the *Sunday Times* Magazine achieves a token emergence by a slight lift of the head (which would be a look at Mr Srinivasan if the eyelids did not simultaneously lower) . . . " – while Mr Srinivasan's "mild but penetrating gaze . . . reveals a readiness to withstand the subtlest insult that an experience-sharpened sensibility is capable of detecting." (Paul Scott, *The Jewel in the Crown*, New York: Avon Books, 1979, p. 175). A second example: the wife's off-hand refusal of the Indian's offer to buy her a drink, and her seconds-later request to her husband: "Order me another of these, Terry, will you?" (ibid., p. 176). Scott is one of the masters of the literary depiction of cultural power exercised in these minute ways.

20 And it doesn't by any means always hope for or even desire that democratization. Nietzsche and Althusser, to take just two examples, are unsparing in their critique of the self-presentation of lived life, without the former's wanting or the latter's seeing any real chance for the eventual triumph of popular critical thinking.
21 Theoretical historians can be interesting exceptions to the rule: for example, Perry Anderson, in part although not the whole of *Passages from Antiquity to Feudalism*, London: New Left Books, 1974; or Barrington Moore in *The Social Origins of Dictatorship and Democracy*, Boston: Beacon Press, 1966. At the same time, to the extent that such historians have themselves an insolence towards the accidental fact, there is a danger in the theorist's reliance upon them for concrete illustrations of a theoretical argument.
22 Such a figure or scene is the logical opposite of the Weberian ideal type, an abstraction from a multiplicity of actual socio-historical details.
23 Karl Marx, *Capital*, pp. 176, 190, 192.
24 Mary Daly's range is more colorful: there are hags and crones and spinsters (women who have exorcized patriarchal ideology from themselves); female tokens or fembots ("women with anatomically female bodies but totally male-identified, male-possessed brains/spirits"; traditional women; and men. Mary Daly, *Gyn/ecology: The Metaethics of Radical Feminism*, Boston: Beacon Press, 1978, p. 57.

6: Point and Counterpoint

1 There is a very large literature on the relationship between thought, action, and social practice, of which Hampshire's *Thought and Action* is only one example. For a few other classic ones, see Peter Winch, *The Idea of a Social Science*, London: Routledge & Kegan Paul, 1970, and Alasdair MacIntyre, *Against the Self-Images of the Age*, New York: Schocken Books, 1971; also MacIntyre, *A Short History of Ethics*, New York: Macmillan Publishing Co., 1966.
2 One finds perhaps the deepest resemblances between loyalist and rebel in families split along political lines in times of social upheaval.
3 See Hannah Arendt, *The Human Condition*, Chicago, Ill.: University of Chicago Press, 1974, especially the chapter on "Action."
4 Feminist dualists, some of whom are cultural and some ontological dualists, run the gamut from Mary Daly to Carol Gilligan. Just a few other examples: Adrienne Rich, Susan Griffin, Andrea Dworkin, Marilyn Frye, Sheila Jeffries, Jan Raymond, and almost all the contributors to Charlene Spretnak (ed.), *The Politics of Women's Spirituality*, Garden City, NY: Anchor Press, 1982.
5 To take just a few random examples, note the "bruised look" in the cosmetic fashion of a few years ago; the obsessive representation of an eroticized female masochism in the advertisements of Paul Marciano clothing, the now infamous album covers for the records of the Rolling Stones, Robert Palmer, *et al.*; movies such as *Night Moves*, *True Confessions*, *Dressed to Kill* (all admittedly made more than a few years

ago – one simply gives up going to "popular" movies after enough like these); reviews of critics like Vincent Canby on *Angel*, *Butterfly*, and *Personal Best*; interviews with the directors of movies like *Personal Best*. With respect to the cult of criminality among avant-garde writers, note Norman Mailer's celebration of Jack Abbot and Foucault's fascination with Pierre Rivière. The contempt for women in "popular" culture is so widespread that no brief reference to a few examples of it can do it justice. The cult of criminality – perhaps a fairer phrase is the flirtation with the idea of the criminal (a flirtation by male intellectuals with the idea of male criminals) – is more specific and contained. Nonetheless, it has its connections with the more general cultural tendency, being an attraction to masculine violence and predation, although this time an attraction in the name of an anarchistic defiance of discipline and order. Arendt's discussion of high society's flirtation with criminality in turn-of-the-century France comes to mind here, although that was a flirtation with criminality as the "diseased," while this is a flirtation with criminality as the "virile." Interestingly enough, homosexuality is a theme in both constructions of the "criminal." See Hannah Arendt, *The Origins of Totalitarianism*, Part One. The criminal as adventurer surfaces again in Part Two.

6 Quotations respectively from Daly, *Gyn/Ecology*, p. 29; Andrea Dworkin, *Our Blood*, New York: Harper & Row, 1978, p. 104; and Susan Griffin, "The politics of rape," in Griffin, *Made from this Earth*, New York: Harper & Row, 1982, p. 44.

7 Lawrence Kohlberg's theory of moral development, of which Carol Gilligan's is the feminist inversion, is the psychological analogue of this socio-political view of the sexes. For Gilligan and Gilligan-on-Kohlberg, see Carol Gilligan, *In a Different Voice: Psychological Theory and Women's Development*, Cambridge, Mass.: Harvard University Press, 1982.

8 John Stuart Mill and Harriet Taylor are of course the classic examples.

9 In his *Philosophy and Social Issues*, Notre Dame, Ind.: University of Notre Dame Press, 1980, Richard Wasserstrom stands at this far boundary of liberalism. It is his unflinching application of liberal individualist ideals to the social reality of male/female, and white/black, power relations that has brought him there.

10 See, for example, Andrea Dworkin's essay "The root cause" in her collection of essays, *Our Blood*. There is one clear, important moment of this essay that is strongly anti-instrumentalist, in which Dworkins makes an argument close to de Beauvoir's: that actual individual women and men are the living expressions of an objective cultural–political system of masculine/feminine, with men no more self-conscious of that system's contingency and conventionality than women. Equally, there is a strong psychoanalytic moment in Adrienne Rich's "Compulsory heterosexuality and lesbian existence," *Signs*, 5: 4 (Summer 1980), pp. 631–60, in which it is men's unconscious wish to return to an unrivalled relation to the mother, rather than any self-conscious intention to dominate, that is seen to stand at the root of the system of male domination.

11 Mary Daly is the crudest but also the wittiest of feminist mechanists.

7: Impositions and Evasions

1 A minor chord in phallocentric ideology is this image's inversion: the vision of the female as lustful, predatory, voracious in sexual appetite – but still an object-for-the-male-subject, not a subject in her own right.

2 Socio-biologists and conservatives see phallocentrism as secondary in its effects; liberal individualists tend to see it as weak in its effects.

3 There can be all sorts of interesting disjunctures between public costume and decoration on the one hand and the course of intimate eroticism on the other. There also can be disjunctures between bodily type, sexual preference, public costume, and private desire. See Esther Newton and Shirley Walton's illuminating little essay on this subject: "The misunderstanding: toward a more precise sexual vocabulary" in Carole S. Vance (ed.), *Pleasure and Danger: Exploring Female Sexuality*, Boston, Mass.: Routledge & Kegan Paul, 1984, pp. 242–50.

4 Once again, we should remember the tradition of black blues and jazz singers, many of whom present a wholly different testimony on heterosexual eroticism than that of woman as subordinate victim of phallic desire. The image of woman as strong sexual subject is strikingly clear in the work of Koko Taylor, Alberta Hunter, Betty Carter, *et al.*, and in some of the work of B.B. King and Johnny Copeland.

5 Rich, 'Compulsory hetrosexuality.' *Signs*, p. 643.

6 ibid., 645. In this quotation and the one above, Rich is drawing on Kathleen Barry, *Female Sexual Slavery*, Englewood Cliffs, N.J.: Prentice-Hall, Inc., 1979.

7 Dworkin, *Our Blood*, p. 104.

8 ibid., p. 105.

9 ibid., p. 107.

10 Andrea Dworkin, *Pornography. Men Possessing Women*, New York: G.P. Putnam & Sons, 1981, p. 69.

11 Dworkin, *Our Blood*, p. 107.

12 Sally Wagner, "Pornography and the sexual revolution: the backlash of sadomasochism," in Robin Linden, Darlene Pagano, Diana Russell, and Susan Star (eds), *Against Sadomasochism*, Palo Alto, Calif.: Frog in the Wall Press, 1982, p. 29.

13 Dworkin, *Our Blood*, p. 54.

14 Dworkin, *Pornography. Men Possessing Women*, p. 185.

15 John Stoltenberg, "Sadomasochism: eroticized violence, eroticized powerlessness," in Linden *et al.* (eds.), *Against Sadomasochism*, p. 126.

8: Power, Desire and the Meaning of the Body

1 Curtis Bill Pepper, "The indomitable de Kooning," *New York Times Sunday Magazine* (November 20, 1983), p. 90.

2 Stoltenberg, "Sadomasochism," in Linden *et al.* (eds), *Against Sadomasochism*, p. 129.

3 For a different kind of presentation of the possibilities of heterosexual desire and the logic leading from one to the next, see Robin Morgan, "The politics of sado-masochistic fantasies," Part III (The parable), in Linden *et*

al. (eds), *Against Sadomasochism*, pp. 117–20.

4 Stoltenberg makes this point in "Sadomasochism." Marilyn Frye makes a parallel one about gay men's appropriation of the feminine in their mannerisms and style of dress in "Lesbian feminism and the gay rights movement: another view of male supremacy, another separatism," in Frye, *The Politics of Reality: Essays in Feminist Theory*, New York: The Crossing Press, 1983, pp. 128–51.

5 For a graphic account, see Pat Califia, "Feminism and sadomasochism," *Heresies*, 123: 4 (1981), pp. 30–4. Also see her "Gender-Bending," *The San Franscisco Advocate* (September 15, 1983), pp. 24–7.

6 These of course are the arguments on which Linden *et al.* (eds), *Against Sadomasochism*, is centered. See also Leah Fritz, "Is there sex after sadomasochism?", *New York Village Voice* (November 1983), pp. 24–5.

7 For a very suggestive discussion of the multiple elements involved in the sado-masochistic erotic theme, see Jessica Benjamin, "Master and slave: the fantasy of erotic domination," in Ann Snitow, Christine Stansell, and Sharon Thompson (eds), *Powers of Desire: the Politics of Sexuality*, New York: Monthly Review Press, 1983, pp. 280–99.

8 In their different ways, Hegel, Freud, and de Beauvoir all make this point.

9 Of course, what counts as "free play" is a real problem which this sentence begs rather than solves. Certainly the acting out of all erotic impulses is not synonymous with it or with emancipation in erotic life.

10 This point works against Dworkin's claim that an emancipated male desire requires men to give up the erection for flaccidity. Nowhere is her tendency to equate facts about the brute physical body with the desire for power on more graphic display. "For men I suspect that this transformation" (of the male sexual model "based on a polarization of humankind into man/woman, master/slave, aggressor/victim, active/passive," *Our Blood*, p. 11) "begins in the place they most dread – that is, in a limp penis. I think that men will have to give up their precious erections and begin to make love as women do together," *Our Blood*, p. 13.

11 Of course, the refusal to respect established boundaries between private and public with respect to eroticism's proper location may be precisely one feature of such a distinct mode of life. See Dennis Altman's "Sex: the new front line for gay politics," *Socialist Review*, vol. 12, No. 65, No. 5 (September–October 1982), pp. 75–84.

12 The emergence of AIDS in the gay male community has had a far from merely negative effect on the pressure gay culture places on the conventional imagination. If the prevalence of AIDS among gay men can seem to confirm entrenched ideas about the rightness of heterosexual, monogamous, and restricted sex, the barrage of journalistic descriptions of homosexual sex in the mass media and of medical advice on how to conduct that sex more safely has brought a multiplicity of hidden sexual practices into public view, with the effect of greatly expanding the universe of sexual possibility (although not always the physical safety, at least for the moment, of that possibility) for everyone.

9: A Regime without a Master

1 Including, among others, Adrienne Rich, Susan Griffin, Andrea Dworkin, Dale Spender, Catharine MacKinnon, and Marilyn Frye.
2 All of the above phrases of Daly's occur throughout *Gyn/Ecology* as her counter-language to the conventional language. Thus I have not provided specific page references for them.
3 MacKinnon, in Keohane *et al.* (eds), *Feminist Theory*, p. 28.
4 Rich, "Compulsory heterosexuality," p. 647.
5 Dworkin, *Our Blood*, p. 85.
6 Frye, *The Politics of Reality*, p. 13.
7 Sheila D. Collins, "The personal is political," in Spretnak (ed.), *The Politics of Women's Spirituality*, p. 364.
8 Hallie Iglehart, "The unnatural divorce of spirituality and politics," in Spretnak (ed.), *The Politics of Women's Spirituality*, p. 406. My emphasis.
9 MacKinnon, in Keohane *et al.* (eds), *Feminist Theory*, p. 21.
10 ibid., p. 6.
11 ibid., p. 28.
12 Collins, in Spretnak (ed.), *The Politics of Women's Spirituality*, p. 363.
13 Rich, "Compulsory heterosexuality," p. 660.
14 Griffin, *Woman and Nature*, pp. 57–61.
15 Griffin makes the same kind of argument in *Pornography and Silence: Culture's Revenge against Nature* (New York: Harper & Row, 1981).
16 Dworkin, *Our Blood*, p. 61.
17 ibid., pp. 82–3.
18 Charlene Spretnak, Introduction to *The Politics of Women's Spirituality*, p. xviii.
19 Thus, to take the most vivid example, Adrienne Rich's essays are populated by women who are victims of male exploitation but who also, to the extent that they have wrested control over their purposes and passions out of men's hands, show loving empathy with other women and antipathy to aggressors and dominators.
20 See Rich, "Compulsory heterosexuality," and "Disloyal to civilization: feminism, racism, gynephobia," in Rich, *On Lies, Secrets and Silences, Selected Prose 1966–1978*, New York: W.W. Norton & Co., 1979, pp. 275–310.
21 Haunani-Kay Trask, *Eros and Power, the Promise of Feminist Theory*, Philadelphia: University of Pennsylvania Press, 1986, p. 162.
22 Dworkin, *Our Blood*, p. 84.
23 Frye, *The Politics of Reality*, p. 114.
24 ibid., p. 122.
25 ibid., p. 123.
26 Rich, "Disloyal to civilization," p. 301.
27 ibid., 282.
28 ibid., 285.
29 ibid., 283.
30 ibid., 292.
31 ibid., p. 300.

32 Certainly, it would not prohibit one from reading the white women's hatred of the black slave as Andrea Dworkin did: as a "good" hatred of her husband misdirected against "those who, like her, were carnal chattel, but who, unlike her, were black." (*Our Blood*, p. 87). It simply would not cut off the possibility that the white woman acted out of passions having nothing to do with her own submission to men; it would require the mustering of evidence that those other passions were not at work in any particular case; it would allow one to conclude that the white woman's hatred of the black had its source in a dynamic of racial power in which white women and white men had distinct but determinant and oppressive parts to play.

33 One still could join Adrienne Rich in noting that, while the male in some particular situation "is charismatic though brutal, infantile or unreliable . . . it is the women who make life endurable for each other, give physical affection without causing pain, share, advise, and stick by each other." ("Compulsory heterosexuality," p. 656). One only would have to remember to scan those pleasing moments of women's solidarity for signs of a less pleasing underside, to draw no general truth about women directly from the specific situation, and to remain on the alert for all the ways in which women might, with as much or as little self-direction as anyone else, make life a torment rather than a joy for one another.

34 One can imagine a third, very different, psychoanalytic account – but radical feminism would be loath to draw on it, as it would imply that men did not know or control central facets of their thought and action, and that their evil agency might not lie behind women's own phallocentric thought and action.

35 See Daly, *Gyn/Ecology*, p. 54.

36 Said, *Orientalism*, p. 3.

37 ibid., p. 49.

38 ibid., p. 2.

39 It was left to Said, writing a quarter of a century after the publication of de Beauvoir's *The Second Sex*, and with Foucault's intervening presence to his advantage, to develop the notion of a consciousness of a dominant group derivative of the dominant discourse, and to elaborate on behalf of this notion an exquisite and detailed defense.

40 I hope it no longer needs to be said that the various means by which a dominant group comes to monopolize reflective learning are not *necessarily* devised with the intention of keeping the pleasures of iconoclastic reflection to itself. The forbidding of literacy to subordinates might be done for the sake of preventing them from acquiring skills to perform high-level, white-collar work; the private academy might be designed as a finishing school in social comportment and intellectual self-assurance.

40 The Western tourist industry, especially in its "popular" package tour guise, has done the latter trick.

Conclusion: On Practice

1 Christine Delphy's concept of patriarchy is an exception, in that she believes patriarchy is monolithic and universal (all men as a sex-class oppress all women as a sex-class throughout all of history and culture) but denies that "men" and "women" mark identities more fundamental than patriarchal rule. The belief and the denial combined together are the cause of a theoretical inconsistency running through *Close to Home*.

2 In the United States, where racial domination and subordination always has complicated sexual power and vice versa, the slave system originally prohibited black men from wielding patriarchal power in the first place. Hence capitalist development and the modern ethos could not signify for them a loss of economic power, or of paternal rule, or of moral authority. For a fine, suggestive, now classic essay that traces out the way in which slavery changed the terms in which sex, gender, and power otherwise would have been fused, see Angela Davis, "The black woman's role in the community of slaves," *The Black Scholar*, 3 (December 1971), pp. 3–15. A different qualification of the point is that differentials in men's and women's pay scales, which were legitimated by the patriarchal principle that women's first and primary responsibilities were in the domestic sphere, functioned to ameliorate this decay of the father's economic status.

3 I have always found Eldridge Cleaver's description of the sex–race types dictated by the system of white supremacy to be highly suggestive, even though Cleaver has no intention of subjecting the dictations of Masculine/feminine *per se* to the same searing political critique. The two masculine possibilities white supremacy elaborates are those of the "Omnipotent Administrator" (which it assigns to the white man) and the "Supermasculine Menial" (which it assigns to the black man). This bifurcation of what Cleaver sees as a naturally masculine whole obviously bears a resemblance to the distinction between mind and body, and to my own distinction between the patriarchal and the phallic principle. Cleaver astutely argues that the great problem such a bifurcation posed for white supremacy was that, in assigning the black man the attributes of the brute body, it accorded him sexual prowess and magnetism. Hence the constant obsession with black male sexuality and the frequent resort to castration as the solution to that problem. The bifurcation of the feminine that white supremacy dictated was one between the "Ultra-feminine" and the "Amazon" – each a diseased figure in opposite ways. For Cleaver, the true solution to the whole conglomeration of sex–race difficulties is the unification of the two masculine halves into a Masculine whole, and the two feminine halves into a Feminine whole. Eldridge Cleaver, *Soul on Ice*, New York: Dell Publishing Co. Inc.: 1970. See especially chapter IV, section 2 ("The primeval mitosis.").

4 Even the military, phallic power's most perfectly matched institution, has begun to treat women and men as formally equal individuals who are able to compete for military positions.

5 And hence those very curious alliances, in which *Playboy* offers its

support to NOW and the ERA campaign, while Women Against Pornography joins forces with the New Right and the Reagan administration to ban pornography.

6 Thus radical feminism is absolutely right to see pornography as a politically crucial issue, against all those who argue that the real problems of women are "material," not "ideological" (i.e. that they have to do with women's economic situation, with actual batterings and rapes, with the organization of child-care, with reproductive choice). But radical feminism is right often for the wrong reason – or rather, the reason it gives when pressed to give reasons for its anti-pornography campaigns often is wrong. It claims that it is against "violent" pornography on the grounds that such pornography causes men to go out and rape and brutalize women – as if images were like physical objects that pressed in on brains and triggered behavioral responses out the other side. The real argument to be made, very differently, is that pornographic representations help constitute and embellish masculine and feminine erotic identities, in always complex, circuitous ways – so that cultural struggles over those representations are politically key. Indeed, radical feminism has been too modest in concentrating its attention on violent pornography instead of on all images of masculine and feminine eroticism in "popular" culture. There are other problems with the details of radical feminism's anti-pornography struggle as well. One is that it pursues the struggle on behalf of a reduced, not expanded, ideal of female eroticism. Another is that it chooses a dangerously centrist strategy when it supports state censorship (which it by no means always does). On the other hand, it is right on target in its anarchic, grassroots strategy of superimposing on dominant public images of feminine erotic identity the public exposés of those images as serving the interests of power: "This advertisement is an assault on women!" For the full set of reasons radical feminism opposes pornography, including the behaviorist one, see Laura Lederer (ed.), *Take Back the Night*, New York: William Morrow & Co., 1980. For a critique of the radical feminist position, see Varda Burstyn (ed.), *Women against Censorship*, Toronto: Douglas & McIntyre, 1985.

7 Even, perhaps, with respect to the resistance of those simple people, the peasants, who Gramsci was convinced needed direction from a revolutionary party. See James Scott, "Hegemony and the peasantry," *Politics and Society*, 7: 3 (1977), pp. 267–96.

8 Radical feminism also vociferously condemns the strategy of a centralized party as authoritarian, elitist, and – its own addition – male. In other ways, however, it speaks its own "party" language, dividing the world into oppressors and oppressed, insisting on the existence of a primary power relation, describing all women as sisters, calling for a global feminism to resist a world-wide patriarchal (or "white capitalist p̈triarchal") rule. Not even the most orthodox Marxist would dream of going, in the dropping of fine distictions, quite so far. And if radical feminism outdoes Foucault in denouncing the will to power behind every discrimination between better and worse modes of thought, and so behind the claim that critical philosophy must help cultivate good sense in

practical life, it is no more able than anyone else to talk about the secret workings of power without distinguishing between thought that is blind to that power and thought that sees it, between thought that has been determined by power and thought that manages to see that determination.

9 I argue very much the same thing in my essay "Hegel's logic, Marx's science, rationalism's perils," *Political Studies*, 31:4 (December 1983), pp. 584–603.

Index